Culture and the Question of Rights

Culture and the Question of Rights

Forests, Coasts, and Seas in Southeast Asia

Edited by Charles Zerner

Duke University Press   Durham and London 2003

© 2003 Duke University Press
All rights reserved
Printed in the United States of America on acid-free paper ∞
Typeset in Stone Serif by Wilsted & Taylor Publishing Services
Library of Congress Cataloging-in-Publication Data appear
on the last printed page of this book.

For Toby Alice and Lucia Xingwen

Contents

Figures

Acknowledgments

The idea for this book arose from work I was engaged in as a fellow at the Woodrow Wilson International Center for Scholars. In 1992 Mary Brown Bullock, then the Asia Program Director of the Wilson Center, asked me about the topic I wished to present at the Center. I was writing about my fieldwork among Mandar fishermen in South Sulawesi, an experience that had given me a sense of the complexity of relationships among languages, performances, claims, and cultural visions of marine nature. In place of an individual presentation, I proposed a colloquium on the topics that I found intriguing and perplexing.

At that time, discussions at the intersections of culture, politics, performance, and nature constituted a new terrain. Part of the excitement of the colloquium that took place in May 1992 was the participants' use of varying optics on nature and the processes of claiming it, including law, cultural anthropology, rural sociology, and ethnomusicology. Our work was also based on richly varied sources and modalities—trance dances, rituals performed in marine and forested environments, erotic poems and oratory, court proceedings, tree plantings, and codifications of customary law.

I am thankful to the participants in that colloquium: Nancy Peluso, Marina Roseman, Anna Tsing, Donald Brenneis, and Jane Atkinson, as well as to Stephanie Fried, who contributed a chapter after the colloquium was convened. Mary Brown Bullock, then Director of the Asia Program, and Charles Blitzer, then director of the Woodrow Wilson Center, supported both my project and the colloquium. I am grateful as well to colleagues and friends whose work, directly and indirectly, has contributed to my understanding of these themes: Michael Watts, Peter Brosius, Ken George, Elizabeth Coville, Kirk Endicott, Karen Endicott, James Boyce, Karl Zimmerer, Michael Wright, Janis Alcorn, Marshall Murphree, Walter E. Coward, Alan Isaacman, Daniel Lev, Fred Myers, Celia Lowe, Peter Riggs, Hasmi Bandjar, Sandra Moniaga, Emmy Hafild, and Roem Topatimasang. Christine Harrington, Director of the Institute for Law and Society at New York University, welcomed me as a Visiting Scholar and supported the formation of a faculty working group on Geographies of Injustice, which allowed conversations on rights-related issues to flourish in the company of Tim Mitchell, Wolf Heyderband, Margaret McLagen, Cesear Rodriguez, and Neil Smith.

Special thanks are offered to Almarhum Pak Mas'ud, his son Darmawan Mas'ud Rahman, and his daughters Haerani and Darmi, who offered friendship and the welcome of their home during fieldwork in Majene and on the sea. On the Makassar Strait, Nuhung Tata, Pak Hadari, Pak Dahalang, and Pua Haji Saniaja provided amazing, safe, and storied journeys on board their craft.

This volume was largely completed during my tenure as director of the Natural Resources and Rights Program at the Rainforest Alliance. I am thankful for the support of Daniel Katz, then Executive Director of the Rainforest Alliance. Louis Putzel, program intern at the Rainforest Alliance, and Ginger Hagan, at Sarah Lawrence College, assisted in preparing the manuscript. I am grateful to cartographer David Lindroth, who generously provided several maps of Southeast Asia, Kalimantan, and Sulawesi.

In different ways this book was nurtured by the memory of my father, Charles S. Zerner, journalist and artist, the creator of Vic Jordan; by my mother, Miriam Alterman, who taught me to swim with joy; and by Florence Volkman Pincus, psychologist and activist.

Culture and the Question of Rights

Indonesia and Malaysia. Map by David Lindroth.

Introduction. Moving Translations: Poetics, Performance, and Property in Indonesia and Malaysia

Charles Zerner

Woodpecker's tap-tap
On the honey tree.
I'm drunk with singing,
But I shan't let go.
Lower down the python's tail
Let it to the ground
Come down laughing ladies
As we shower you with gold.
—Meratus Dayak honey hunter's song

In the dark of night, in the forested Meratus Mountains of southeast Kalimantan, a young man crawls out along the branch of a tree known as "Where He Fell" to reach a honeycomb. Suspended high above the forest while excited men, women, and children wait below, he begins to sing, in the hope that his verses will keep the bees from stinging. When his song is finished, he swipes his torch against the beehive, releasing a shower of "gold" sparks "that floats down in a spectacular display."[1] Hoping the bees will follow the sparks, he severs the honey-drenched brood comb from the rest of the hive and descends.

In the Makassar Strait, coursing between Sulawesi and Kalimantan, Mandar fishermen in pursuit of flying fish tell stories of bees and swallows flying out to sea and becoming, in their confusion, schools of flying fish. Shouting Rabelaisian verses, these fishermen seek to cajole, entice, and arouse the spirits of the flying fish into their traps. In coastal coves, sweet bananas and clove cigarettes are offered to spirit guardians, said to be like regional government officials watching over their jurisdictions, in need of flattery, bribes, and "sweet things."

The chapters in this volume explore terrain at the intersection of performance, poetics, and the politics of claiming nature and property.[2] Like the mountaintop trails traversed by Meratus cultivators of southeast Kalimantan, this is a ridge runner of a book. It crosses ambiguous, shifting topography that confounds analytical moves to fix and "root" certain kinds of cultural performance as religious or poetic, on the one hand, or to articulate performance, poetics, and environmental practices as political expressions of property, rights, and rules of access, on the other hand.[3] These crossings raise questions. When, and under what conditions, do poems and performances become claims to nature? How are these translations and articulations made? Which ones are effective and why?[4]

In the context of threats and seizures of land and resources by state-sponsored projects, private-sector invasions, and rapid in-migration, what strategies of articulation are available to fashion claims from a panoply of existing cultural materials—songs, verses, trances, and memories, as well as customary property rights marking practices?[5] How are the politics of interpretation and cultural representation linked to the transformation of poetic tropes into property? How are performances and culturally distinctive families of imagery refracted in ways that may yield a claim of right? What particular combination of circumstances—historic, political, and cultural—determines audience reception of these new articulations? When do performances and other cultural practices and representations become valid evidence for claims to property?

Central within the stories presented here is the drama of translation. The word *translate* itself contains three related meanings, each of which has relevance to these chapters: "to bear or carry from one place or condition to another"; to "turn into one's own or another's language"; and "to change the substance, form, or appearance." The authors of these chapters and their multiple subjects—middle-class lawyers, honey hunters, Durian tree planters, flying fishermen, and trancers—as well as a web of national and international environmental, human rights, and indigenous peoples organizations, are all engaged in acts of translation.

Fashioning these translations is a strategic journey. The meanings and intentions of a diverse group of communities are being transported from one political and cultural context to another. This is the first sense of *translation* as a carrying, a portage from one stream of meaning to another. At the same moment, a mutable body of practices—flying-fishing, honey-hunting and tree-minding, trance-dancing and dream-telling—are being converted into texts. This transformation constitutes the second meaning of *translation*, creating a linguistic entity. They are texts with a twist, a turn toward meanings that have purchase and "legibility" within a larger force field of legal and political interpretation.[6] As Stephanie Fried shows us in her chapter on the Bentian Dayak, "Writing for Their Lives: Bentian Dayak Authors and Indonesian Development Discourse," the gaze of the state legal apparatus—its culturally peculiar legal forms, development ideology, and environmental discourse—constitutes a terrain of articulation to which these texts are linked and tuned. In the political and cultural crucible in which these practices are refracted, there is a "transformation in substance, form, or appearance," the third aspect of *translation*. What emerges from this process is something new.

There are losses, as well as gains, entailed by these translations. As Anna Tsing remarks in her chapter, "Cultivating the Wild: Honey-Hunting and Forest Management in Southeast Kalimantan," we must "take very seriously other ways of understanding and making 'rights' and 'forests' " (see page 27). Tsing argues against the facile assimilation of particular cultural logics of relationship—to nature, power, and property—into the property rights grids and environmental cultures of national governments, global commodity markets, and the development juggernaut.

Both kinds of claims need to be advanced at the same time. Given the political-economic context in which these communities are situated, a strong case for translation as transformation should be made. Since the meanings of cultural representations are invariably fashioned, strategically, in contexts of power, recent translations of these practices as evidence of property, claims to territory and rights, constitute the latest twist in a complicated history of interpretation of customary law, practice, and ritual.[7]

There is more than one reason to support the claim that these practices and performances are being precipitously rendered and dissolved into the universal logic of the Western property rights grid. It is not nostalgia for the culturally specific logics of nature that animates our concern for the loss. It is the conviction that community rights to forests, seas, trees, and coves might be argued more forcefully on the basis of their own particular logics and sensibilities. Why convert to advocate when arguments based on long-term local practices, poetics, occupancy, and historical relationships may be more persuasive *on their own terms*? Perhaps these highly specific modes of expressing and embodying relationships to nature—myths, stories, dances, and the panoply of performance modalities described in this volume—constitute the basis of powerful property claims in their own right, on their own ground.[8]

There is a fourth aspect of the idea of "translation" that needs to be mentioned here: these translations must be *moving* translations—not only in the sense of conveying a burden of meaning from one site to another, but moving in the sense of stirring an audience's sense of rightness, conviction, and moral compulsion. This is the realm of morality, as well as aesthetics. These translations are being forged in situations of danger and distress. They are being strategically rearticulated in ways that resonate with the sensibilities of state officials, judges, and provincial forestry experts, as well as the complicated, sometimes interconnected communities of non-governmental groups, international "publics," and "public opinion."

These translations are being forged on the anvil of competing sensibilities. I am reaching for a notion of translation that is integrally linked to the central thesis of this book: that poetics and performances—the forms that animate and move the sensibilities of specific audiences—are deeply connected to the politics of reading nature and making persuasive claims.[9] This goes beyond James Scott's valuable idea of "legibility"—the formal simplifications produced by state representations of nature, law, and order, on the one hand, and the seemingly illegible, irregular "squiggles" of common property, customary claim, and "messy" local agricultures on the other hand.[10] State officials, "expert" consultants, and timber-firm employees, intentionally or unintentionally, ignore the signs of local relationships to nature, including claims to property—whether they be offerings of coconut and ginger left on the surface of the sea near a specific promontory, the writing of a legal text that codifies practices, or the planting of durian trees in a protected nature area. Non-governmental, scholarly, and local community efforts to translate and rearticulate these forms are often attempts to communicate messages that move the hearts, minds, and sensibilities of multiple, culturally disparate, and not always receptive audiences.[11]

Behind, but not hidden from this already complicated interpretive scene, are the ethnographers, sociologists, lawyers, and musicologists in this volume, who, as part of progressive networks of transnational professionals engaged in "writing culture," constitute part of a skein of boundary-crossing translators, mediators, presenters, and advocates.[12]

While the intersection of environment, politics, performance, and culture constitutes a large terrain, the geographic scope of this volume is more circumscribed. The chapters that follow are all based on fieldwork conducted by the authors in Indonesia and Malaysia from the late 1980s to the mid-1990s. Individual chapters refract the terrain of property and performance through distinctive disciplinary optics. What emerges is a cross-country traverse across the oceans and forests of Indonesia and Malaysia that provokes questions and reveals connections. This book also contributes to the debate on three themes: the cultural production of nature as a material artifact; the cultural production of nature as idea and ideal; and the politics of representing relationships to nature, resources, and territory.

Although the stories these authors tell about cultures of nature and cultures of rights differ in their particulars, they share concerns with the political force and consequences of state and private-sector claims upon land, trees, forest gardens, and fishing sites used, remembered, and claimed by local communities and individuals. Whether on the periphery or at the center of these narratives, these claims—and often seizures—are driving strategic changes in the ways communities represent a variety of relationships, including customary practices linked to nature. These are preeminently stories of the cultural production of local relationships to nature and property rights under conditions of intense political, cultural, economic, and sometimes paramilitary pressure.

At a time of resource greed, corruption, and gross disparities in political power in Malaysia and Indonesia, these chapters articulate itineraries in self-fashioning and self-defense, inasmuch as they present journeys across terrestrial and marine realms. Each "articulation," to use Stuart Hall's helpful term that evokes the double sense of "to speak" and "to link," provides clarification through rendering into language and linking to larger worlds of power, discourse, and institutional allies.[13] In the political hurly-burly over resource control, legal authority, and rights of access, strategies of self-representation and interpretation are often potent tools. Within the arena of resource wars and competing property claims, cultural representations constitute a rich field of potential resources for politically weak communities seeking allies, access to networks, and leverage.

As several chapters in this book show, the poetics of nature embody social relationships to nature.[14] The reader is cautioned against reducing concerns with performance, perception, and metaphor to mere exercises in nature appreciation or comparative cultural aesthetics. None of the communities or individuals portrayed here is imprisoned within a romanticized, reified zone of rural culture: all are able to move between pragmatics, aesthetics, and legal-strategic modes of articulation, depending upon the circumstances. The poetics and performances analyzed here are keys to understanding how communities position themselves, in relation to nature and to other ethnic groups, the state, and the resource-extraction industries, at a particular historical moment in Indonesian and Malaysian history. Rural communities and cultures of nature are not the sole focus of this volume. The cultural production of ideas of nature and property by national governments, colonial surveyors, and state technical experts are analyzed in chapters by Anna Tsing, Charles Zerner, Marina Roseman, and Stephanie Fried.

The Cultural Fashioning of Nature

The Context

In the mid-1990s, concern with ideas and images of nature, normative visions of nature management, and the cultural invention and legacy of "wild" nature, effloresced into a veritable garden of scholarship and provocative rumination. In *Landscape and Memory* (1995), Simon Schama's masterful excavation of Euro-American cultural ideas of nation, nature, and human relationships to landscape, he demonstrated that German, American, and English ideas of landscape and the wild—coupled with the potent, sometimes lethal, potential of Romanticism and the cult of the wild—provided majestic, sometimes disturbing accounts of the cultural force of landscape visions. William Cronon's pathbreaking work, *Changes in the Land: Indians, Colonists, and the Ecology of New England* (1983), altered our understandings of how landscapes change by demonstrating the cultural and material force of native peoples' and colonists' cultural practices in shaping the landscape of New England. Archaeological, ethnobotanical, and anthropological research in Africa, Asia, and Latin America demonstrated that forested landscapes popularly assumed to be pristine were culturally fashioned forests— produced and modified by a variety of practices, intentional and unintentional, for decades, centuries, and, in some cases, millennia.[15] The forest as a material presence is as much artifact as it is an embodiment of wild, non-human "nature."

The appearance of William Cronon's *Uncommon Ground: Toward Reinventing Nature* in 1995 marked a further, radical expansion of the cultural lens on nature-making and un-making. Through the diverse optics of natural scientists, cultural historians, and anthropologists, the book advanced the thesis that nature is a culturally imagined terrain of values, images, beliefs, and practices, and a site marked by the historically specific impress of cultures. By reexamining the scientific and cultural foundations of nature conservation, *Uncommon Ground* questioned the goals of a "mission" focused on "wild" or "pristine" nature. Nature became as much a cultural construction and site of interrogation as a site "out there" for intervention.[16]

Ecologists, environmental historians, and geographers, including Benjamin Botkin, Donald Worster, and Karl Zimmerer, at roughly the same time, were reviewing the history of ecological thought and science. Questioning the presuppositions of several decades of ecological theory, they argued that ideas of stable communities of organisms existing in equilibrium or homeostatic relationship with particular ecological niches were no longer justified.[17] Instead, chance, unpredictability, complexity, and human history played major roles. To the historicization of nature that emerged from these studies—and the recognition of nature's cultural fashioning that grew out of research in the humanities and social sciences—Donna Haraway intervened, conjuring a provocative vision of nature as a dynamic, boundary-crossing, shape-shifting fusion of nature/culture that she has called "Cyborg."

This volume contributes to the discussion of the material and symbolic ways in which nature is culturally constructed. It shows how the forests and coasts of Indonesia and Malaysia have been materially transformed through cultural practices. These accounts provide culturally nuanced analyses of the insight that few, if any, of the "natural" habitats popularly viewed as "pristine" by global environmental organizations are actually what they seem to be. Rather, rainforests as well as reefs and coastal seas are sites with histories, both human and natural. They are landscapes and seascapes whose features have been shaped over time by complex and varied interactions with human societies.

How nature is materially made, shaped, modified, and cared for by particular peoples is vividly illustrated in several chapters. In arguing against a romanticized view of Meratus Dayak cultural beliefs and knowledge, Tsing describes the ways in which particular communities "reshape" the forest to accommodate the major honeybee of the Meratus Mountains, the *indu wanyi* (*Apis dorsata*). Her analysis of governmental and local practices of making, managing, and mapping the forest creates the ground for a critique of the Indonesian government's timber-management policies and practices (including "commodity-property" claims) as equally exotic and more environmentally destructive than those of the Meratus Dayak.

While Tsing's account of Meratus Dayak forest practices reveals forest-making on the scale of individually named, claimed, and cared-for trees, Fried offers a vista of community-level forest-making on a vast scale. Fried provides a glimpse of the forest-shaping agro-ecological practices of Bentian Dayak cultivators who have transformed large regions of "wild" forest into a patchwork of half-wild, partly cultivated forest gardens.[18] These intricately fashioned rattan gardens, cultivated over generations, form a striking coun-terimage to the international icon of the pristine, green, and wild "rainfor-est." Bentian Dayak forest-fashioning practices have socialized a portion of Kalimantan, preserving much of its "wildness," enriching biological diver-sity, and permitting the capture of a tidy profit at the same time.

Nancy Peluso's account of the Bagak Salako in "Fruit Trees and Family Trees in an Anthropogenic Forest: Property Zones, Resource Access, and Environ-mental Change in Indonesia" demonstrates the transformation of the "natu-ral forests" of West Kalimantan into patches of intensively managed areas of fruit production. Peluso's historical account of the changing composition of the forest, and of the political-ecological forces that drive that change, pro-vides another example of how forests are not only managed but also cultur-ally produced. While Fried discovered that Bentian Dayak groups consider their rattan-forest gardens to be their "bank accounts," a metaphor suggest-ing a view toward management for profit, Peluso shows how Bagak Salako forests have been intentionally created as *production* forests: cultured forma-tions that articulate well with changing regional and global market opportu-nities.

Two hundred miles across the Makassar Strait from Kalimantan, Mandar fishermen have affected river flows and drainage patterns in estuaries and have selectively altered the stocks of freshwater, estuarine, and coastal fish-eries. And across the Malacca Strait from the island of Borneo, Temiar horti-culturists, through the planting of manioc, hill rice, maize, and millet, as well as fruit orchards, and through the selective harvest of non-timber tropical forest products, have also shaped nature as landscape and as ecosystem for centuries.

Cultural Representations of Nature

Before it can even be a repose for the senses, landscape is the work of the mind.
Its scenery is built up as much from strata of memory as from layers of rock.
—Simon Schama, *Landscape and Memory*

"This is how we see the world," Rene Magritte argued in a 1938 lecture explaining his version of La Condition Humaine in which a painting has been superimposed over the view it depicts so that the two are coterminous and indistinguishable. "We see it as be-ing outside ourselves even though it is only a mental representation of what we experi-ence on the inside." What lies beyond the windowpane of our apprehension, says

Magritte, needs a design before we can properly discern its form. And it is culture, convention, and cognition that makes that design, that invests a retinal impression with the quality we experience as beauty.—Simon Schama, *Landscape and Memory*

All the chapters in this volume explore the culturally variegated ways in which landscape is the work of the mind. Tsing demonstrates how state-sanctioned, developmentalist cultural conceptions of a dichotomy between "culture" and "nature" serve to split forest representations—on maps and in practice—into strictly separate realms. And this peculiar cultural dichotomization has serious consequences: viewing vast expanses of forest in Kalimantan as wild, Tsing asserts, ratifies a statist vision of the forest as a pristine, unused, uninhabited, raw realm. It is a realm awaiting its state-appointed end: development, modernization, stabilization, and violent extraction.

Tsing's chapter challenges the familiar cultural terrain of state-enforced cartographies and wild nature/culture dichotomies by contrasting these articulations with Meratus cultural visions of the forest and relationships to it:

> Meratus relations with bees and honey trees also refuse the dichotomies that make the forests, and their fauna, wild. . . . Are honey trees and honeybees wild? Meratus claim, protect, and prepare honey trees, and they sometimes even plant them. They imagine a relationship with particular migratory honeybee swarms whose descendants, they say, come back year after year to the same trees. . . . In place of the wild–domestic divide, . . . Meratus ecological discourse on bees calls up imagery of travel, trade, and marriage. (see page 32–33)

Tsing offers a challenge: "Only if we expand our ecological analyses to take in such alternative frameworks can we begin to imagine varied relationships between people and forests." What might a Meratus vision of human–honeybee relationships look like? A mobile, dichotomy-crossing vision of the forested landscape of the Meratus Mountains is offered:

> Migration is central to Meratus understandings of indu wanyi. Sometimes people say that the bees have their own land, where they farm rice swiddens like Meratus, in a distant place where the *pau janggi* trees grow. Only when a fragrant season of flowers beckons do the bees cross the River of Changes to fly into the Meratus Mountains as bees. This is a model that acknowledges the long-distance mobility over irregular vegetation and seasonality that these bees require. (see page 39–40)

The vivid center of Tsing's chapter is a description of the nighttime ascent of honey hunters. Tsing tracks, as if she were following the floating sparks of the honey hunter's torches, the meanings of images sung by the honey hunters—images of seduction, reciprocity, trade, and travel. She reveals a culturally distinctive landscape of relationships between people, bees, and forests, one animated by personal prowess and charisma.

The Mandar fishermen depicted in my chapter, "Sounding the Makassar Strait: The Poetics and Politics of an Indonesian Marine Environment," are engaged in establishing a variety of personal relationships with the objects of their quests—flying fish, tuna, and huge schools of scad. Their marine performances—the casting of silent spells, the arrangement of magically charged flowers and herbs, and the broadcasting of erotic marine oratory—reveal multiple cultural sources of ideas about politics, power, and poetics. Fishing in the Makassar Strait is an exercise, in part, in how to move fish corporeally, how to stir their own spirits and the spirits that control them. The representations deployed by Mandar fishers in their marine oratory are made from images of distant kingdoms, as well as images of flight, desire, and flattery.

The vision of Mandar marine poetics, property, and politics that emerges is a variegated terrain. It is as much the creative product of contemporary political-administrative discourses and practices of the bureaucratic state as it is an embodiment of religious views antedating the arrival of Islam in the fifteenth century. Although a topography of shallow waters, reefs, coasts, and promontories is believed to be inhabited by unpredictable, shape-shifting spirit guardians, these same spirits and their jurisdictions are also reviewed through the lens of the Indonesian bureaucratic state. Promontory spirit guardians are analogized to "district officers," while a primary spirit who "grasps all the other authorities" is conceived of as a spirit "regency head" or "president." Given the multiple cultural screens or templates placed upon Mandar marine nature, the chapter makes the case for complex, historically layered understandings of nature and of human relationships to it. By exploring the contexts in which particular kinds of representations of nature are deployed, the essay emphasizes the politics of cultural representation: the strategic selection of particular representations and differential emphases on certain elements within each image.

Trees, landscapes, and their changing meanings form a connective tissue among the essays by Tsing, Peluso, and Roseman. Peluso's essay traces the interrelationships between the biological characteristics of particular trees, the political history of the Bagak Salako peoples of West Kalimantan, and the

cultural meaning of certain trees. Peluso explores the ways in which durian trees' biological characteristics—uncertainty about when the fruits will
ripen and the multigenerational longevity of durian—intersect with cultural
interpretations, practices, and valuations. Like young men and women who
are considered adults in Bagak Salak society only *after* they have children, durian trees are given proper names only after they have begun fruiting.

Roseman's contribution to this volume, "Singers of the Landscape: Song,
History, and Property Rights in the Malaysian Rainforest," makes the most
radical interpretive claim linking cultural visions of the landscape and performance with property. Temiar trance performances, in which spirit mediums travel across the Malaysian landscape, embody a world of nature imagined, known, named, and ultimately claimed by the Temiar:

> Temiars map and mediate their relationships with the land and each
> other through song. Landforms traversed or cultivated become land-
> marks named and recorded in the songs Temiar receive from the souls of
> the landscape, its flora and fauna. . . . Temiar mediums are singers of the
> landscape, translating the rainforest environment—jungle, field, and
> settlement—into culture, as inhabitant spirits emerge, identify them-
> selves, and begin to sing in dreams, and later, in ritual performance. The
> forest becomes a social space when networks of association are estab-
> lished between humans and spirits. . . . Songs are termed "paths," a po-
> tent image for people living in dense rainforest. . . . As the singer stands,
> vocalizing and dancing, his or her voice is now the voice of the spirit,
> singing of its visions as it flies above the forest canopy, alights upon
> mountain crests, scans the horizon, finds and returns dislocated souls of
> patients brought to be healed. (see page 123–24)

Roseman's analytic lens is not solely focused on articulating the politics
and poetics of Temiar representations. She also foregrounds perceptions of
the jungle by Malay peasants, who cleared permanent, jungle-covered lands
for rice fields and called it "live land," thereby contrasting it with the surrounding jungle, which they called "dead land." Similarly, Roseman analyzes the cultural world of a British mining engineer and shows how his carefully wrought map, driven by "the lines of colonial interest in economic
resources," is a cultural-political document as distinctive and unusual as any
performance by Temiar shaman. By turning her lens toward representations
of the early-twentieth-century rational, natural-scientific cartographic re-

gime, Roseman reminds us of the culturally specific conceptions and mythic topographies of technocratic representations:

> Orang Asli areas lurk beyond the fringes on Doyle's map: note the "JUN-GLE" enscripted in curves at the map's edges where detailed tin mines, gardens, and footpaths peter out into the aboriginal absent presence. Just beyond the map's Chinese temples and Christian chapels, placed at the forest's edge and mountain's feet to serve genealogically and cosmologically outlying spirits, short curved lines trace the mountains' perimeters. . . . The montane, upstream territory of the forest peoples looms like the ocean's edge of medieval and early renaissance maps: what strange beings lie in wait in the blank space at the crest of Bukit Assam Kumbeng (Assam Kumbeng Hill) bordered by the scalloped cartographic symbols so often used for coastlines? (see page 114)

Roseman's fastidious yet rhapsodic analysis of Temiar sound and performance also serves as an act of impassioned, scholarly protest against the state-sanctioned silences that have been imposed on Temiar spaces, places, and claims.

Representing Relationships to Nature in a Time of Danger: Performance, Poetics, and Rights

The tradition of the oppressed teaches us that the "state of emergency" in which we live is not the exception, but the rule.—Walter Benjamin, *Theses on the Philosophy of History*

Accommodating the luxuriant variety of customary land tenure was simply inconceivable. The historical solution, at least for the liberal state, has typically been the heroic simplification of individual freehold tenure. . . . Just as the flora of the forest were reduced to *Normalbaume,* so the complex tenure arrangements of customary practice are reduced to freehold.—James Scott, *Seeing Like a State*

Backed by state power through records, courts, and ultimately coercion, these state fictions transformed the reality they presumed to observe.—James Scott, *Seeing Like a State*

James Scott's reflections on the imaginative and material simplifications imposed on the landscape of customary tenure form a useful frame from which to behold these several instances of forest management, claims, and performances. Each essay in this volume recounts the ways in which relationships to the land or seas are idiosyncratically conceptualized, performed, and claimed, and, in most cases, the ways in which representatives of the state fail to perceive these performances as embodied symbolizations of social relationships to land and resources.

Beyond Scott's image of the topographic diversity of customary land-tenure arrangements and practices, the "jogs and squiggles" straightened out and eventually obliterated by the techniques of the state surveyor and the processes of cadastralization, these essays convey the complexity and ambiguity of boundary-crossing customary practices and performances. The play of strategy and imagination in performing, proclaiming, and translating ritual practices and poetics into claims to nature needs to be emphasized. In many cases in this volume, representations of relationships to nature seem to occupy both sides of a conceptual divide at one and the same time. Although performance, poetics, politics, and claims of rights are implicated in all the essays, what they mean and how they come to mean what they mean—to performers, claimants, government officials, and scholars—is a more complicated story.[19]

Peluso, in her account of Bagak Salako resistance to a Dutch plan to convert the upper slopes of a mountain into a watershed-protection area, shows how locally defined ways of signifying property rights claims in a landscape—the planting of productive tree crops as well as swidden fields—were used as stakes, botanical and symbolic, to reclaim areas within the protected-watershed zone. Peluso tracks Bagak Salako resistance to forced relocation, abandonment of ancestral forests and lands, and threats of criminal penalties:

> The villagers have continued to "push back" the border in less organized, informal ways. Villagers harvest rubber, durian, langsat, rambutan, angkaham, cempedak, and other fruits planted by their parents and other ancestors within the border. During the Japanese occupation (1942–45), the Indonesian revolution, and the early years of Indonesian independence, villagers made swiddens within the reserve boundaries and planted rubber and fruit in the fallows. . . . By planting productive tree crops, people were also staking their claims in the control of the hillside's upper slopes, negotiating new forms of old territorial and resource claims. (see page 193)

Tsing stakes out her ground in a movement that renders, in stark relief, the dominant but "problematic framework: the classification of forest resources as natural commodities." Disenfranchisement of Meratus Dayak communities from their forest lands and livelihoods rests upon two culturally alien conceptions, the dichotomous characterization of landscapes as either "wild" or "cultural" on the one hand, and the imposition of "commodity-property" claims to forest resources on the other. By classifying vast regions of forest within which Meratus Dayak live, work, and cultivate as "wild," Indonesian forests become fair game for commercial exploitation. Forests are made, Tsing reminds us, and relationships to nature, including ideas of control, access, and property are seen through cultural screens. To the extent that Meratus visions of the forest are outside of or different from the dichotomous conceptions imposed by the Indonesian State Forestry Corporation or the Forestry Department, Meratus are excluded or marginalized.

Rather than reinterpreting Meratus views of their relationships to honey-tree claims within the "commodity-property" perspective, Tsing contrasts that system, with its emphasis on impersonal, context-free transferability within a universal, cadastral grid of property rights, with the charismatic claims of Meratus honey hunters and tree owners:

> Honey-tree claims are "charismatic," not "bureaucratic.". . . Claims tap and create skills of bravery, travel, magic (to climb trees), heroism, social networking, and narration. There is an economic theory here that has nothing to do with rights to benefit from and distribute products. The theory is that abundance is attracted to prowess. The man who can hold a claim can make honey plentiful, not just for himself but for others. In that sense, he is a "charismatic" owner, calling up an abundant liveli-hood and an active community through his own attractiveness. When the climber courts the bees in his songs, he is doing more than pacifying them; he is enticing them into his sphere of influence. The point is not, as in the commodity-property systems with which we are more familiar, to define natural objects that establish social relations by the exclusivity of social access to them. (see page 46)

Tsing turns the ethnographic gaze away from Meratus particularities and highlights the features of the Western property-rights grid, its assumptions about "commodity-property," its environmental and developmental ideologies about power and relationships to nature and resources. In her resolute affirmation of the Meratus theory and practices of relations to nature, Tsing

challenges the development communities, global conservation organizations, and economists engaged in expanding and enforcing universal property grids to recognize culturally different theories and forms of claims.

Fried tells a story of resistance through convergence. Tracking changes
in the articulation of Bentian Dayak customary land tenure, or *adat*, over a
fifteen-year period (1985–99), Fried demonstrates how timber concessionaires, accompanied by military-security personnel and forestry "experts," in-
vaded Bentian territory and ran roughshod through hundreds of hectares
of "invisible" rattan gardens, familial gravesites, and swidden plots. In response, Bentian lawyers, educators, and provincial-government officials
sought to find and fashion successive versions of Bentian adat land tenure
that would be recognizable and legitimate from the perspective of state law
and Indonesian development ideology. We witness, through a progression of
documents on customary land-tenure practices, a series of attempts to make
Bentian ownership and agroforestry practices visible and, in James Scott's
terminology, "legible."

Stuart Hall's idea of articulation is helpful in understanding the process of
Bentian cultural and political attempts at fashioning versions of their adat:

> Articulate means to utter, to speak forth, and to be articulate. It carries
> that sense of language-ing, of expressing, etc. But we also speak of an "ar-
> ticulated" lorry (truck): a lorry where the front (cab) and back (trailer)
> can, but need not necessarily, be connected to one another. . . . An artic-
> ulation is thus the form of the connection that *can* make a unity of two
> different elements, under certain conditions. It is a linkage, which is not
> necessary, determined, absolute and essential for all time. You have to
> ask under what circumstances can a connection be forged or made? (Hall
> 1996: 141)

The story recounted in Fried's essay is, in large part, an effort to reconstruct
the "nature" of Bentian customary land tenure—to fashion, in Hall's sense,
an "articulation" that is politically and culturally viable. The lawyers, educators, and provincial-government officials who were fashioning this adat articulation were struggling to create a new cultural entity: a collective right
whose "front end" articulated neatly with already recognized government
regulations and property rights forms, while its "rear end" remained rooted
in Bentian claims and soil. These articulations permitted linkages between
Bentian Dayak customary law and land management practices on the one
hand, and state-sanctioned ideas of development, environmental manage-

ment, and property rights on the other. Fried's strategy, like those employed by Bentian academics, lawyers, and the non-governmental activists she describes, is to emphasize the similarities between Bentian Dayak property rights claims and statutory rights to land recognized under Indonesian agrarian and forestry laws.

While Fried tracks changing articulations of local customary law in texts, demonstrating strategies of convergence, Roseman presents the reader with unfamiliar modalities and materials—trance transcripts, songs, and fragments of narrated dreams—to demonstrate Temiar relationships and claims to the jungle in which they live, work, and travel. Roseman's analysis is extraordinarily daring because it leaps from Temiar trance rituals in which social relations to Temiar nature are performed, embodied, sounded, and danced—the phenomenological data of dream and personal narratives of spirit possession, even flight over the jungle landscape—to a jural modality: the assertion of claims and rights to access and ownership. Unlike the history recounted in Fried's account of Bentian Dayak fashioning of a given land adat into progressive articulations, Roseman performs an act of translation by hermeneutic fiat: "What might sound like 'merely a song' to a Malay precolonial peasant, British colonial speculator, or Malaysian postcolonial administrator, is both map and history text to Temiar singers. . . . Charting a different history than the maps of colonial typographers, Temiar songs trace their experience and relationship with the land areas across which they historically ranged; this is one form in which they record their entitlement: their 'title' or 'deed' to land" (see pages 124–26).

Roseman's contribution, like those of Zerner and Tsing, directly engages the proposition that aesthetics and politics, sensibilities and statecraft, are inextricably linked. Roseman analyzes trance narratives as the performative equivalents of a cadastral map: a flight map, as it were, and a template for a Temiar territorial-legal vision of rights and claims. For Roseman, trance narratives are simultaneously expressions of distinctive cultural poetics and relationships to the forest and evidence of jural claims to forest territories.[20]

Interpretive Strategies in Times of Danger

There is another interpretive strategy available in the search for legitimizing relationships between peoples and their environments. Rather than reducing, for example, the culturally distinctive, poetic, rhythmic, oneiric "otherness" of Temiar trance flights to the uniform, state-sanctioned grid of

Malaysian cadastral maps, and thereby asserting a fundamental equivalence between two strikingly dissimilar modalities, one might begin by asserting that radically different cultural logics and imageries form the substratum of relationships to land, self, history, and resources. There may be strategic gains in shaping arguments for recognition of rights to landscapes, resources, and territory in the culturally distinctive logics, metaphors, and modalities that are examined in these essays. Analysts grounding claims based on *difference* would not then have to demonstrate underlying parallels, congruencies, and equivalencies.

But collective claims to Indonesian and Malaysian forests and seas are being made to counter the claims of timber concessionaires, mining corporations, and globally powerful fisheries conglomerates—the raw-resource extraction juggernaut—who invade, claim, seize, and in many cases, destroy any possibilities for local livelihoods. If the state turns a blind eye to the cultural specificities of local relationships and claims to nature, resources, and territory, then advocates for these local communities may be forced to refashion representations of local relationships to nature into "legible," state-recognized forms of property.

State-sanctioned forms of property and territorialized claims are not the only forms of the procrustean grid into which culturally distinctive forms of relationships to nature, including property rights, are being embedded. In the effort to articulate counterclaims for local communities, many advocates of environmental justice and community rights have discovered a countergrid of collective rights, institutions, and territorial management known as "community-based resource management."[21] In the 1920s and 1930s a generation of liberal, Dutch scholars of customary law, interested in defending community lands and livelihoods from impending state and private-sector encroachments, fashioned images of community, lands, and governance that were based in the idea of territorial, village-based republics. Since the 1970s, social and environmental non-governmental groups, as well as common-property scholars, have built upon and deployed similar images. Visions of just, village-based republics, environmental-access rules, sanctions, management institutions, and collective property rights are put into play in contemporary political struggles. Such a strategy may promote opportunities for negotiations with national governments, multilateral financial institutions, and international conservation organizations, based on recognizable, if different, ideas of property, territory, and title.[22]

Rights discourses, especially those couched in languages and forms recognized by the state, become salient at those situational "edges" where conflict and competition over places charged with memories, histories, and meanings are most intense. At these "edges," state-sanctioned ideologies of exploitation ("development"), jural grids, and cultural meanings of landscape, nature, and environment are put into play in the service of the development juggernaut. There, in the presence of the state security apparatus, Walter Benjamin's reflection seems germane: "To articulate the past historically does not mean to recognize it 'the way it really was' (Ranke). It means to seize hold of memory as it flashes up at a moment of danger" (1969: 255).

At the edge of the forest, as the surveyors' lines are laid and the bulldozers move in on ancestral graves and family honey trees, local visions and versions of relationships to nature are seized and transfigured. Performance becomes transformed into customary law, and ancestral custom becomes a means of signifying rights. In the face of power, these strategically fashioned versions of the past, of custom and culture, performance and poetics, are put forth as primary evidence, embodiments of rights, claims, and territories. They are momentary codifications of a kaleidoscopically changing, uneven landscape of cultural forms.

That the traces of cultural transformation, newly refracted articulations of a terrain of meanings and practices, are visible does not devalue these feats and facts of translation, their translators, or the project of advocacy and strategic transformation. The concept of an "original" culture has always been a fiction, a strategic fabrication deployed when needed.

Within the contexts of danger and environmental destruction, amid the desolate ruin of timber clear-cuts, mine tailings, and mercury-laden streams, the poisonous havoc wrought on reefs and on divers' bodies by cyanide fishing,[23] beside the intimidation of the military-backed, state security apparatus, the acts of cultural self-fashioning and articulation recounted here become acts of creativity, craft, and courage. It is the Indonesian and Malaysian governments, their military-security apparatus, and the private-sector timber and fisheries extraction firms that have twisted the landscape and its meanings, leaving desolation in their wake—the traces of violent, extortionate demands made upon nature and communities.[24]

Turning multiple cultural representations against the lathe of power and advancing, by acts of creative advocacy through complex political fields, these translators—fishermen and forest cultivators, lawyers, provincial officials, ethnographers, trance dancers, and non-governmental advocates—are engaged in attempts to fashion, and to carry with them into the future, cultural representations yielding some form of traction over intensely disputed lands, coasts, seas, and selves. They are deploying translations of culture in politically dangerous terrain, seeking to move meanings and audiences—at home, in national capitals, and abroad—by rendering their relationships to nature, to historical memory, and to specific landscapes—visible, audible, and valid.[25]

Notes

1 Tsing, "Cultivating the Wild: Honey-Hunting and Forest Management in Southeast Kalimantan," this volume, pp. 25–55.

2 On the poetics of place-names and their relationship to Apache perceptions of landscape, see Keith Basso's (1984) pioneering work. On ethnographic explorations of poetics, aesthetics, and cultural aspects of the experience of place, see Feld and Basso (1996). On cultural perceptions of marine nature among sea cucumber fishers in the Togean Islands, Indonesia, see Lowe (1997). See Nabhan (1997) on poetics, seeds, and landscape in North America. See Feld (1982) and Scheiffelein (1976) on explorations of aesthetics, emotions, and sound, and see Attali (1989) on the political economy of music. See Acciaoli (1985), Volkman (1990), and Pemberton (1994) on intersections between ritual performance, the politics of culture, and cultural representation in Indonesia. On relationships between property, persuasion, performance, and culture in North American cultural contexts, see Rose (1994) and Nedelsky (1990).

3 Although the analyses offered in this volume do not explicitly address the question of legal pluralism, they cross terrain that implicates debates about multiple legal orders. If these essays seem to point toward legal pluralisms, they are pluralisms that constitute a multifarious conjunction of practices, beliefs, and conceptions of nature and social relationships to it that are selected, articulated, and deployed in relation to specific historical, cultural, and political contexts. The kinds of performances, conceptions of order, and articulations of rights examined in this volume cannot be satisfactorily reduced to jural discourse, rules, and conventional notions of legal pluralism characterized by Merry (1988: 870, citing Pospisil 1981, Griffiths 1986, and Moore 1986) as "a situation in which two or more legal systems coexist in the same social field." For an attempt at a culturally broad definition of Indonesian *adat* (local practices or customs) from a legal perspective, see Fitzpatrick (1997), who characterizes customary law as a "body of adat rules [which] are quite detailed, sometimes written, and exhibiting such a high degree of predictability, application, and adherence that they take on many of the characteristics of "law." This definition assumes the cultural features of stability, "pre-

dictability," and "adherence" which are placed in question by the changing tactics of interpretation and articulation exemplified by the cases in this book. On the Dutch adat imaginary, see Li (2000: 159), who states: "The Dutch colonial authorities played an important role in ethnicizing or traditionalizing the Indonesian interior. . . . The Dutch concept of the adat law community *(masyarakat hukum adat)* assumed, as it simultaneously attempted to engineer named, bounded, and organized groups." See Merry (1988), Von Benda-Beckmann (1988), Griffiths (1986), Burns (1989), and Von Benda-Beckmann (1993) for theoretical reviews of conceptions of legal pluralism. On legal pluralism in Indonesia, see Fitzpatrick (1997), and see Peluso and Vandergeest (2001) on legal pluralism in Malaysia, Indonesia, and Thailand. On the political construction of tradition in Indonesia, see Bowen (1986). See Chanock (1985) on colonial interventions and interpretations of customary law in Malawi and Zambia.

In emphasizing the role of performance and poetics in the articulation of relationships to nature, I do not wish to suggest a romantic reification of "performative" cultures on the one hand, and "textual" cultures on the other hand (Ong 1977, 1982; Hibbets 1992). Formulations of legal pluralism need to take into account the variegated, non-unified, non-systemic character of cultures, as well as recent theoretical understandings of culture as ensembles of strategically selected, articulated, and deployed representations (Hall 1996; Li 1997, 1999, 2000, 2001; Tsing 1999). These authors emphasize how political and cultural contexts are, in part, shaping the ground in which local communities select, refract, and deploy representations of relationships to nature, including rights: they demonstrate how the "facts" of each case are being remade, and, in this politically creative process, how poesis and performance may become rearticulated as map, right, rule, and property claim. The study of the conditions under which those refractions are made, mobilized, communicated, and received constitutes one of the more exciting avenues of inquiry in legal and cultural theory. The contributions to this volume, although they nominally focus on the cultural practices and representations of rural communities, do not privilege rurality by locating culture in the hinterlands alone.

4   When the honey hunters of South Kalimantan climb the forest giants one hundred feet into the air, singing seductive songs to lull fiercely stinging bees, is this performance to be interpreted as a dramatic, culturally specific embodiment of Meratus beliefs about the politics of pleasure, friendship, or seduction—relationships that are more akin to sensibility and social affinity than to the category of the jural? If these songs constitute ways of manifesting Meratus power and prowess over groups of honeybees or honey trees, might they also be considered as evidence of authority and rights—to sites, to specific creatures, to regions? Is the oratory of Mandar flying fishermen simply an example of the fantastic, Rabelaisian

cultural repertoire of these salty-minded, deep-sea fishermen? Is there a single politics of Mandar marine nature, a master theory of social relations to the sea, its creatures and currents, embedded within Mandar marine verses, practices, and beliefs? And how do local expressions of cultural relationships to nature articulate with state ideologies of resource extraction, nature conservation, development, and environment? Are cultural representations of local relationships to nature— bees, trees, seas, and jungles—disjunct from, or emerging in dialogue with and resistance to, state and private-sector claims?

5   On the history of state policies toward indigenous peoples of Malaysia, see Denton et al. (1997). See Colchester (1990) on the status of native customary claims in Sarawak.

6   See James Scott (1998) for a masterful analysis of the ways in which state-sanctioned, simplified forms of property, agriculture, and village settlement form have been inscribed on and over more idiosyncratic forms of common property, forests, gardens, and settlements.

7   On the cultural and political history of customary claims and their interpretation in Indonesia, see Burns (1989), Fitzpatrick (1997), Lev (1972), and Hooker (1991). See Moniaga (1993) for a nongovernmental articulation of customary law, community territory, and their relation to state policies and legislation. For a critical examination of representations of community and customary law, see Brosius et al. (1998). On the multilayered history of conceptions of customary law, village republics, territory, and ethnicity, see also von Vollenhoven (1981), Bourchier (1997), and Zerner (1998).

8   Recent jurisprudence in Canada (De Palma 1998: 1) and elsewhere suggests that property rights claims based on these alternative modalities and culturally specific logics of and relationships to nature may be increasingly recognized by courts as legally valid. The Supreme Court of Canada recognized Gitxsan claims to an extensive region of the Province of British Columbia by holding that "orally recited tales and myths of the Gitxsan peoples" are "legally binding evidence that can be used, along with other histories, to support Gitxsan claims to as much as 222,000 square miles of British Columbia's remote interior." Although the issue is often articulated as a question of whether local groups have legitimate property rights claims to vast sections of Indonesia's forests and coastal seas, the critical issue is what procedures are used to validate facts. As Stanley Fish (1980: 338) asserts, "What is at stake in a disagreement is the right to specify competing visions of the truth, based on competing versions of 'proof.'"

9   This line of argument builds on Dove's (1983) idea of the "political economy of ignorance": the willful failure of governmental and private-sector actors to perceive and recognize evidence of local communities' positive management of forested environments.

10 The idea of legibility/illegibility in Scott (1998) is itself a perspectival notion, rooted in different perceptions and presuppositions about order/disorder on behalf of differently positioned observers. Scott's contrast between legibility and illegibility is not, in my reading, grounded in an essentialist notion of order/disorder inherent in the object of perception itself.

11 On the willful ignorance and self-interested "blindness" of Indonesian officials in viewing the environmental effects of swidden agriculture, see Dove (1983). On property, local cultures of communication, and customary claims among miners and other resource users in the North American context, see Rose (1994).

12 On the history and political significance of transnational issue networks, see Keck (1995) and Keck and Sikkink (1998). On transnational social movements in Latin America, see also Brysk (1994, 1996). On the history and interrelationships between international human rights, indigenous peoples, and global legal institutions, see Tennant (1994) and Kingsbury (1998) for a constructivist account of indigenous and minority peoples' rights.

13 On the concept of articulation, see Hall (1996).

14 On the historical links between British landscape aesthetics and the politics and poetics of imposing a national park system on British colonies in Tanganyika, see Neumann (1995, 1996); on links between the production of toxic landscapes and landscape descriptions in the United States, see Kuletz (1998); on cultural images of the marine sphere and its links to conceptions of space, territory, and resources, see Lowe (1997, in press); on political and cultural dimensions of landscape in Western European societies, see Mitchell (1994).

15 For critical historical analyses of the cultural fashioning of African forests, see Fairhead and Leach (1996) and Leach and Mearns (1996); on the anthropogenic nature of Latin American forests, see Padoch and Pinedo-Vasquez (1996), Alcorn (1981), and Roosevelt (1980, 1997, in press). On the cultural making of Indonesian forests, see Michon et al. (2000), Padoch (1994), Peluso and Padoch (1996), Tsing (1994), Padoch and Peters (1993), and Potter (1987a,b).

16 See Pollan's (1991) meditations on weeds, gardens, and American social history for an account of the cultural consequences of the American cult of the wild.

17 On the insights and implications of the "new ecology," see Zimmerer (1994), Worster (1990), Botkin (1990), and Pickett, Parker, and Fiedler (1992). See Zimmerer (1998) for an insightful analysis of the lessons of the "new ecology" for conservation theory and practice in developing countries.

18 On forest fashioning in Sumatra, see Michon and de Foresta (2000) and Michon et al. (1999).

19 I am indebted to recent work by Anna Tsing (1999) and Tania Li (1999, 2000, 2001), building on Stuart Hall's (1996) concept of articulation.

20 Roseman has executed a variety of transformative operations in making her asser-

tions that trance narratives are the equivalent of culturally distinctive territorial claims: she has made transcripts, translated them into English, then performed an exegesis of the English-language transcripts. Her process involves translation in all four senses: conveying, language-ing, transforming, and moving.

21 On indigenous peoples and recognition of territorial claims, based on the idea of collective territories and spatial perimeters, see Lynch (1992) and Moniaga (1993). On community-based resource management and collective property rights more generally, see Lynch and Talbot (1995), Birkes (1989), McKay and Acheson (1987), National Research Council (1986), Bromley (1989), and Wright and Western (1994). See Zerner (1994a, 1999, 2000) on more general concepts in international environmentalism and environmental justice. For assessments of community-based natural resources management, see Brosius et al. (1998), Li (2000, 2001) and Goldman (1997, 1998).

22 See Zerner (1994a) on non-governmental imageries of Moluccan communities and customary environmental law, and links to earlier Dutch adat scholarship. On the shared assumptions of common property scholars, see Goldman (1997). See Li (2000) and Tsing (1999) for astute analyses of the way in which the "tribal slot" and the tribal imaginary have been articulated and deployed as both sword and shield in the context of development. See Li (2001) for an analysis of the risks and concerns that campaigns for land-rights recognition based on a "politics of difference" rather than a discourse of citizenship may pose. On the dangers posed by these campaigns linking space and ethnicity, see Malkki (1992), Zerner (1994c).

23 On the effects of cyanide fishing on the reefs and fish of the Indo-Pacific, see Johannes and Riepen (1995). See Lowe (1997, 2000) on the dynamics of cyanide fishing and international conservation efforts in the Togean Islands of Sulawesi.

24 See Peluso and Watts (2001) for political-ecological perspectives on violence and resource extraction in a variety of geographic and political-economic contexts.

25 See Hale (1994) on historical memory and contested notions of land rights among the Miskito peoples of Nicaragua. See Boyarin (1994) generally on the politics of memory in time and space. On cultural performances in public spaces, fashioned as a form of resistance to state acts of terror, see Taylor (1997) and Schirmer (1994). The marches of the Mothers of the Plaza de Mayo were, in part, a way of making the memory of "disappearance" of the victims of Argentina's dirty war palpable.

Cultivating the Wild: Honey-Hunting and Forest Management in Southeast Kalimantan

Anna Lowenhaupt Tsing

Chopping tumeric, crushing tumeric
Chopping on a bamban leaf.
Ladies don't sting us,
For aren't we together in the forest?

Clinging to a tree branch high above the ground in the pitch dark of a moon-less night, a Meratus honey hunter raises his voice to sing verses like these to charm and calm the bees. In the Meratus Mountains of southeastern Kali-mantan, Indonesia, migratory bees make their combs under the carefully cleaned branches of great rainforest trees, perhaps one hundred or more feet off the forest floor. Brave young men scale the trees to harvest the combs in the dark of moonless nights. Before they approach the comb, while perched in the dark high above the ground, they sing to the bees to keep them from stinging. Between the danger, the song, the beauty of the fireworks' sparks that drive away the bees, and the sweetness of the honey afterward, these were nights for all of us there to anticipate and remember.[1]

The excitement of honey hunting involves more than a good story. The ex-citement reminds us that we are dealing not just with things but with mean-ings. Popular and scholarly economists and ecologists have worked hard to obscure the fact that resource use is always a matter of aesthetics in its broad-est sense: feelings, sensibility, moral vision. Instead, economic production and environmental resource use are said to be neutral matters of efficiency, natural capacity, and profit margins. This convention of thinking hides, but does not stop, the making and affirming of cultural frameworks in all human activities. It also hides attempts to export particular cultural frameworks globally under the guise of neutral knowledge. In this essay, I am concerned with a powerful set of conceptual frameworks through which the environ-ment is explored, managed, converted, and conserved. I argue that these frameworks get in the way of understanding not just Meratus honey hunt-

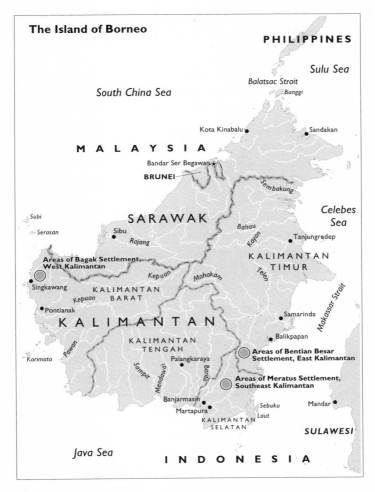

Meratus Settlement Area, Kalimantan, Indonesia.

ing, but also Meratus—and other—alternatives for creating long-term associations between people and forests. In the process, I must theorize both the excitement of those Meratus nights and the blinding magic of the international economic and ecological projects that separate scientists, activists, and policymakers from Meratus insights.

When European naturalists walked into the great forests of Borneo in the last part of the nineteenth century, they thought they had found a profoundly stable natural resource that would remain in all its immensity for as long as they could imagine.[2] Their predictions, perhaps unwittingly, played a small part in legitimating a now still-accelerating process of forest destruction. A century later, environmental scientists and advocates have found these same forests dwindling, precarious, and fragile. Plywood and construction-wood timbering take down vast tracts daily. Plantation and peasant agricultural expansion clear many hectares of new fields. Hydroelectric power dams flood once-forested valleys. Transmigration and resettlement projects gnaw at the remaining edges of the forest. Conservationists fight to save a few forest parks, as national policymakers remind them of the human needs forest conversion serves. But only recently has international attention been drawn to both the social needs and the ecological knowledge of the communities of shifting cultivators and foragers who have lived in these forests for a very long time.

An awareness is growing among environmentalists, scholars, and progressive policymakers that the indigenous inhabitants of forest environments deserve a great deal more recognition than they have been getting: first, they have established rights to forest resources, which national governments and transnational corporations must learn to acknowledge; and second, they know a lot about the long-term coexistence of people and forests, which policymakers and environmental scholars could well afford to learn from before all the forests are gone. Indeed, these two elements of recognition are inseparable since one must appreciate local forest-use practices to understand local resource claims. But because governments, corporations, policymakers, and scientists are best trained to absorb information through already familiar frameworks, the question of how to acknowledge the resource rights and learn from the knowledge of forest-living communities is not a simple one. If we do not want to impose inappropriate cultural standards and their associated environmental practices (And haven't these so often proved destructive?), we must take very seriously other ways of understanding and making "rights" and "forests." Yet this stimulates the difficult process of self-reflection in which we glimpse the limits of our most familiar assumptions about humans and nature. This chapter crafts tools to build respectful multicultural conversations on long-term human management of tropical forests.

My approach works to avoid two analytic pitfalls that characterize much recent literature on the knowledge of indigenous peoples of the rainforest. One could call these pitfalls a "dematerialized aestheticism" and a "deaestheticized materialism."[3] The former approach contrasts the values of forest-living peoples—taken as a bloc—and those of "modern," industrial peoples; too often, it only reaffirms conventional urban prejudices (positive or negative) that forest-living peoples, like forested nature, are holistic and spiritual against an imagined technical and instrumental modern consciousness. It exoticizes and romanticizes the wild.[4] In contrast, the latter approach treats forest landscapes as sites of nonculturally defined natural resources that are to be managed rationally, as commodities on the world market. Forest-living people and urban people are assumed to be the same in their desire to maximize benefits from natural resources; if the former have some useful know-how, it should be easy for the latter to mine this technical information. This approach discourages its experts from considering how diverse groups of people conceptualize natural resources and economic values. In this, it overgeneralizes from familiar cultural values and then pretends those values do not exist.[5] To avoid these pitfalls, we must formulate new ways of addressing both where to look and how to look at human–forest relationships.

Where to Look: Between Systems and Resources

Sometimes a small ecological detail can illuminate a broad field of inquiry. For Meratus Dayaks of South Kalimantan, honey-hunting, while not unimportant, is only one of many ways to use, transform, and conserve forest resources. Meratus Dayaks are shifting cultivators whose major crop is rice. In focusing on the cultural ecology of a minor forest product, my approach here contrasts with scholarly attempts to capture the total cultural and ecological systems of forest-living peoples. Such "total systems" approaches can overemphasize a group's major subsistence activity and neglect the historical particularities of other subsistence forms.[6]

My approach also contrasts with the other pole of scholarly insight: the universalization of market economy definitions of resource elements. In contrast to studies of major subsistence systems, most studies of cash crops and forest products define resources through their entry into networks of world trade. These studies have paid too little attention to the local meanings and practices in which crops and forest products are defined and renegotiated as they make their way to local, regional, and international markets; instead, resources are described as nonsocially determined natural objects, prefit as world-market commodities.[7] Yet natural resources are cultural resources; commodities are both cultural and natural objects. Trade involves forest-living communities in cultural negotiations with other resource managers. Their interactions define and create conflicting environmental technologies of knowledge and use.[8]

For centuries, Meratus Dayaks have sold forest products and cash crops (including, in various eras, rattan, rubber, resins, incense woods, bamboo, peanuts, pepper, and much more) at regional markets, from which the products have been transported to globally dispersed buyers.[9] Honey and beeswax, which I describe here mainly as they circulate without monetary value among Meratus, are also sold to regional buyers when they are plentiful enough.[10] Yet products do not become commodities in the same way in New York, Jakarta, and the Meratus Mountains. Commodities are made within *local* as well as global economies. Histories of trade, as well as of forest administration and coercion, are also histories of cultural and political negotiation. Trade does not create homogeneous cultural worlds or egalitarian political positions. The challenge for both advocates and scholars is to create a fuller recognition for the local cultural processes obscured by the imagined naturalness and universality of the market.

How to Look: Evading Powerful Tendencies in Thinking about Forests

Two powerful tendencies in popular and scholarly ecological thinking about forests correspond in some ways to the pitfalls of "dematerialized aestheticism" and "deaestheticized materialism." In the first tendency, forests are outside the realm of human culture and cultivation: forests are *wild*—and thus mysterious, unpredictable, Other to human knowledge. It is the wildness of forests that makes for the strength of agendas to tame and convert—and thus destroy—forests for human uses; it is also wildness that environmentalists want to protect. In the other tendency, forests are like any other set of resources available for human use; forests are a storehouse of natural commodities. Commodities are owned, traded, conserved, or converted, according to their market value, and thus forest protection or destruction is a market question. These two tendencies affect environmental scholarship and policy making because they draw upon long-standing traditions in European and North American thinking about nature. Yet neither of these ways of understanding forests allows us to understand the ecological knowledges and practices that have allowed people to live in forests over long periods—at least those people I know best.

What are the implications of thinking of forests as "wild"? In much European and North American writing about forests, whether literary or scientific, forests are wild spaces as opposed to settled spaces; forests are wild plants harboring wild animals, as opposed to the domesticated products and places of agriculture and stock-raising. Forests are nature as opposed to human creation.[11] The sets of contrasts that make forests wild are multifaceted, particular, and sometimes contradictory. Forest wildness takes on idiosyncratic, unexpected shapes as it is negotiated in specific projects of environmental scholarship and policy.[12] Yet familiar wild–settled distinctions reemerge across the globe as they are carried with international projects of "civilization" and "development." In Kalimantan, forests are timbered, converted to permanent farmland, or flooded in dam projects precisely because they are wild nature, waiting for development. The logic of development requires raw nature to be turned to the purposes of progress, culture, and human well-being. Kalimantan forests, from the perspective of national development planners, *are* that raw nature.

This classificatory framework has a long history in the region. European merchants, settlers, and colonial agents differentiated environments and peoples they considered settled versus wild and dealt rather differently with each. Postcolonial governments have tended to follow colonial precedence in creating different policies for settled versus wild peoples and places. In late-twentieth-century Indonesia, the "wild" people were *masyarakat terasing,* "isolated populations," who were (and are) targets of coerced resettlement and "guidance" into state-approved norms of civilization. The wild places were mainly *hutan,* "forests," which, by virtue of such classification were controlled by the national government and managed by the Ministry of Forestry.[13] Until recent environmentalist-led contests, community forest use and management have been constrained by the dominance of national resource priorities over customary and community-based claims; from the perspective of national managers, these are wild places. Yet the process of making forests appropriately wild has not been simple. In the Meratus Mountains, for example, mapping practices in the 1970s, when the country was "opened" to investment, overestimated primary forest; logging company reports from this period found all their territories uninhabited. Classified as masyarakat terasing, the local forest-living people, the Meratus Dayaks, became "nomads" with no political rights or land claims.[14] Through such processes, forests became officially nonsettled, wild. This is a framework that disenfranchised forest-living peoples, denying their very existence except as ragged refugees headed for resettlement camps.

The classification of forests as wild does not always operate as a legitimation for forest destruction. Environmentalists have championed the protection of wild places; forest conservation is high on environmentalist agendas. But perhaps commitments to this framework help explain why it has taken environmentalists so long to recognize the dilemmas facing forest-living peoples. Many powerful conservation organizations still consider people who live in or near forests to be the main enemies of the wild. Furthermore, advocates for forest-living peoples have been sorely tempted to portray "natives" with the same vulnerable and big-eyed endearment with which conservationists portray endangered animals. Yet the need for new frameworks has become apparent. Environmentalists have increasingly begun to look for new ways to imagine forests that are not just "wild" but instead accommodate human uses.[15]

The most easily available tools to do so are those of an equally problematic framework: the classification of forest resources as natural commodities. Like the concept of wildness, the concept of natural commodities does not automatically disenfranchise people like the Meratus Dayaks. Many activists and policymakers have tried to extend commodity-oriented property rights over natural resources, and even knowledge about natural resources, to include forest-living peoples.[16] However, this task is not simple, because resources as natural commodities (like wildness) are *created* within a particular cultural and economic system. To the extent that Meratus are excluded or marginalized from this system, and to the extent that they have different understandings and practices involving nature, there are different kinds of cultural-natural objects in Meratus forests. The claims over these objects are not commodity-property claims. If we take the idea of the *rights* of forest-living people seriously, we must stretch our ideas about resource claims rather than look for easy matches with familiar international conventions.[17]

Commodity standards for resource claims are taken for granted by most environmentalists, scholars, and policymakers. Their attributes seem so "natural" as to seem almost silly to bring up at all—until one thinks about just whom they exclude. Governments build commodity standards into their legal systems of property ownership, thus creating new, state-enforced objects: commodity-property. Claims on resources must take this particular form for state protection.

Two elements are important for this discussion. First, commodity-property claims divorce claimed objects from social context and personal aura. Commodity-property claims are "bureaucratic," to borrow a term developed for talking about politics: claims must be impersonal, passive, context-free, and transferable to be enforced by the state. Commodities are defined by their market value even if they are held for reasons other than sale; commodity-property claims are assessed and enforced in relation to impersonal transferability. For example, we might think about the importance of *visual* cues as property markers (a sign, a fence); aural cues (telling one's claims) tend to be much more context- and person-dependent. Furthermore, the demands of these conventions of property holding are even more pressing as one attempts to claim resources on the "wild" side of the settled–wild divide. One does not need to post a "No Trespassing" sign on a house or a monocropped field to legally warn others off; on a forest or meadow, one must have a fence or a sign.

A second element of the definition of commodity-property claims is equally important in thinking about natural resources: rights to distribute the product are the basis of rights to management. It is the ability to sell an object that defines an owner's commodity-property rights. The owner's right to control the preservation or conversion of the resource is derivative from this market right. Furthermore, in many cases, when governments devolve natural resources to private interests, they expect the "improvement" of those resources, that is, their conversion for profit. In the United States, for example, one can claim an antique just to admire it, but no one gets a license to use resources in a national forest unless he can show that he plans to benefit from his chosen product. Certainly, these are conventions that have often encouraged the destruction of forests.

They are not familiar conventions everywhere; take, for instance, Meratus Dayak relations with honeybees and honey trees. Meratus stake claims over many forest resources, including the forest trees on which honeybees may make their nests. Honey trees are valuable claims. They may be bought and sold, and the price is high. But notions of commodity-property are far too blunt a tool with which to appreciate the specificity of Meratus claims that allow management over long-term forest resources.

It might be useful to consider Meratus claims on honey trees to be "charismatic" rather than "bureaucratic" claims, in Weberian political language. Honey-tree claims require a great deal of personal activity; one must constantly visit, clean, watch, climb, and—most importantly perhaps—narrate one's claims. Without these activities, a man "forgets" and loses his trees. Furthermore, honey-tree claims do not offer the claimant even a better share of the honey and larvae harvested from the tree. Honey is distributed to neighbors, kin, and visitors; everyone who asks or, better yet, comes along on a honey hunt gets a share. "Honey claims," which require sharing, are thus organizationally and conceptually separate from "honey-tree claims," which call for management. What the tree claimant gets is not so much rights over the product as the rights to be the organizing center of a social circle. He calls the honey hunt and pours out the honey shares; he becomes a social initiator. The complex of Meratus honey and honey-tree claims thus fits simultaneously but awkwardly into classifications as individual and common property. The problematic issue is not the unit of ownership, but the kind of claim. Meratus honey-sharing claims spread widely and democratically within an unbounded and expansive social network. They depend on but are not synonymous with honey-tree claims, which focus on rights to social management, not on rights to benefit from the product. Honey-tree claims are personal and active. In these ways, they can force us to see beyond standard commodity-property conventions.

Meratus relations with bees and honey trees also refuse the dichotomies that make the forests, and their fauna, wild. Meratus live with forests; in this sense, they refuse these dichotomies, "cultivating the wild." Are honey trees and honeybees wild? Meratus claim, protect, and prepare honey trees, and they sometimes even plant them. They imagine a relationship with particular migratory honeybee swarms whose descendants, they say, come back year after year to the same trees. Yet in neither of the cases of bees or honey trees does it make sense to say that these are "domestic" animals and plants. The division between domestic and wild charts relations to plants and animals in a binary opposition between full human control and no human influence; the cases I am discussing do not fit neatly on either side. To call bees and trees "semi-domestic" merely hides the inappropriateness of the framework. Instead, we need an analysis that can appreciate other ecological frameworks. In place of the wild-domestic divide, which rests on the supposed stability of family households (that is, the "domestic") as the social relation that guides thinking, Meratus ecological discourse on bees calls up imagery of travel, trade, and marriage. Bees are visiting trading partners and in-laws, not family dependents. Meratus imagery brings in focus the long cycles, irregular activities, and wide forest spaces that are intrinsic to the Meratus economy. Only if we expand our ecological analyses to take in such alternative frameworks can we begin to imagine varied relationships between people and forests.

Animal Lovers?

Before I move further into the details of Meratus relationships with bees, it is important to clarify that, in attending to the rhetoric of bee talk, I am not describing some kind of primitive "nature worship." The idea that forest-living people, unlike urban folk, always know nature in spiritual and human, rather than technical, forms is unfortunately more prevalent than ever. To the contrary, Meratus Dayaks know a great deal more about the technical features of their forests than any of the "experts" I met in the region. And every Western scientific and nonscientific treatise on nature I have read *requires* a social rhetoric and cultural imagination in order to pick objects of knowledge and techniques of analysis. Environmental practices in the most "developed" cities and countrysides of the world all involve treating plants, animals, and elements of the landscape "as kin"—that is, in ways that are related to people's understandings of human society.

This is particularly easy to illustrate in discussing bees.[18] In the European imagination, bees have been a troubling yet "good to think with" natural object. In relation to the line between the domestic and the wild, honeybees have required multiple reaffirmations. Honeybees are a problem: unlike more fully domesticated animals, they do not require human provisions for their sustenance; and, despite recent advances in artificial insemination, honeybees can mate and reproduce outside of human supervision. Although European honeybees (*Apis mellifera*) have often been content to live in human-prepared hives, they have always been likely to "abscond"—to fly off with the queen to build a hive somewhere else. For many centuries, European peasants had the idea of banging kitchen utensils and hearth implements such as pans, kettles, spoons, and fire shovels to keep the bees from absconding. It is not clear whether the bees cared. However, the symbolism seems clear: the bees are reminded of their appropriate "domestic" orientation. One might also think about the nineteenth-century English custom of "telling the bees" when a death or a marriage in the human smallholder family occurred. By treating the bees as part of the family, the family hoped to keep them so.

European and North American beekeeping practices advanced toward greater domestic control in the nineteenth century, particularly after the 1851 invention of the movable-frame hive, which allowed beekeepers to harvest honey without particularly disturbing the reproduction of the colony. The rise of new concepts of property and labor in the late nineteenth century moved these stabilized bee colonies in a new, "industrial" direction: bee colonies became interchangeable economic investments as well as domestic sources of honey, pleasure, and wisdom. Twentieth-century U.S. capitalism elaborated this far beyond nineteenth-century imaginations; migratory fleets of trucks shipped out hives by the thousands to pollinate agribusiness fields. The rhetoric of beekeeping here merged with that of low-wage migrant labor—with its fears of undercutting prices, unfair competition, and the spread of bad hygiene and disease.

A particularly dramatic development occurred with the spread of African-derived bees—the so-called killer bees—into the United States from South and Central America.[19] African bees are the same species as the European races that have colonized North America; they hybridize readily. The human social subtext is hard to miss in talk of these new bees, as newspapers, agricultural officers, and bee scientists write of their fears of "racial mixing," the out-of-control reproduction of the Africanized populations, and the heady sexuality of the African males who threaten gentle and productive European races. The swarms catch illegal rides across the border, hanging on to the bottom of trucks with all the other dangerous mulatto and mestizo aliens, and it becomes difficult to separate the agricultural and immigration officials who hunt each species down to its hiding places under bridges and in junkyards.

My point is simple: people know nature through cultural frameworks. Meratus Dayaks are no different.

Visitors and Signposts in Meratus Forests: Bees and Trees

The Meratus Mountains are a rainforested area, but they are not the "forest primeval" that so impresses Western visitors. Comparatively speaking, the forest looks scrubby and mixed. Secondary and mature forest interpenetrate, and even the largest sectors of mature forest are marked by multiple human uses. Rather than discouraging international interest, it seems to me that this kind of forest, the product of long-term human management, is of exceptional importance for thinking about the future of human–forest associations.

Since the 1970s, the Meratus forest has come under considerable pressure as transnational timber companies, dams, resettlement projects, and pioneer farmers from other areas have made rapidly increasing claims.[20] As far as the national and regional government is concerned, this was unclaimed forest. Activist attempts to establish community-based or customary claims on the Meratus forest have had limited success, at least up through the end of the twentieth century.

Meratus communities differ a great deal from one area to another, and the forms and procedures of claims over resources are one of the most variable features of Meratus social life. I found all the kinds of land-rights systems reported for Dayak groups across Borneo—and more—in various Meratus areas. Border areas are perhaps the most creative, as Meratus respond to the urgent competing claims of immigrants, commercial resource concessions, and government officials. In this essay, I focus on the area that is most removed from these competitions, the central mountains. My "ethnographic present" is the period of my initial research in the area, the early to mid-1980s, when most of this area—while in no sense primordial and isolated—was relatively out of the way of immigration, resettlement, and transnational timber cutting.

Meratus Dayaks of the central mountains are shifting cultivators who grow

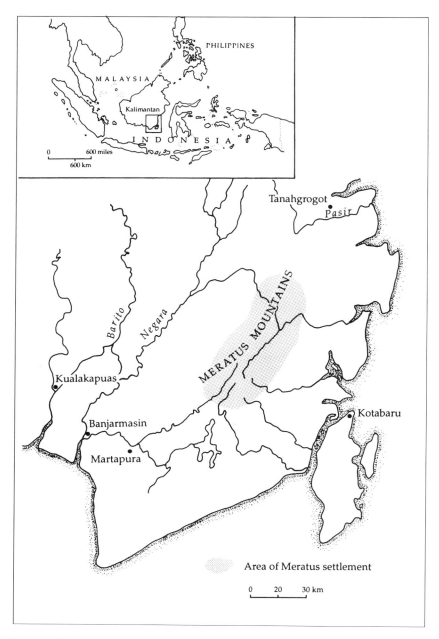

Figure 1. Meratus Settlement Area, Southeast Kalimantan, Indonesia.

upland rice and a large variety of vegetables in small, scattered swiddens surrounded by forest. Forest–swidden cycles range from five to fifty or more years. This is not an area in which forests are managed as bounded plantations, set aside for perpetual wood and fruit production. There are places that have not been farmed within historical memory and places that for varied reasons seem inappropriate for farming. Yet the managed landscape is an unstable, ever-changing patchwork marked by forested former and future swiddens.

Claimed trees, including *linuh,* or "honey trees" (these are the trees on which honeybees make their nests), are saved and protected in making swiddens and thus dominate regrowing secondary forest. Because a large variety of tree species are each sparsely dispersed across the landscape, saved trees are important sources of seed dispersal for species reproduction. Fruit and honey trees, as well as rattans, rubber, and other long-period crops, are also planted in swiddens; these become important components of the regrowing forest. Stumps left in clearing the swidden often resprout to become part of the new forest. Spontaneously growing trees in ex-swiddens are also differentially protected and encouraged as the new forest grows up. These are some of the ways in which the forest can be considered "managed."

Meratus livelihood strategies foster personal familiarity with large tracts of both secondary and mature forest. The forest is not per se a frightening place for Meratus, as it is for many other Southeast Asians. Instead, familiar forest is part of a person's daily haunts as well as personal history. Everyday travels through familiar forests remind people of their past experiences. And people tell stories of their past by recalling their movements across the forested landscape.

Trees are key to social understandings of the landscape here. Even the most unimportant secondary forest trees are seen in relation to histories; their species and girth mark the time elapsed since an area was once a swidden. Mature forest trees are recalled in relation to sites of resource use and travel. Claimed trees are most significant of all. Claimed trees of any stature tend to have not just species names, but individual names: "the Lime Creek Durian," or "Bent Bachelor Fig." Named trees are signposts by which people identify locations. Meratus talk about the landscape by mentioning the relevant trees. The forest landscape is thus always a *social* landscape, not a "wild" place.

In contrast to the long-term stability of the big forest trees, most animal resources in the Meratus forests are transient and mobile. Perhaps the most important meat source in the mountains is the migratory wild pig; constant forest travel keeps potential hunters alert to the signs of the pigs' irregular routes. Similarly, Meratus frameworks for use of other animals are attuned to mobility and irregular seasonality. First, Meratus recognize the finely differentiated niches of forest fauna and make full use of their diversity. Second, personal familiarity with the tree-marked vegetational landscape allows attention to particular sites and their seasonal changes. Mindfulness of diversity accumulates knowledge of floral and faunal associations and builds recognition of the heterogeneity and specificity of particular sites. Grounded in tree-based knowledge of sites and attuned to the mobility and seasonality of animal visitors, Meratus forest use offers a technology of localization that moves beyond appreciation of abstract niches to *place*-particular natural histories.

Meratus attention to resource species and niche diversity is clear in their use of bees. Although only one kind of bee is a major honey producer in the Meratus Mountains, the honey of three other minor producers is also gathered. Stingless bees (*kalulut,* probably *Trigona iridipennis*) provide sweet-sour honey and a sticky wax resin used for musical instruments and noisemakers. Kalulut form a lumpy comb of irregularly shaped honey pots in hollow spaces, such as bamboo nodes with an entrance crack. Meratus sometimes set up hives for these bees, hoping some will settle there. But kalulut nests are most commonly found incidentally while walking in the forest.

The smallest of the true honey bees are *indu bantal* (*Apis florea*), or "pillow bees," named after their semicircular combs built hanging from branches, which are reminiscent of small pillows. Meratus harvest the combs of indu bantal when they find them. There are also *manda luang* or *indu luang* (*Apis cerana*), or "hole bees," which build their nests in the hollows of trees. In other areas of Asia, a beekeeping industry has been built with manda luang, but Meratus instead watch for their nests as they pass the likely locations they know from previous travels. They smoke the bees out to gather the honey.

Attention to these minor honey sources increases a traveler's knowledge of forest heterogeneity. In contrast, the forest is reshaped to accommodate the major honeybee of the Meratus Mountains: *indu wanyi* (*Apis dorsata*). Indu wanyi build single combs hanging from the branches of tall forest trees—the linuh "honey trees." Unlike European honeybees, they prefer good exposure, giving access to the sky by which they orient their dancing. Meratus prepare trees to make them attractive to indu wanyi by cleaning off overhanging vines and felling surrounding small trees and brush to create light around the tree. Bees are most likely to build nests on cleaned and prepared trees, although they also find their own sites. To the extent that the bees prefer prepared locations, it is possible to speak of mutuality in the relationship of indu wanyi bees, honey trees, and people. Human activities encourage both honey trees and bees, as all three coexist in the forest.

The great forest emergents with tall straight boles and wide-spreading crowns make the best honey trees. The tallest tree of the Bornean rainforest, the *mangaris* (*Koompassia excelsa*), is such a popular site for bee colonies that in some Bornean languages this tree is just called "honey tree." A single well-built mangaris can support over fifty colonies. But many other tree species also grow into good honeycomb sites. Large wild figs and the dipterocarps that are the dominant giants of Bornean forests make good honey trees, and even a tropical conifer (*Agathis beccarii,* Meratus *mampiring*) can occasionally support bees' nests. My Meratus friends easily listed a dozen tree species that commonly supported bees. The best individual trees have colorful names: "The Bachelor *Jalamu*," "The Stooping *Salang'ai*," "The *Mangaris* Where He Fell."

Meratus expect bee colonies to settle on their honey trees irregularly, following the season's flowers. The nests do not last long; as bee foraging returns diminish, the colony migrates to a better site, closer to abundant flowers. Some years, no bees settle in a given area at all. Meratus know the qualities of honey produced from different flowers: the sweet-sour honey made from the flowers of litchi-like *siwao* and *maritam* fruit trees (*Nephelium* spp.); the fine light honey made from the white-blossomed *irahan* vine (*Spatholobus ferrugineus*). But flowering seasons are somewhat irregular in the Meratus Mountains, and men must keep their eyes peeled as they walk through the forest following game or gathering bamboo shoots, watching for the coming of bees.

Migration is central to Meratus understandings of indu wanyi. Sometimes people say that the bees have their own land, where they farm rice swiddens like Meratus, in a distant place where the *pau janggi* trees grow.[21] Only when a fragrant season of flowers beckon do the bees cross the River of Changes to fly into the Meratus Mountains as bees. This is a model that acknowledges the long-distance mobility over irregular vegetation and seasonality that these bees require.[22] Both humans and animals, Meratus say, travel freely to "follow their luck."

An Expedition to the Tree

A Meratus honey hunt is a thrilling expedition that is quite different from beekeeping in a household or commercial economy. In place of the frugal beekeeper of traditional European imagery, there is a daring hunter leading a giddy and expectant group of kin and neighbors to the honey tree. Brave young men become heroes as their midnight ascent into the treetops is watched with bated breath. And everyone is rewarded with honey. These aspects of the honey hunt—its ability to animate a wide but flexible social network, its moment of fame for focal individuals, and its insistence on equal and widespread sharing—are important features for understanding the more general shape of the Meratus economy. Honey hunts are also fun.

When a good honey season begins, the word spreads quickly. Hikers walk with their necks craned, searching for the black combs dripping from high branches. Bee news is on everyone's lips: Ma Icit's binuang tree on Long Ridge has eleven swarms; Ma Tiwas's tree above Lime Creek has eight, but one is on a knotty growth and can't be reached. Bees begin to make their presence known even around houses, where they venture inside the door to drink from bamboo water tubes. By then, preparations for honey-hunting have probably already begun with the carving of bamboo stakes to climb the tree, the cleaning of kerosene cans and bark baskets to hold the honey, and the making of vine ropes, rattan strainers, and other paraphernalia.

A honey expedition begins in the afternoon as a party of honey lovers departs for the tree carrying cans, vines, stakes, baskets, and fat bamboo tubes to carry the honey home. Usually only men climb the tree; women and children come along for a share of the honey, the larvae, and the excitement. The tree is scaled by hammering bamboo stakes at intervals along the trunk and fastening thin bamboo poles, end to end, to form a scaling ladder. The actual gathering of honey must wait until absolute darkness (see fig. 2). Any source of light, even a fire at the base of the tree, orients the bees so they know where to sting. No honey can be gathered if the moon is up, as these bees are very light-oriented and even forage on moonlit nights.

Figure 2. Hammering stakes to scale the tree at dusk. The actual gathering of honey must wait until absolute darkness. Photograph by Anna Tsing, 1986.

At the base of the tree, the designated climber mutters spells for strength and self-protection during his climb. Carrying a palm-hair torch, a cigarette lighter, and a can or basket for the honey, he begins the ascent up the bole and on to the branch from which the honey hangs. Perhaps a hundred feet off the ground, he may have to crawl an additional fifty feet out along the branch to reach the comb. And all of this is in total darkness.

Sitting on the branch in the darkness so far above the ground, a climber begins to sing to the bees.

> A split rock, a fractured rock,
> The split rock at Miyambut.
> Here they come from across the divide
> The ladies powdered with dew drops.

The ladies from across the divide are the bees. The song has the form of a *pantun,* a four-line verse with a message about courtship. The first two lines create an image from nature, often a metaphor for the love sentiment; the second two lines offer the message directly, enhanced by rhythms and rhymes hard to preserve in translation. Young men and women tease each other with such verses. In bee songs, the climber "courts" the bees, hoping to charm them.

> Chopping tumeric, crushing tumeric,
> Golden slivers on a tray.
> These bees won't sting us—
> For we're betrothed to the bee children!

> The bubut bird and the squirrel
> Both nest in the pelajao tree.
> As my voice drifts to the ground
> May the comb be big as a Chinese jar.

Bee songs are sung to charm the bees, not only as lovers but also as children, pleased and calmed with a lullaby. Although they follow the courtship verse format, bee songs are called *timang,* classing them with the songs used to comfort and amuse babies. Just as lullabies calm a child's crying, Meratus hope bee songs will keep the bees from stinging.[23]

Bee songs also artfully describe honey hunting itself. In these next verses, the woodpecker's tap is the sound of stakes hammered into the tree trunk and the snake's tail is the vine that lowers the honey to the ground. The verses capture some of the excitement of the event.

> Woodpecker's tap-tap
> On the honey tree.
> I'm drunk with singing,
> But I shan't let go.
> Lower down the python's tail,
> Let it to the ground.
> Come down laughing ladies
> As we shower you with gold.

When the climber finishes his songs, he lights the palm-hair torch he has carried into the tree and wipes it across the comb. The torch emits a shower of sparks that floats down in a spectacular display (see fig. 3). (These sparks are the gold of the verse above, as well as the golden tumeric of the earlier verses.) As the sparks fall, the bees follow them. A low droning hum that seems to have no source fills the air. When the torch is put out, most of the bees have followed the sparks to the ground.

What remains is to cut off the comb, separating the heavy, irregularly shaped, honey-filled "head" from the traylike brood comb beneath it. The cans of honeycomb and baskets of brood comb can be lowered to the ground with vines (the "python's tail") or carried down by climbers. When a climber arrives back at the base of the tree, everyone is anxious to taste the honey.

Sometimes things do not go quite so easily. On one of my trips, the climbers were stalling because the bees were stinging badly. Then the moon began to show and there was a last mad rush to get some remaining honey before the darkness was broken. In his hurry, an older climber dropped a whole kerosene can of honey from his perch on the branch. The honey flew out in every direction, and the can was smashed beyond use. But spirits remained high. We split the honey and brood and lit dammar torches to find our way home through the dark forest—over treacherous holes and troops of fiercely stinging ants. Only a few hours remained before the sun's reappearance would mean work to do, but when we arrived home, people were up waiting to revive our spirits again with their enthusiasm for our stories.

After the long trip home through the darkness, an arriving honey party

Figure 3. As the sparks fall, the bees follow them. Photograph by Anna Tsing, 1981.

brings excitement to a lightly sleeping household. Whatever the hour, people get up for honey-tasting and bee gossip and preliminary honey distributions and the telling of adventures and mishaps until everyone is satiated with sweetness and stories.

Management and Sharing as Resource Claims

Honey distribution is very wide. Everyone who attends the honey hunt gets a full share. Shares are sent to close kin and neighbors. And anyone who arrives for a visit also gets a share. Larvae spoil more quickly; they are distributed along the same lines but limited to those who can get to them and consume them in a few days. Most of the wax, used for candles and sometimes sold at market, tends to stay with the honey-hunting party who receives first divisions of the comb; the more-valued honey is poured off for further shares.

The distribution of the products of honey hunting is independent of the system of claiming honey trees. Yet tree claims are important. A man claims a honey tree by being the first to find and prepare it. He must also keep up his work, continually visiting it, cleaning it, and harvesting the honeycombs on it. Meratus say that bees do not return to sites with unharvested, abandoned combs. If a man loses interest in a tree, someone else may claim it.

Meratus tree claims are inherited as a shared resource by the children, male and female, of the claimant. Honey-tree claims differ somewhat from other kinds of tree claims, however, because of the work required to keep up the claim. None of the women I knew were active enough in honey hunting to hold honey-tree claims; they maintained an interest in honey shares but left the claims to their brothers. Not all men are active claimants either. Unlike fruit trees, for which the sharing of claims is very important to people, honey trees tend to be discussed as having singular claimants, usually the man who most actively cares for them and climbs them or organizes climbs.

Men who claim trees talk about their claims. The men I knew were eager to list their honey trees for me, telling their specific location and condition. Such tellings slip into ordinary conversation as men discuss their comings and goings in the forest. The importance of narration in establishing claims became particularly clear to me in the contrast between two older men I

Figure 4. Everyone is anxious to taste the honey. Photograph by Anna Tsing, 1981.

knew, both of whom could no longer climb. Pa'an Suran had fallen out of a honey tree, miraculously lived, but lost feeling from his waist down. He could still farm, but he was no longer interested in bees. He told me he had forgotten the locations of all his (once many) trees. They reverted to unclaimed forest resources. In contrast, Ma Alun had developed a condition in which he could not walk, but he still hoped to be cured. He listed his more than fifty honey trees with more detail and intensity than any other account I was offered. Narrating was a means to holding his claims. This is equally true for healthy, active men.

Here, I return to the notion that honey-tree claims are "charismatic," not "bureaucratic." Holding a claim involves a great deal of personal action, most of it involving what one might call "prowess," following Jane Atkinson's (1989) terminology in discussing male leadership among the Wana of Sulawesi.[24] Honey-tree claims tap and create skills of bravery, travel, magic (to climb trees), heroism, social networking, and narration. There is an economic theory here that has nothing to do with rights to benefit from and distribute products. The theory is that abundance is attracted to prowess. The man who can hold a claim can make honey plentiful, not just for himself but for others. In that sense, he is a "charismatic" owner, calling up an abundant livelihood and an active community through his own attractiveness. When the climber courts the bees in his songs, he is doing more than pacifying them; he is enticing them into his sphere of influence. The point is not, as in the commodity-property systems with which we are more familiar, to define natural objects that establish social relations by the exclusivity of social access to them. Instead, the point is to draw both human and non-human agents of luck, livelihood, and activity into a beneficially focused network.

At particular ceremonies, communities build a pole with dozens of wooden disks hanging from its branches to represent a honey tree laden with nests. The shaman chants and dances to spread the community's social networks in spiritual directions. As in other ceremonies, the abundance-attracting charisma of the shaman—his vitality, well-being, and the breadth of his human and supernatural ties—brings abundance to the entire community. Similarly, the charisma of the courageous, agile men who know the forest and climb and claim its trees reaches an abundance-bringing focal point around each honey tree in its season.

Human and Animal Agency in Long-Term Forests

This leads me into the other wing of my argument. The form of resource claims develops together with local ecological models. The possibility of human–animal relationships requires understanding animal behavior in relation to models of agency that humans and animals are expected to share. Thus, Western models of the domestication of animals depend on a conceptual nature–culture divide in which animals are appropriate for human retraining, breeding, and enclosure because they can be made to approximate subordinate human family members. In contrast, Meratus relations with bees are forged around a model of mobility of both humans and bees in the forest.

Let me return to Meratus bee songs to describe the kinds of agency bees and people are seen to have in common—and thus their possibilities for relationship within forest mobility. First, the bees are both marriage partners and affines. In one bee song, the bees are said to be the hunters' third cousins (*dangsanak datu*), or, as Europeans might say, "kissing cousins." (It is not inappropriate in the Meratus Mountains to marry a same-generation cousin. The relationship of those descended from common great-grandparents is considered by some to have the right mix of romance-forming distance and trust-forming closeness for a marriage.) As an alliance between kin or affines, the bee–human relationship is seen as both open and enduring, with no need to bring the bees home for "domestication."

The songs also portray bees and people engaged in trade. The bees bring their "pillows" (honeycomb), "woven mats" (brood comb), and "twisted needles" (stings) to exchange for "gold"—the gold sparks of the torches used to drive the bees from the comb.

> A spice spoon, a spoon of spice,
> Spread it on a mango sprout.
> We'll buy your pillows and your mats,
> But take your twisted needles home.

As trading partners, bees and people are engaged in a long-term but only sporadically intense relationship:

> The flowers, so sweet smelling,
> The leaves drifting down.
> Come back, friends, with your pillows and mats,
> Come back again each year.

The song is an elegantly romantic statement of the expectation of sustainability. Yet such expectations in themselves cannot guarantee ecological mutuality. The trade motif celebrates social equality. Trade is defined as equal, but often enough this definition masks asymmetry. Certainly this is true in Meratus relations with human traders, who offer cheap cloth and trinkets for exorbitant prices and buy forest products for little. What about the bees, who, after all, aren't really interested in Meratus gold?

As far as I can tell, Meratus honey-hunting does not destroy the swarm. Both the queen and the workers fly away and move on to other nesting sites. Ecologists have done so little work on *Apis dorsata* migration and colony reproduction that it is impossible to compare scientific and folk views about these matters. But taking the honey and brood comb cannot help the bees; they would probably reproduce more quickly if people stopped bothering them. At the same time, bees do reasonably well in the Meratus Mountains. Meratus never harvest all the combs, many of which are in inaccessible places. Furthermore, the continuing availability of foraging and nesting sites in the Meratus forest is key. As long as Meratus maintain the forest, the bees will not suffer too badly.[25]

I am not arguing that Meratus are ecological geniuses destined to save the planet. Lots of things my Meratus friends did—like cut down all the *garu* (Borneo aloes wood) in sight when the market price was high—seemed a rather bad idea for conserving biodiversity. (Unlike honey, garu has no local uses but is harvested only as a commodity to sell at market. Irregular market pricing encourages booming sales at those moments when the price is high.) But the relationship maintained between people, honey trees, and bees is one promising example of the kind of open-ended, semi-autonomous management relations that make it possible for people and forests to live together over time. Furthermore, this three-way relationship is central within a particular set of Meratus ecological ideas and practices that offers a challenging alternative to European models. The flexibility of Meratus management of migratory bees would be difficult to achieve with an ideal of domestication; indeed, North Americans have tried to hive *Apis dorsata* without success. Instead of domesticating the bees, Meratus trade with them. Meratus bee management involves an ideal of social networking that includes both humans and bees in focused interactions. This management style aims to draw *more* social/natural resources into a person's charismatic reach. It works through the independence of management claims and product distribution schemes, which allows common needs to be met at the same time that individuals deploy their most entrepreneurial talents as managers of social and natural resources.

Many conservationists assert that the best way to keep Meratus forests in existence would be to move the people out. This, indeed, is the rhetoric of government agencies that justify the resettlement of Meratus Dayaks because it is assumed that Meratus shifting cultivation and forest foraging destroy the forest. In fact, certain Meratus forest-management practices conserve the forest in a way that may allow people and forests to live together. These are practices that are difficult for Western-trained environmental scientists to grasp because they cut across the dichotomy between domestic husbandry, on the one hand, and protection of the wild, on the other. I am suggesting that attention to local cultural ecologies may give us more tools to think about forest conservation in regions of human settlement. Furthermore, if we are even to make alliances in support of forest-living communities, we need to have a good sense of the cultural shape of their political and economic strategies before we start imposing the cultural logics we take for granted. We need a better appreciation of varied ecological models through which people live with rainforests.

I am not recommending the commercialization of *Apis dorsata* honey in the Meratus Mountains as a means to empower Meratus Dayaks. Michael Dove (1993a) has offered a scathing critique of environmentalist strategies for the mass commercialization of rainforest products. He argues that such strategies, to the extent of their commercial success, will take more forest resources out of the hands of forest-living communities rather than offering these communities more economic and political options. If honey were to become a profitable business, according to this argument, regional, national, and international business interests would not let the Meratus Dayaks control its production and distribution. Dove reminds us not to lose sight of the political weakness of forest-living communities. Pointing to the usefulness of Meratus ecological models, as I have done here, does not combat Meratus political weakness, but it does attempt to illuminate some of the lines of difference where this weakness should be challenged.

It also may point to some possibilities for environmentalist alliances with Meratus attempts to hold on to their forest livelihoods. Most advocacy for forest-living groups has begun with bounding property rights to land; this is an important cause, but not always the one local people choose. Thus, when some Meratus in one area of the well-populated western foothills were forced to respond to new incursions by timber companies in the mid-1980s, I expected at first a struggle on the logic of property boundaries. To my surprise, boundaries were not invoked; instead, two strategies were taken. First, people swamped the timber company with demands for compensation for claimed trees destroyed in logging and road making. Most of these claims were unsuccessful. Timber company officials would not compensate the large number of trees for which Meratus petitioned; they also were unwilling to recognize claims over the wide range of claimed tree species. Most forest trees, according to the timber company, are "wild" and therefore unclaimable. Yet, from the Meratus viewpoint, forest trees are not "wild." Timber company officials and Meratus claimants saw different "forests."

Second, people began to organize against the timber company by calling it—following the rhetoric of the 1940s Indonesian revolution—a "colonialist" invader. (Ironically, the company was Indonesian—and had used its national status to overcome watershed-protection logging restrictions.) Meratus opponents of commercial logging defined the problem with the timber company not as a transgression of community terrain; instead, they suggested that the timber company was an improper kind of forest-resource claimant, an unsuitable center of power and social management. Those who harangued against "colonialist" companies argued not that their own forest claims were exclusive but that some social managers, that is, claimants, are more appropriate than others. I tend to agree.

Notes

1   Papers sometimes take a long time to emerge. The ethnographic sections of this essay were first drafted in the mid-1980s—close to the period to which they refer—and then filed away. Charles Zerner kindly gave me the opportunity to use these descriptions in addressing "culture and the question of rights" in the 1992 Wilson Center symposium on this topic. Final revisions of this essay were then made in 1993 and 1994; this is the period to which the literature I cite refers.

Research in South Kalimantan was supported by fellowships from the National Institute for Mental Health and the Social Science Research Council and sponsored by the Indonesian Institute of Sciences under the direction of the late Dr.

Masri Singarimbun of Gadjah Madah University. I am grateful to James Fox and
Charles Frake who each, now quite a long time ago, encouraged me to write about
Kalimantan honey-hunting. Jane Atkinson, Don Brenneis, and Paulla Ebron have
also offered comments and encouragement. Finally, the current version of this essay took shape through conversations with Charles Zerner, who not only organized the Wilson Center symposium but also took the time to offer detailed and
substantial comments on my drafts.

2 See, for example, Beccari ([1904] 1986).

3 I first heard these terms from anthropologist and Southeast Asia scholar Shelly
Errington.

4 See, for example, Banuri and Marglin (1993), which offers a dichotomous scheme
through which to learn from forest-living peoples: there is "modern" knowledge
—individualistic, instrumentalist, disembedded, and rationalist—and there is
"nonmodern" knowledge—all the opposites of modern. This dichotomy pushes
us to learn but also constrains the nuance and range of what we might learn.

5 This is the cluster of approaches taken by most of those, whether social scientists,
natural scientists, or policymakers, considered "natural resource experts." They
identify resources and—untroubled by questions of the cultural systems that define "resources"—figure out how to use them. One illustrative example is the mi-
croeconomics approach to natural resources as explained by Anthony Scott
(1973). The political power and cultural legitimacy of such approaches can also be
seen by the way they are adopted, as science, even by those who are trying not to
universalize capitalism; it is thus possible to fall simultaneously into both the pitfalls I have outlined. For recent work on environmental justice and tropical resource extraction that conceptualizes resources as culturally defined objects, passing through what Arjun Appadurai (1986a) has called "regimes of value," see
Zerner (1999, 2000).

6 "Total systems" approaches have come to play an important role in environmental advocacy. Recent cultural/ecological scholarship has highlighted the dilemmas of indigenous peoples for whom whole ways of life are indeed in danger.
Bringing together systems-oriented approaches in ecological science (which
brought the discipline beyond the classificatory boxes of natural history) and the
cultural holism of anthropology (which moved beyond the shreds and patches of
earlier approaches to "custom"), this work has often been both academically illuminating and politically effective. However, it can come too close to that metro-
politan projection in which indigenous peoples and wild nature retain the "total-
ities" that have become fragmented in "modern" urban lives. Here, I show how
we might hold on to the important idea of the systematic interconnectedness of
elements without an overcommitment to a historically simplifying totality.

7   One illuminating example is the explicitly commerce-oriented report on forest products in Borneo written by students of the Harvard Business School (Dixon, Rodoti, and Silverman 1991). More research-oriented studies of forest products also tend to list forest resources as unproblematically "natural" objects (e.g., Dunn 1975).

8   Scholarly work on conflicts between different communities of forest users is best developed in analyses of elite and state attempts to enclose, regulate, and manage forest use; thus, for example, E. P. Thompson (1975), Ramachandra Guha (1990), and Nancy Peluso (1992c) each analyze situations in which peasant smallholders resisted attempts to cut off their use of forests. Donna Haraway's *Primate Visions* (1989) is particularly useful in theorizing the historically changing and politically contested cultural construction of natural objects.

9   For further discussion of this history, see Tsing (1984).

10   Honey, like rice, is too important within Meratus livelihood standards to sell at regional markets unless there is more than enough to go around locally. Honey is brought to market only in the very best honey seasons, and it tends to be available there, from Meratus sources, only for short periods and then unpredictably.

11   Robert Harrison's *Forests: The Shadow of Civilization* (1992) explores Western literary constructions of forests. Neil Evernden's *The Social Creation of Nature* (1992) is one of many good discussions of the construction of ideas about "nature"—in opposition to "culture"—in Western thought; Evernden's analysis is particularly illuminating about those aspects of "nature" that have come to be seen as "the environment."

12   Simon Schama's *Landscape and Memory* (1995) offers a sense of the historical particularity of national forest aesthetics in Europe.

13   The control of forest land in Indonesia has become a very much contested issue, as the question of community customary claims has been brought into national discussion by environmentalists. Zerner (1992a) discusses late-twentieth-century legislation that created a basis for community customary claims on forest land. Zerner (this volume) also explores the contested status of oceans as another state-controlled "wild" place. My discussion in this essay considers the situation in Indonesia under President Suharto, who formed a center-focused authoritarian government between 1966 and 1998.

14   For a discussion of land-use mapping in the Meratus Mountains, see Tsing (1993), which describes the effects of the classification of Meratus Dayaks as masyarakat terasing in the 1970s and 1980s. More recently, some Meratus have organized to oppose timber company logging; see, for example, "Dayak Meratus Tolak Rencana Kodeco," *Banjarmasin Post,* 6 March 2000.

15   Peter Brosius (forthcoming) has written incisively about environmentalist por-

trayals of the Penan of East Malaysia, in which the Penan are romanticized as endangered "nature"; see also Tsing (1990). Anthropologists with cross-cultural experience have not always been particularly helpful in showing alternatives to the wild–settled framework that has gained international legitimacy. French structuralism, for example, is based on the supposed cognitive universality of a familiar nature–culture dichotomy. In Borneo studies, ethnographic reports that showed the decent, orderly nature of Dayak social life were particularly common in the 1950s and 1960s; showing that Dayaks knew the difference between society and the wild was one strategy here. Geddes (1957), for example, argues that Land Dayaks of Sarawak contrast the safety and order of secondary forest "countryside" and the danger of mature "jungle." Geddes, like other ethnographers of his time, stressed rice farming to show a basis for settled land claims and played down Dayak forest use. Recent work on Dayak forest use throughout Borneo, however, has challenged familiar domestic–wild distinctions; see, for example, Nancy Peluso (this volume), Michael Dove (1993a), Jessup and Peluso (1986).

16 Oran Young (1981) reviews the depressing results of the Alaska Native Claims Settlement of 1971, which gave native corporations rights over natural resources. The settlement was an attempt to recognize native resource rights within familiar U.S. economic conventions. Yet the settlement stumbled over a contradiction: from the first, it was unclear how to run a corporation for the benefit of native welfare. Indeed, during the period covered by Young's study, none of the corporations either made money or improved native life.

17 Some activists argue that their work best focuses on the other direction of change: instead of stretching international concepts, their goal is to stretch forest-dwelling peoples' concepts until these latter can pass as internationally familiar. Thus, customary claims are brought into alignment with national legal conventions (Tsing 2002). Activists rush to place stones at newly imagined "boundaries of native lands" before national mappers can get there to record ancient custom. It is not the purpose of this essay to detract from this creative and important work. However, it is important to recognize the flexibility and dynamism of national courts as well as of local customs. Thus, for example, environmentalists' struggles to get adat ("customary law") claims over resources recognized and protected in contemporary Indonesia have required changing official meanings of adat; this is not just a matter of bringing already existing national laws and local customs into the light (Tsing 1994, 2002). Divergent local voices, however nicely retrained in dominant codes, will never be heard without improving national and international frameworks for listening.

For the purposes of this essay, which aims to provide tools for those who would advocate for forest-living communities, I am leaving aside one of the most important problems in recognizing local forest claims: the political powerlessness of these communities. Politically powerless people tend to get relocated whatever the cultural or moral standing of their claims. However, I do not want to make their political powerlessness seem an unchangeable fact.

18 The culture of North American beekeeping is discussed further in Tsing (1995).

19 Twenty-six African queens escaped from an experimental hive in Brazil in 1956 and within a few short years managed to "Africanize" the entire honeybee population of Latin America. By the 1980s, they began to cross the border into the United States with some frequency (see Tsing 1995).

20 For further discussion of regional economic and environmental issues, see Dove (1986b). One piece of the South Kalimantan transmigration program is described in Levang and Marten (1984).

21 In the Meratus discussions in which I took part, *pau janggi* was the species name of a tree found in a particular distant place. For Malays, the pau janggi is the "double coconut" (*Lodoicea maldivica*) found growing in the wild only in the Seychelle Islands. Malay sailors occasionally encountered the fruits floating in the ocean; they said the tree grew at the lands near the navel of the sea (*pusat laut*). It makes sense that Meratus have used this species to describe a tree on the other side of a water divide. And, while it is unlikely that the *Apis dorsata* of the Meratus Mountains make it to the Seychelles, Meratus lore reminds us that the migration distances of these bees are impressive—and still largely untracked by Western-trained ecologists.

22 The specificity of the Meratus model as a forest-management conceptual framework becomes clear in contrasting it with the framework that guided a U.S. attempt to capture *Apis dorsata* as a private economic investment. In an era of exuberant imperialism at the end of the nineteenth century, U.S. beekeepers decided they wanted the biggest and best bees—and that these might be available in South and Southeast Asia. In 1899, the journal *Gleanings in Bee Culture* commissioned an American missionary named Rambo to catch the bees in India. Yet each time he captured a swarm and placed it in a hive, the bees absconded. Indeed, despite patriotic exhortations, competitions, and rewards, the attempt to bring the giant bee into the American hive—tamed to the model of beekeeping they knew—was a failure. Refusing a sedentary existence, the bees preferred the lofty trees of the forest.

23 For many years bee scientists believed that bees do not hear airborne sound. More recent research, however, suggests that bees are sensitive to air-particle movements, rather than the pressure oscillations that most vertebrates detect (Towne and Kirchner 1989). Furthermore, bees detect sound transmitted through solid media. Bees use sound extensively in their own communication system. For ex-

ample, *Apis mellifera* (European honeybees) transmit a great deal of information through sound: virgin queens identify and challenge each other with noises called "tooting" and "quacking"; foraging workers recruiting others emit low-frequency pulses of sound whose length is proportional to the distance to the food source; and disturbed workers produce a "piping" sound that helps quiet the colony. Could the songs of Meratus honey hunters help calm the bees? It is possible, although there is no clear evidence. Colin Butler has observed that a person's loud singing can cause bees (in this case, *A. mellifera*) to freeze (Butler 1974). The cross-cultural prevalence of beekeeping customs using sound to calm bees, such as the European "tanging" of kitchen implements I mentioned earlier, certainly suggests that sound may have some calming effect.

24 Atkinson extends O. W. Wolter's use of the term "prowess" to describe the specific forms of male leadership among the Wana, whose social forms are similar in a number of ways to those of Meratus Dayaks.

25 Commercial logging in the 1990s destroyed honey trees, and the honey harvest, on the east side of the Meratus Mountains. At the beginning of the twenty-first century, the central mountains are threatened by the same logging company that destroyed the east side.

Sounding the Makassar Strait: The Poetics
and Politics of an Indonesian Marine Environment

Charles Zerner

The way in which the word conceptualizes its object is a complex act—all objects, open to dispute and overlain as they are with qualifications, are from one side highlighted while from the other side dimmed by heteroglot social opinion, by an alien word about them. And into this complex play of light and shadow the word enters—it becomes saturated with this play, and must determine within it the boundaries of its own semantic and stylistic contours. . . . And an artistic representation, an "image" of the object, may be penetrated by this dialogic play of verbal intentions that meet and are interwoven in it; such an image need not stifle these forces, but on the contrary, may activate and organize them. If we imagine the intention of such a word, that is, its directionality toward the object, in the form of a ray of light, then the living and unrepeatable play of colors and light on the facets of the image that it constructs can be explained as the spectral dispersion of the ray-word, not within the object itself (as would be the case in the play of an image-as-trope, in poetic speech taken in the narrow sense, in an "autotelic word"), but rather as its spectral dispersion in an atmosphere filled with alien words, value judgments and accents through which the ray passes on its way toward the object; the social atmosphere of the word, the atmosphere that surrounds the object, makes the facets of the image sparkle.—M. Bakhtin, *The Dialogic Imagination*

To articulate the past historically does not mean to recognize it "the way it really was" (Ranke). It means to seize hold of a memory as it flashes up at a moment of danger.
—Walter Benjamin, *Illuminations*

E . . . Raja! O, beautiful one! Heavenly Soul Guardian! Lord!
Arrive here all of you
Those in the south, those in the north
Those below and those above
Your ancestral drum has been launched, Lord
The drum of ancestral ways, the heirloom
There is nothing else that [you] desire

Nothing else [you] need
Let it happen!
—Pak Hadari, on board the *Rachmat*,
somewhere in the Makassar
Strait, August 1985

Introduction

Sulawesi, Indonesia's orchid-shaped island whose peninsulas point to the Flores, Celebes, Molucca, and Java Seas, has always been linked through oceans to distant worlds of ideas and practices. South Sulawesi's coastal peoples, the Bugis, the Makassarese, the Konjo, and the Mandar, are known throughout the region as long-distance traders, boatbuilders and fishermen. This essay focuses on the Mandar people of Majene Regency, on Sulawesi's southwestern flank (see fig. 5). It is from this region of poor soils and small landholdings squinched between infertile hills and the Makassar Strait, which cuts between Kalimantan and Sulawesi at depths greater than six thousand feet, that Mandar fishermen set out to wrest a living from the sea, casting their throw nets and sounding or broadcasting their fishing calls.

In South Sulawesi, between 1970 and 1995, international markets for

Figure 5. Indonesia. Map by David Lindroth.

flying-fish roe, ornamental shells, seaweed (*agar-agar*), fresh frozen tuna, and luxury markets for shark fins for export to Taiwan, Hong Kong, Singapore, and the United States, grew dramatically. National and regional markets for marine protein from scad, mackerel, and red snapper and other kinds of fin-fish, have brought outsiders or their representatives into waters formerly fished by Mandar fishermen.[1] Mandar fishers' ideas of resources, and the practices that they use to obtain them, are rapidly changing. Small-scale entrepreneurs from Java and South Sulawesi now travel the well-paved roads up the coast from the port city of Makassar, showing picture albums of seashells to villagers—men, women, and children—who they hope will collect, clean, and sell the shells to them. Local Mandar civil servants dream of harvesting new resources, such as "spiny lobster," eels, tuna, and red snapper, which they hope to ship down to Ujung Pandang, where burgeoning domestic demand and an international tourist industry fuel consumption of significant quantities of marine creatures, recently conceptualized as resources, in fresh, fried, pickled, grilled, and dried forms. Former government and military officers concoct schemes in which Mandar practices, such as raft fishing, are enveloped as "plasma" in large-scale, plantation-like marine "nuclei" focused on freezing and air-shipping local tuna to Taiwan, Japan, and the United States (Zerner 1991b, 1997).[2] And local fishers are conceptualized as targets for fisheries "development" and "explanations" about modern fisheries techniques (Escobar 1995).

Fisheries resources, like forests, are governed by an overarching national mandate: "Land, water, and their natural riches are controlled by the state and are to be utilized for the maximum prosperity of the people" (Article 33, Constitution of the Republic of Indonesia, as cited in Moniaga 1993). Supported by multiple sources of authority, including national and regional fisheries development policies, laws, and licenses, as well as the authority of the national judicial system, parastatal and private-sector fisheries operations have unparalleled access to local waters and resources.[3] Large- and medium-scale fishing craft known as "pole and liners" now enter local coves and inshore waters, capturing hundreds of tuna in the time it takes a Mandar fisher, trolling with a feathered lure, to capture one fish. New resources are being conceptualized and local practices are being modified and reshaped, with considerable ingenuity, to respond to new market opportunities.

Where new fishing technologies compete in local waters for the same

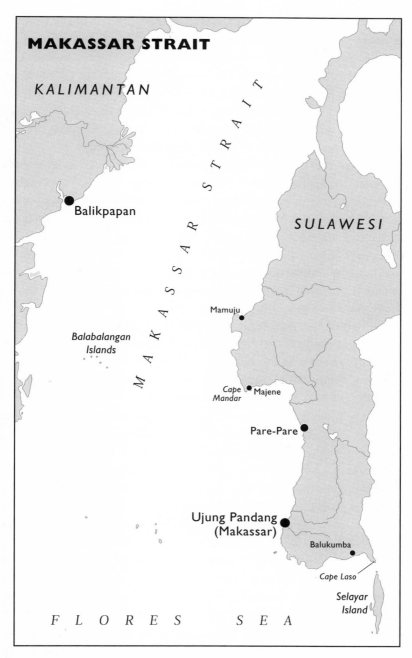

Figure 6. Mandar and the Makassar Strait, Indonesia. Map by David Lindroth.

resources historically captured by Mandar fishers, conflicts erupt. Arguments over resources, rights, and relationships to the marine environment are being forged at these sites of conflict and contestation. Where resistance to outsider intrusions is hot and active (as accounts of burnings, knife brandishings, rock wars, and public protests attest), local fishermen's images of their historical practices and emerging ideas of their rights and relationships to the marine environment are being fashioned, in part, by seizing the past "as it flashes up at a moment of danger" (Benjamin 1969: 255).

In this essay, I hope to broaden the political–ecological analysis—the study of the intersections and social and environmental consequences of conflicting levels of claims, institutions, and interests[4]—by taking seriously the notion that poetics—the study of how images and discourses are constructed —and aesthetics—the investigation of the ways in which images and discourses are felt, sensed, and perceived—penetrate and inform environmental politics. Cultural discourses, images, analogies, and tropes about the environment—the way(s) in which the world is constituted and reconstituted through talk, back-talk, and cross-talk—create the basis of new alliances, realignments of "interests," and new forms of imagining the marine realm, authority, and struggles over access and control.

By auditing the sounds, cadences, and concerns of fishermen, jurists, and capitalizers, fishing the Makassar Strait for meanings, rights, sites, and creatures in the late 1980s and early 1990s—I hope to evoke the polyphony, the overlapping and mirroring, and the back-talk that scuttles across these seas and shores, and the emergence of new ways of imagining authority and asserting rights to the marine environment.[5] The poetics and performance of Mandar soundings—how their images are constructed and delivered, and how Mandar practitioners of these arts believe these images reach and move men, spirits, fish, and ancestral authorities—are important aspects of Mandar politics and poetics in the marine realm. In extraordinary performances of calling flying fish as well as larger, pelagic fish such as tuna, tone, pitch, pacing, and poetics are part and parcel of the politics of power and the exercise of authority over the seas.[6]

In the first part of this essay I will explore the marine imaginary of contemporary Mandar fishers through their calls, fishing stories, and practices. Next, I will examine the politics and poetics of a 1988 district court ruling that nullified a system of customary marine property-rights practices on the

Figure 7. Sulawesi, Indonesia. Map by David Lindroth.

Makassar Strait. I then will examine the ways in which Mandar fishers expressed their agitation at the intrusion of a capital-intensive fishing craft into waters they considered their own. As Donald Brenneis acutely observes (this volume), the ways in which authority is established by Mandar fishers searching for flying fish contrasts sharply with the way Indonesian judges constitute their authority in rulings made in a local district court. While flying fishermen use a remarkable variety of soundings—"calls"—as well as prayers, exhortations, and instrumental performances to lure flying fish to their floating traps, the district court uses visual metaphors and texts to construct and to legitimize national authority over the seas and marine resources. The striking contrast between the sonic performances of flying fishermen and the visual metaphors of the district court's written decision embodies an important distinction between charismatic authority and performance, on the one hand, and bureaucratic authority, on the other hand.

But we should resist the temptation to create boundaries that codify, reify, and classify the practices of flying fishermen in opposition to the state. This essay is as much about the crossovers, strategic borrowings, the echoes and reverberations between sources of metaphor and models of political power and administration as it is an explication of contrast between dry court talk and charismatic fisher calls. Like the changing configurations of a kaleidoscope in motion, the beliefs and practices of flying fishermen contain the traces of complicated historical conversations and accommodations with Islam, as well as with contemporary Indonesian political life, language, technologies, and institutions. A landscape of shape-shifting local Mandar spirit guardians who inhabit coastal promontories exists side by side with a more limited, less place-specific, powerful group of spirits known as the Nabi. For many Mandar fishers, almost all of whom are Muslim, Allah is believed to exercise complete and ultimate power over the fate of men as well as the creatures, weather, and currents of the marine realm.[7] Diverse forms of authority overlap, coincide, and conflict.

Against this idea of pure autochthony and a simplistic before-and-after version of Mandar fishing conceptions, practices, and beliefs, I propose a vision of borrowed metaphors and turns of phrase, of boundary-crossings and appropriations of political and poetic discourses that intersect with the marine environment. Contemporary Mandar discourses about the marine realm are as much the creative product of conversations and overhearings, of reconfigurations of political-administrative structures, discourses, and etiquettes of the bureaucratic state as they are the products of an ongoing dialogue with Islam.[8]

Local beliefs about power in the marine realm are being constantly refigured. As we shall see here, a fishing companion explains his behavior (placing offerings, speaking with deference, giving the "news") toward a guardian of a point as analogous to his behavior toward a district official (B.I. *camat*) upon entering a new district (B.I. *kecamatan*).[9] At the same time, the Indonesian telecommunications satellite known as Palapa, hovering in orbit above a three-thousand-mile-wide archipelagic nation, provides a fertile source of metaphor for explaining fishermen's communications with spirit authorities. Mandar fishermen employ satellite imagery to explicate and amplify the processes and technologies they use to send prayers to the spirits of the flying fish. Older political and poetic models of explanation, including myths written on *lontar*-palm manuscripts during the eighteenth century, continue to be invoked as explanations of the extraordinary powers of the flying fish (*Cypselurus* spp.), as well as the remarkable rapport between Mandar society and this fish. Interactions between an undersea kingdom's ruler and a terrestrial monarch and his son, said to have taken place hundreds of years ago, are cited by contemporary fishermen as the charter for their relationships with particular kinds of fish.[10]

In the second part of this essay I focus on a single jural ruling invalidating the practice of Mandar customary marine tenure. I use this case to heighten the contrast between state-generated forms of authority (textual), imaginaries (visual), and genres of authoritative, powerful speech (bureaucratic-legal) with local forms of charismatic authority (oratory), imaginaries (aural), and genres of Mandar flying-fisher soundings. The example I draw upon is one judicial response—legal, political, and cultural—to a specific marine-property-rights dispute in the Mandar raft fishery.

The exercise of jural authority by the district court in 1988, however, constitutes only one limited and relatively recent instance of the exercise of bureaucratic authority over the Mandar marine realm. There is a long history of central authority's attempts to control the movement of people, goods, and vessels in the Makassar Strait. Mandar traders sailing the Makassar Strait en route to Ambon and other Moluccan islands, as well as to Java, Sumatra, and Singapore, have been governed by multiple institutional authorities and regulations including written commercial codes governing the shipment of goods.[11] In precolonial times, terrestrial petty kingdoms on the Mandar coast formally maintained that their boundaries extended out to sea (Muis Mandara, personal communication 1989). Dutch regulations on interisland trading, taxation, and conservation, as well as post-Independence levies on marine produce, trade, and fisheries all constitute part of the historical layering of state-based attempts to impose authority over seas, peoples, and the movements of goods (if not over the movements of flying fish). If the district court decision shifts from sound to sight, as Brenneis suggests, we need to remember this long, layered, and complicated history of political-legal authority within the Makassar Strait.[12]

The third part of this essay explores the varied responses of Mandar fishers to the intrusion of a devastatingly efficient contemporary fishing technology, "pole-and-line" tuna fishing in local waters. In defending what some fishers believe to be their rights and territories, a discourse has been fashioned that strategically borrows from and builds upon two streams of talk and practice. One stream of discourse ingeniously appropriates contemporary Indonesian national discussion about rights, justice, and fairness. For these fishers, the issue is one of gross unfairness or disproportionality between non-local, medium-scale technologies and small-scale, low-capital, local technologies. Other fishers, faced with the same sight—a boat capitalized from afar that captures hundreds of tuna in the time it takes a Mandar troller to catch a single fish—draw upon concepts, practices, and beliefs about local marine landscapes, histories, and relationships that resonate with the soundings discussed in the first part.

These latter fishers reconfigure the intimate, personal, charismatic relationships with the marine world embodied in the performance of Mandar soundings, and they transform them into the beginnings of novel legal arguments based on custom, culture, and history.[13] Ritual offerings at particular places, dream appearances, repeated exchanges with spirit authorities, and historic relationships with particular regions of coast, shore, and sea are described as "heirlooms." In Mandar discourse, the term *heirloom* (B.M. *assimemangan*) denotes a template for action passed down from ancestors or revealed by contact with ancestral spirits. In Indonesian, the use of the term *heirloom* (B.I. *pussaka*) also suggests, as it does in Anglo-American jurisprudence, an inheritance, a piece of property. These senses of *heirloom*—as a charter or principle for action and as a concrete bit of property—are linked, in some of these discourses, to emerging ideas of "our [local] territory," "our rights," and "our [customary] law." These conceptions of historic territorial rights and cultural authority are contrasted with national fisheries regulations based on the ideas of open-access for all Indonesian citizens. At times of crisis, at least some Mandar fishers have begun to weave multiple sources of authoritative discourse, from the national political center as well as from soundings performed at local promontories, into ways of talking about and defending their rights to livelihood, territory, and cultural authority.

Voices on the Sea

Jurisdictions: The Several States of Nature

"There is someone who moves up and down on the edge of the sea. She is different from the one on the seas and from the ones on the promontories. She once met me, the one on the land (B.M. *potana'*) and she spoke to me saying: 'If we want to meet, light incense for me which is in the form of a circle, then mention my name.' She is a woman and the wife of the one on the seas, the one they call Nabi Heder. I asked for her name and she gave it to me. I asked her: 'If I wish to call upon you, who am I going to call you?' She said: 'I Sabaria'" (Kamma' Nuri, personal communication, field notes, 1989).

The edge of the land, the promontories that jut out into the sea, and the sea itself are inhabited by an impalpable population of spirits—conceptualized alternatively as family, lovers, a hierarchically organized kingdom, or a regional governmental administrative unit. The inhabitants of these regions —"those who are not earth people"—constitute a fractious, powerful, unpredictable population with whom boat captains and crews must establish a relationship each time they "go down to sea." On the edge of the sea, in the sands just above the high-water line, I Sabaria, the "guardian of the edge," wanders nervously up and down the shore. At the beginning of the flying-fish season, it is she who is given an offering, buried in the sand where she wanders, of sticky rice and miniature cigarettes.

"Who knows whether the guardian of the edge will pass, right? The one who always walks each day and night, always moving, the one who walks on the edge. . . . She moves, up and down the length of the coast, she is always in motion" (Kamma' Nuri, personal communication, field notes, 1989).

While the edge of the sea is haunted by a restless, ceaselessly moving female spirit, the shallow waters, reefs, coasts, and promontories are inhabited by unpredictable, shape-shifting guardians. These regions are watched over and governed by potentially cruel spirits known as the "guardians of the points" (B.M. *pakammi tanjung*). In seeking safe passage past dangerous promontories and guardians, Mandar fishermen are not merely navigating through a threatening seascape; they are negotiating, through speech, conduct, and offerings, with a loosely linked family of local spirits that are often conceptualized as an invisible but powerful group of siblings. "All the promontories—Ngalo, Lariang, Batu Roro, Labakang, Rewata—have guardians. They are all male except for one. They are all friends or siblings. I suspect they have one father and one mother. So, there are five brothers and one sister" (Pak Nuhung, Luoar village, field notes, 1989).

Soundings from a Floating Polity: Pointillist Politics

The fate of each boat is negotiated through offerings conceptualized as "shares" placed on the surface of the sea, on the beach sands, or on hooks, traps, or nets, by the *punggawa lopi*, or boat boss, as well as by the *sawi*, or crew. There is no central broadcasting station: each boat's boss and crew negotiate their boat's individual fate every time they go to sea. Once the boat has left the shore, it becomes a single floating polity among hundreds of others, as many as there are vessels at sea on a particular night or day. Each crew makes its own soundings to the spirits, unheard by other boat crews. Boat bosses murmur communications "within their mouths," so that they are not overheard by other crew members as they attempt to establish contact with spirits whose regions they are traversing. Coastal navigation is simultaneously a geographical, social, and political endeavor. Following are excerpts from my field notes of August 1985:

> 7:00 AM. We are nearing another point, Tanjong Rorro (Rorro Point). Nuhung, recently appointed Imam of his village, takes care of all offerings and communications. As we pass the point, crossing shallow waters, the currents are particularly treacherous. The water below our boat becomes an increasingly lighter shade of blue until it is turquoise. Nuhung reaches into the hold, gathers up several creme wafers and a Bentoel Biru cigarette and places them in a coconut half-husk, carries these gifts to

the bow, kneels, and bends low. Reaching out, he places the coconut husk and gifts gently on the water surface, on the right-hand side of the boat, and lets the offering drift away. He watches the offering for a while and then rinses his hands.

As Rorro Point recedes to our south, I talk with Nuhung about these offerings, the intentions which underlie them, and their audience.

Charles Zerner: Do you make offerings at every point?

Pak Nuhung: No. I only make offerings at points which have a spirit guardian. This point is the most feared of all points. There is no one who passes this point who does not fear it. We are not afraid now, as we pass this point; we are not worried, or nervous or confused, because we are already known by the guardian. I met him in a dream. I was sleeping on a boat when he appeared.

Charles Zerner: Did you have a conversation?

Pak Nuhung: Yes. But I cannot tell you about our conversation or what happened. We are afraid to talk about things like that before we ask permission from him. The guardians are like the district heads [B.I. *camat*]. When we come into their areas, we must report to them and announce our intentions. We talk to them, tell them what we are doing, and ask their permission to enter the area.

In negotiating safe passage with unseen local authorities, Mandar fishermen not only announce their presence and make offerings, they also make requests or demands in exchange for the "share" laid out on the ocean. Kamma' Nuri, a fisherman in his eighties, explained that, in his fishing days, he poured a few drops of fragrant oil on the water as he passed the promontories, a practice handed down within his family, while saying silently:

Here is your share
Don't you do anything
[To me or] my children [or] my grandchildren
Give [them] safe passage if they pass by [here]
This is what is asked

The seascape of the Mandar coast is a world in which power and authority are unevenly distributed: families of spirits or singular spirit guardians inhabit only certain points. Their temperaments are differentiated and vola-

Figure 8. Pak Nuhung observes an offering to a local spirit guardian he has just placed on the sea. Photograph by Charles Zerner, 1985.

tile. The areas around particular points are viewed as "places" (B.M. *oro*), a term which Mandar translate as spots, jurisdictions, or territories (B.I. *wilayah* or *daerah*). As one enters into a guardian's district, special precautions must be taken. As the boat travels through the guardian's district, anything done or said can be detected, heard, or seen by the guardian.

> Kamma' Nuri: Don't tell certain kinds of stories or speak of certain things. . . . He knows, the guardian, he knows, he hears.

Guardians can also shift their shape, appearing in the form of a fish with unusual shapes or markings, as a many-tentacled squid or octopus, or as a large shark. If a guardian follows a boat in one of these shape-shifting forms, it is often hard to tell whether one is looking at a fish or beholding a spirit.

> Pak Nuhung: If it circles the boat as if it were a person with a purpose, this is a sign it is not ordinary. If it appears to have a purpose, we feed it. It's like the police. They can pass us in a vehicle, or on foot, and not have any business with us. They ordinarily pass us and do not bother us if we are not in their precinct. They do not control the area we are traveling through. But if it is not an ordinary creature, we feed it red [palm] sugar

with our hands. We are not afraid. We put our own hands right into its mouth. But if there have been disturbing words on board which angered it, which upset its feelings, then not even offerings will do any good.

Lasting personal relationships between fishermen and spiritual authorities are established through visitations of "those who are not earth people," in the form of dreams or guest appearances while one is at sea. Conversations may take place and gifts may be offered in the form of esoteric knowledge that can be deployed to move the world: revelations of the secret, personal preferences of spirits for certain foods, or the recitation of a particular passage of the Koran at a particular time of day, and revelations concerning their secret names "in heaven." Fishermen who have received this knowledge through personal visitation are given the means to contact these fearsome and benevolent characters, to call them up and to converse with them, and to help themselves in tough times by moving the spirits.[14]

Kamma' Nuri recounted his meeting with Nabi Heder:

> Kamma' Nuri: Once I met him, the first of the old people, bearded, bent over, and walking on the surface of the ocean. He looked like us, his face was like ours, but his beard was long.
>
> Charles Zerner: Did you speak with him?
>
> Kamma' Nuri: He spoke to me. I was on my raft, reading Surat Yasin from the Koran. I had just finished twilight prayers [B.I. *shalat Magrib*] and he arrived. He limped. On his shoulder he wore a sarong. But he wore short pants, like the kind I wear now and this is what he did: he walked on top of the water, came over to my boat and immediately said "Assalmu Alaikum." Then I answered "Waalaikummussalam." Then he stepped aboard my boat. . . . He sat down and took [out] a long sword and faced me. Then we stepped upon the blade, each one of us on a por-tion of it . . . then [he] clasped me as if I were a person [being] married and gave me his cloak. . . . It was a large Arab cloak used by Haji. After I received it he said, "Receive this, it will not again be known . . . but within your heart you will see [me] as before [in the form of] mankind."

Ethnicity, History, and Relationships to the Marine Environment

Relationships to the marine environment are also linked to ideas of ethnicity, language, and historical familiarity with the local marine and coastal landscape.[15] The guardians of particular promontories, like the inhabitants of particular regions of South Sulawesi—the Bugis, Makassarese, and the Mandar—speak local languages and respond to their speakers. Strangers traveling through Mandar waters are subject to a higher level of danger than are local persons. Iron-hulled Dutch ships that cruised Mandar waters carrying passengers and copra during the 1920s and 1930s were often stranded on shoals and beached on reefs. While they had charted the coordinates of every known reef and atoll in the Makassar Strait, the Dutch knew not who lived below the reef, who followed them and listened to their babble of foreign speech while they cruised through the local guardians' jurisdictions. In August of 1985, while sailing north toward Mamuju, I continued my conversation with Nuhung aboard the Rachmat. We were passing Tanjung Rewata, or Spirit Point:

> Pak Nuhung: This is the most feared of all points.
> Charles Zerner: Does everyone fear this point equally?
> Pak Nuhung: We all fear it. But non-Mandar people, strangers from outside this area, must take special precautions. When the big Bugis ships—the *pinisi* and the motor-driven, iron-hulled ships—pass by this point, they make special offerings of chicken eggs because they are strangers. These waters and coasts are not their area.

The guardian of this point speaks Mandar. When an iron-hulled ship runs aground on the coral, only the ritual practitioner knows how to get it loose. He speaks to the guardian in Mandar, he releases a living chicken, and he tells him to let the ships go.

On the Open Ocean: The President of the Sea

When Mandar fishermen sail toward the open seas and skies, they turn to Allah to secure their safety and good luck (B.M. *dalle*). They also turn to the prophets (B.I. *nabi*).[16] It is the Nabi who "control the seas from the edge of the village to Mecca—the seas everywhere on earth" (Pak Amidung, personal communication 1989). Dominion of the seas is divided into two regions, each ruled by its Nabi. The lowest levels of the water column, the very bottom of the sea, "where the anchor lines lead and the anchor rocks lie," are said to be governed by Nabi Nuh. Vast regions of the open seas, the upper reaches of the water column, are governed by Nabi Heder, the Prophet of Fish. Unlike the feared guardians of the points, whose power is localized, Nabi Heder seems to be everywhere at once. He lives upon the surface of the waves whose foaming crests rise and fall, and far below where deep-sea creatures swim and mate. "No one knows where Nabi Heder lives, his place is the sea." Nabi Heder is the guardian (B.I. *pengembala*) of all fish, dwelling everywhere and nowhere at once. "He rules the seas—the waves, the wind, and the movements of fish from Mandar to Mecca."

Nabi Heder is the authority to whom flying fishermen pray when they seek to draw schools of flying fish, scad, or tuna, to their traps. It is he, the "president of the sea," who directs his charges to the boats of individual fishermen, the way a young "goatherder directs his flock as it moves along the road" (Kamma' Nuri, personal communication, 1989). Nabi Heder controls the seas, the movements of weather and waves, the currents and clouds.[17] "We make our requests to him, the prophet of the water (B.M. *Nabinna uwaio*), because he owns the fish, controls all the fish, knows everything about the fish. Our old people (B.M. *to mawuweng*) understood this, that Nabi Nuh manages and controls all the fish in the sea. So if we want to catch fish, it is necessary to make requests to Nabi Nuh, through the knowledge [B.M. *pa'issangang*]."

Requests are directed to Nabi Heder, whose relationship with the guardians of the points is often likened to that of a government head's relationship with district officials, using the model of contemporary Indonesian governmental organization:

> As for Nabi Heder, his authority is extensive. He grasps all the authorities at the promontories, the guardians. As for the guardians, their power is limited. The administrative unit analogous to the promontories is the RT [B.I. *rumah tangga:* domestic household], while Nabi Heder is analogous to the Regency Head [B.I. *Bupati*]. (Nuhung Tata, personal communication, 1989)

In my field notes, two old fishermen, Pak Amidung and Pak Janjang, proposed another administrative analogy:

> Nabi Heder is the President of the Sea! He controls things from Sabang to Merauke![18] Everyone obeys him. The promontory guardians are like district officers [B.I. *camat*], they follow the orders of the regency head and the president. And the fish follow his orders too.

Appealing to Authorities

In 1989, along the Mandar coast and on the Makassar Strait, shares of food would be offered in exchange for safe passage past dangerous promontories and for prosperity, luck, and full holds of fish—in nets, on hooks, and in the traps, as catches of large, silver tuna or masses of slender flying fish drying salted on the deck, as skeins of translucent, red-orange eggs "glowed from the sails like the light on one's boat at night." The spiritual authorities of the sea, like humans, are said to be responsive: they are sensitive to the character of the offerings proffered, to behavior on the boat, and to the kinds of talk between sailors. A wrong word or phrase uttered among the crew—"there are none" (B.M. *andiang*)—and no fish will appear. These authorities are also responsive to the kinds of speech made directly to them, in the form of prayers, spells, and calls or songs (B.M. *ilongi*). Those "who are not earth people" delight in speech that honors them, that raises them above normal ranks, and that uses high-ranking titles. Marine spirits also delight in speech that is erotic, that stimulates them, incites them, even goads them to act.

Spells and prayers (B.M. *pa'doangan*) are treated as secret instruments or gear (B.M. *parewa*) to be used on fishing trips, and they are passed down through families, from fishing father to fisherman son, or between intimate friends. The transmission of such heirlooms (B.M. *assimemangan*) is an exchange shaped by ancestral templates for action (B.M. *ussul*). The indiscriminate transfer of a spell is believed to dilute or "bleed" (B.I. *luntur*) the spell's strength, just as the colors of a new batik sarong, clear, bright, and sharp in the sun, will, with repeated washings, fade and lose their fullness. Secrecy also pervades the speaking of these spells—their transmission or broadcast on the sea is done silently, in the mouth, or quietly—so that the secret speech will not be overheard by another member of the crew and its strength diluted.

Ilongi, or calls, in contrast, constitute a form of men's speech that is generally known and publicly acknowledged throughout Mandar villages. At my request, some fishermen and young men would shout these calls on land, and they often did so, exploding with laughter, before a gender-mixed audience.[19] Several older fishermen refused to utter the calls on land or in the presence of women, insisting that such uses were inappropriate, or *porno*. They said that the sea was the region for sounding ilongi, and that, on a boat, they are murmured, called, or shouted, by night or day, in a great variety of tones, rhythms, and times. At sea, unlike spells and prayers, ilongi are not diluted by their public performance. Rather, ilongi are built through the crews' participation, in adding conventional as well as newly improvised phrases, until the call becomes a subversive, unpredictable trajectory of sound and imagery.

The Authorities Respond: Shares and Equity

Mandar fishermen keep track of individual contributions of labor and capital on fishing voyages through *bare,* or share systems.[20] Until the 1970s, when capital contributions for increasingly expensive engines and factory-manufactured gear began to drive fishing crews to seek capital from outside investors, fishing voyages were capitalized entirely by the crew, each member receiving an equal return on the catch.[21] Even today, at sea, the personal and collective relationships of Mandar fishermen to the spirit authorities of the sea, the fish, and the coastal landscape—one of indebtedness and thankfulness, of power, permission, and politeness, and of fair returns and exchanges—are configured and negotiated through shares. Indeed, each time Mandar fishermen go to sea, the relationship of that boat crew to the powers of the sea is established, renegotiated, or commemorated through offerings of speech and food, as well as through respectful, appropriate conduct and mindfulness. At the same time that bare offerings—a small coconut half-shell filled with sweet foods or clove cigarettes—are being laid upon the surface of the sea, an exchange is being negotiated. Shares are provided to spirits who yield, in turn, fish, safety, and prosperity.[22]

As Pak Janjang and Pak Amidung float out of sight of land on the Makassar Strait, their bamboo, barrel-shaped, flying-fish traps drift behind them, graced with a bare offering for Nabi Hader, and they shout to him:

> Come here!
> Your food is on the right!
> Pinang on the left!
> Pinang on the left!
> Sticky rice on the right!
> With bananas!
> Here, come here and take your share![23]

Within their jurisdictions, promontory guardians decide whether one will pass safely. An angered guardian could "attack the boat" with waves and destabilize or capsize it. Or worse, he might shift from shape to shape (B.M. *ma'minra minra*), appearing as a giant squid, a shark, or large fish that persists in following the crew, paying altogether too much attention to them. In order to avoid their attacks, Mandar fishermen negotiate their safe passage past the promontories through gifts or shares of food. Although promontory guardians generally prefer to receive "sweet things," respectful speech and conduct, the terms of such exchanges are frequently personal and may be passed down through the family as heirloom practices or promises (B.M. *ussul* or B.M. *assimemangan*) that are the fruit of negotiations with spirit authorities. Kamma' Nuri, a fisherman in his eighties, carries a little chest containing fragrant oil on his boat. In times of danger, as he passes a promontory guardian, he has often poured a few drops of the oil on the ocean, saying:

> Here is your share
> Don't you dare do anything [to me]
> Together with my children and my grandchildren
> Give me safe passage if we pass by [here]
> This is what is asked

Failures of Reciprocity: Theft and Danger

When one fishes, whether at sea or on the coasts, one offers shares to Nabi Heder and the invisible fish-soul guardians (B.M. *manurun*). Failure to tell the one in control that one has arrived, to tell it the daily news, that one is fishing or traveling, and to make requests—whether for fish, for full nets, for shark, tuna, or squid—is to steal from the guardian spirit. To make requests of the spirits that you wish to catch fish is to obtain fish properly by first asking for permission. Failure to provide adequate requests or appropriate food may provoke a spirit's rage: high waves may suddenly arise although there is no wind, boats will be overturned, fishermen may drown or drift helplessly. To take more than one's share of fish and be greedy is to risk an angered spirit's response, as my friend Nuhung, a flying fisherman shaken by an experience at sea, recalled:

> I was on the sea [Makassar Strait] near Kalimantan. We were near a boat using a purse seine. Their net was in the water, and so full with fish and

heavy that they could not haul the net into the boat. They requested help. I dove, swimming inside the purse of the net and reaching out for tuna. As I reached out for the fish, I began to lose consciousness. I remember calling out, "Help me!" I woke up on deck, exhausted. My crew had rescued me. I know now that it was the spirit of the flying fish that was scolding me for reaching out for more than my share.

Going Fishing: Contact, Connection, and Communication

For Mandar fishermen, who sometimes describe fishing as "going to war," the struggle to catch fish is the problem of how to meet fish at sea, how to concentrate and attract creatures dispersed in the seas below them, "sleeping on a rock mattress" or "playing on the foam." Fishing is an exercise in how to move fish: how to stir their spirits, transporting them by affecting their feelings, stimulating their appetites, and goading them to strike. If one is a flying fisherman, once the fish have gathered, a second problem is how to lure them into entering the floating trap. If one is trolling, dragging a silver hook bedecked with bird feathers, the problem is how to get reef fish to rise to the surface, to incite their passions to bite, how to get them angry and hot enough to swallow the hook hidden within the bait wholeheartedly, like "a sarong around one's body." In part, these are technical problems in the design, construction, and operation of gear—the lines, knots, leaves, and feathers that are used to lure fish into the trap, into the open net, or onto the hook.

But Mandar fishers have designed and deployed other "gear"—fashioned of sounds, phrases, calls—in the form of prayers (B.M. *pa'doangang*), spells (B.M. *pa'issangang*), and songs or calls (B.M. *ilongi*), as well as instrumentalities made of plants, perfumes, and oils that are intended to act upon fish and their soul guardians. From the moment a man wakes in the morning to the moment he casts his net at sea, seeking to set his hook in a tuna "as large as a coconut tree" and approaching his bait "shining far below the surface," he attempts to influence the course of his fate. He tries to gather fish in his net by first gathering them in his mind—as visual images—or with figures of speech, the silent or sounded tropes of his heart and the explosive, extravagant, erotic calls sounded from his boat.

During the month of April on the Mandar coast, slender boats called *sande'* and *pangkur* are drawn up on shore and prepared for the impending flying-fishing season. Flying fish are caught in drum-shaped bamboo traps known

Figure 9. *Buaro,* or flying fish traps. Photograph by Charles Zerner, 1985.

as *buaro* that float several hundred yards behind the vessel.[24] At the entrance to each buaro, the tapered tips of bamboo stakes face inward: flying fish may enter easily, but exit is impossible. The entrances to the "drum," as the buaro is called, are garlanded with a variety of leaves that hang down into the water like tresses. These leaves simultaneously disguise the traps and attract spawning flying fish to them as sites on which to deposit their roe. The trap is likened to ancestral drums and to beautiful women, each comparison with its own appeal. As flying fishermen busy themselves with untying and rebinding knots at every crucial juncture in the fishing boat, "because the flying fish knows," they stash small clusters of especially potent plants, known as the boat's medicine (B.I. *paulina lopi*), within these joints.

Before fishermen can draw breath and open their mouths to call the gliding fish to them, their boats are already making submarine broadcasts, beckoning to flying fish with their names, fragrances, and botanical forms that permeate the waters below their boats. The sweet odor of jasmine emanates from the outriggers, diffusing through the waters below; the multiplicity and density of *dui-dui,* the "thousands"; the capturing, grasping qualities of the *malapau* plant, the "grasper"; the latching-on capacities of *kai-kai,* the "one with the tendency to hook"; and the sheer prolixity of the *punaga* and *apar apar* plants—these potent bouquets are the botanical equivalents of calls evoking and prefiguring the desired event: that flying fish will gather from afar and concentrate about the boat and that they will deposit massive quantities of their roe on the long-leaved, enau-palm "hairs" (B.M. *bulu*) of their "ancestral drum," the buaro. These bouquets constitute a semiotic profusion of shapes, names, fragrances, and structures, botanical countervoices to the fishermen's calls.[25]

Seated on the outrigger, Jahmal had begun to compose his handful of Mandar plants for the interstice between the outrigger arm and the outrigger. "Why do we fishermen use jasmine and other powerful medicines when we go flying fishing?" I asked. Nuhung explained: "This particular fish needs more flattering, seduction, praising than any other fish. It knows what we think, even in our hearts."

Out of sight of land, somewhere between Sulawesi and Kalimantan on the Makassar Strait, at the moment before launching a flotilla of leaf-bedecked bamboo barrel traps, Pak Hadari, the captain of the *Rachmat*, knelt before the mast, his hand upon the line leading to the lead trap, and uttered:

> E . . . Raja, Lovely One! Heavenly Soul Guardian! Lord!
> Those in the South, those in the North
> Those below, and those above
> Your drum has been launched, Lord
> The drum of ancestral ways, the heirloom
> There is nothing else that you desire
> Nothing else [you] need
> Let it happen!

Pak Hadari's prayer was addressed to the flying fish's soul guardian. He exhorted the flying fish to arrive in droves about the traps—from the north, the south, from above, from below. A floating speck in the center of the Makassar Strait, the boat was thus transformed by means of the prayer's imagery into a broadcasting center, the site of Hadari's appeal. Hadari's prayer described the bamboo traps as ancestral heirloom drums associated with spirits, with stories of the origin of flying fish, and with drummers capable of producing sounds that would "rise to heaven," drawing the spirits to them.

Nuhung, my friend and fishing companion on that voyage, explained Hadari's prayer and other forms of Mandar evocation in terms of Indonesian telecommunications satellites, constructing a striking cultural translation that is not only vivid and attuned to its audience, but that mirrors the diverse array of "goods to think with" that are available to Mandar fishermen[26]:

> Pak Hadari's [the *Rachmat*'s captain and owner] prayer is like a shortwave radio broadcast, because shortwave broadcasts are not heard by other people. Of course I can hear you if you are speaking out loud. But there are other ways of making words [B.M. *mapau*]. . . . I can call within my mouth and you cannot hear me. . . . Shortwave radios have a cable, right? Hadari has a line connected to the fish traps. The line from our boat to the buaro is like the shortwave cable. So Hadari holds the rope and speaks with his mouth [closed]. His calls cannot be heard by other people and he doesn't have to use an audible voice [B.I. *suara kasar*]. When you make a silent prayer like this, it is like whispering. You can communicate, but other people do not hear what is being said.

Why does Hadari need to make silent prayers? I asked.

> It is done to make a direct voice connection with the raja [the flying fish]. It isn't possible to live without a connection. And all connections must be made by instruments. We use cable to make the connection. And only then is the connection direct. It's like the broadcast of radio messages from PALAPA [the Indonesian communications satellite].

Not all connections are made silently, however, through whispered words or silent spells "within the mouth." Mandar men also seek to move flying fish through space and concentrate them about the traps by moving their feelings. These movements, simultaneously sentimental and corporeal, are engendered through an interpersonal process known as *ma'pangara'*, which may be translated as "to stimulate, to goad, or to influence by engendering strong feelings such as anger, shame, or sexual arousal." Nuhung explained:

> You can ma'pangara' anything that lives—fish, wind, men or water buffalos. If you want to goad a man into action to use his hot fishing magic [B.M. *pa'issangan lopa'*], just ask him why he's not catching any fish

Figure 10. The crew lowers the sail on a *sande'*, or double outrigger.
Photograph by Charles Zerner, 1985.

today! When you ma'pangara', you push somebody into doing something. The flying-fish calls have the same effect as cheering "Yeh yeh
yeh!" at a soccer game. The calls give "support" for the raja fish to come.
They enlarge the soul of the fish, they make it feel good, they flatter it.

At sea, before the flying fish are sighted, or if they are sighted as a distant
mass of flying, gliding creatures on the horizon, Mandar fishermen call to
them in verses that prefigure their concentration about the drum-shaped
barrel traps likened to ancestral drums:

> O . . . Raja
> Those from Bone
> Those from Jawa
> Those from Kaili
> Those from Bugis
> Gather here now
> This is your ancestral drum
> It knows no satisfaction
> Smack into it, enter en masse!

Fishermen suggest that this call evokes the attributes of the remote former
Sulawesian kingdoms of Bone and Kaili, as well as the kingdoms of the even
more remote Java, with their dense populations, lively inhabitants, and
well-coordinated, swiftly moving armies.[27] Linking remote kingdoms with
Mandar fishermen on the sea, calling flying fish to "mate" with their women,
evokes images in which the Mandar region and Mandar fishing craft drifting
in the currents of the Makassar Strait become the centers addressing geographical and political peripheries—the areas of former polities in Kaili, Toraja, Bugis, and Java—from which flows of persons, goods, winds, and fish
are drawn. In sending out these metaphor-studded invitations, Mandar
fishermen seek to yoke flying fish, through politically and erotically compelling tropes, into their floating trap.[28]

When a swarm of spawning flying fish reach the trap, fishermen shout to
them, "Don't just play around, bang on your ancestral drum [the *buaro*],
smack into it, and enter it!" As the fish come closer to the traps, some entering, others covering the long masses of dangling *dui-dui* leaves with gelati-
nous rings of pale pink roe, the imagery of the calls mixes evocations of dis-

tant kingdoms and polities, exalted titles of high nobility, with unmediated images of vigorous sexuality—copulations, ejaculations, and the banging, lively, repetitive rhythms of sex.

O Raja!
Strike hard entering your heirloom drum, O Lord!
The one with the dense hairs
The cunt like the *butir* fruit
The moist one, beautiful
Stuff it in tightly, the spice-pounder in the mortar
Sink down into it, like a rock in water
Entering, make a juicy liquid sound!

The calls themselves act as copulae, packing images together, densely and promiscuously, producing a cross-fertilization of meanings and semantic trajectories. Further, both the imagery and intensity of the calls change from relaxed, intermittent evocations to shouts and commands, many fusing the erotic with the political and historical in a manic melee of images, a profusion of tropes hurled across the waters and at the fish in an attempt to make sure "they don't just play around." At this point, the work of the calls is likened to that of "stir-frying chili peppers in a wok," as one old salt put it, evoking the heat, bustle, and sounds of red and green chili peppers crackling in a black wok.

A Makassarese fisherman vividly recalled his days calling for the fish for me: "They come like a black house, a dark cloud on the horizon. Our calls are like trumpets or drums. Sometimes we even take a *kacapai* [South Sulawesian string instrument] out on the boats to call them. They love it!" (Abdul Halik Paete, personal communication, 1985).

By evoking multiple images of flying fish in midflight intercourse with the winds of the west monsoon while gliding over the Makassar Strait, of desired local women, of the massing of distant armies and the formations of daring men, of dense swarms of honeybees lost at sea, and of massive flocks of sparrows hungrily descending upon fields of ripe rice, the calls themselves are an incitement to action, a politics and a poetics of desire and compulsion. Ilongi are Rabelaisian mid-ocean copulae, producing improbable semiotic unions, unstable transpositions, and cross-fertilizations of meaning, shouted, crooned, and commanded in the middle of the Makassar Strait in order to entice a group of flying fish into a floating trap.

Figure 11. A crew member climbs the mast to help lower the sail of a *sande'*.
Photograph by Charles Zerner, 1985.

Figure 12. Pak Hadari, the captain of the Rachmat. Photograph by Charles Zerner, 1985.

A Voice of the State

Mandar fishers' concepts of sea rights depends upon the kind of gear they use, the kind of fishing they do, the geography of the sea sites in which they fish, and the political-historical context of particular kinds of fishing. The rights to certain sites, for example, are applied to fixed gears, while the general notion of "freedom of the seas" (B.I. *laut bebas*) is used by fishers using mobile gear when they troll for tuna. Three kinds of stationary gear were and, in certain sites, continue to be operated in inshore waters: *roppong*, fish-aggregating devices; *jaliq*, V-shaped fish corrals; and *bagan*, lift-net platforms.

Although it looks like an unclaimed watery expanse, the Makassar Strait contains recognized, monitored, and culturally claimed sites, not unlike patches of swidden farming within the vast forested landscapes of Kalimantan and Central Sulawesi.[29] "The sea," a Mandar woman once explained to my wife, "is our garden" (Volkman 1994). As our boat sailed further out to sea, and the majestic, clove-tree-studded hillsides and forested mountains of central Sulawesi receded from sight, a lively seascape loomed: the Makassar Strait is populated with hundreds of individually or collectively owned and marked roppong.

Roppong are rafts of lashed and layered bamboo anchored in the Makassar Strait by lines of braided rattan and polypropylene in depths ranging from several hundred to six thousand feet. These long cables link the roppong to massive anchors made of rocks and limestone chunks. Near the surface, fronds of bright green banana leaves are attached to the undersides of rop-pong, where their undulating presence attracts schools of scad and tuna. Schools of fish are surrounded and netted in purse seine nets several hundred feet long. Mandar fishers have constructed roppong since at least the late nineteenth century.[30] Spiked palm fronds are lashed onto the sides or posts of each roppong, as if gesticulating, up, out, or down. If recently attached, these fronds are a bright, vivid green, while if they are months old, they are tan skeletons, beaten and bleached by the Makassar Strait and its storms. When a roppong is launched, these fronds are tied to its vertical posts, constituting a vivid, idiosyncratic alphabet of possession and individuation. Each botani-cal wrapping marks the roppong to which it is attached, signaling the iden-tity of its owners and its location at sea (see fig. 13).[31]

A roppong can be installed anywhere on the Strait of Makassar and, for most Mandar fishers, the strait is conceptualized as a vast, open-access fish-ery. Although roppong fishers, like other Mandar fishers, affirm a general ide-ology of open access, their roppong fishery is predicated on rights established on particular sites. Once a roppong is anchored securely on the sea bottom, its owners control the rights to that site and an approximate area of two to five kilometers of sea around it. Many Mandar fishers claim that new rop-pong, at least through the 1970s, were launched "as far away from an already anchored roppong as the eye could see." Should a drifting or an intruding roppong interfere with the operation of an already anchored roppong, or be-come entangled in its lines, the owners of the first roppong on the site have the right, by customary practice, to destroy it or to cut its lines and set it adrift. When a roppong is carried by currents into another roppong's terri-tory, the destabilized roppong's lines frequently become entangled with the stable roppong's lines. The abrasion of anchor lines, under great tension,

Figure 13. A fishing raft, or *roppo,* at dusk on the Makassar Strait.
Photograph by Charles Zerner, 1989.

may sever one or both roppong from their moorings. Mandar recognition of priority rights to owners of already anchored roppong protects the labor and investment of fishers who were first in time to establish a secure site for their roppong.[32] The right to destroy the intruder roppong, however, is limited. Primary owners may not unilaterally sever the lines of the intruding roppong unless they have first convened a meeting with the intruding raft's owners, boat boss, or capitalizers, and attempted to devise a mutually acceptable solution (Kallo 1988). Until the mid-1970s, conflicts between entangled roppong were infrequent.[33] By the early 1980s however, there was a dramatic expansion of the numbers of scad roppong built, launched, and fished in the waters off the Mandar coast. By 1989, in the waters off the Mandar and Mamuju coast, more than two hundred roppong were owned and operated.[34]

In June 1986, a crew of roppong fishers towed a new roppong, capitalized by a retired Mandar army officer living approximately two hundred kilometers south of Mandar Province, in Ujung Pandang, out into the Makassar Strait. As the crew passed the vicinity of a successfully anchored roppong, the crew of the anchored roppong raised a flag, signaling danger and warning the approaching crew not to drop the new roppong's rock anchor. The arriving crew noted the flag, ignored the warning, and launched the new roppong approximately five hundred to a thousand meters from the previously anchored roppong.

Launched close to the "eye of the current," the new roppong drifted closer to the primary roppong. While the crew of the new roppong caught bountiful quantities of fish, those on the primary roppong caught few fish. When the new roppong drew closer, presenting an imminent threat of entanglement, the original roppong's owner sought to convene a meeting with the men who installed the intruder roppong. No meeting ever took place.

On the afternoon of 16 June 1986, following fishing and completion of Ashar prayers, the crew of the original roppong sailed the short distance to the new roppong, severed it from its anchor lines, towed it far out to sea, and set it adrift on the Strait of Makassar. That roppong was never seen again. These incidents were reported to the new roppong's owner and capitalizer, who, in turn, reported the incident to the local police. The distant owner, a former military officer, filed charges against the crew in district court. At issue in the complaint were damages for the lost roppong and criminal charges for violent destruction of another person's property. In the ruling on the case, the district court took the opportunity to rule on the validity of Mandar customary law for roppong, to assert its jurisdiction over previously remote areas of sea on the Makassar Strait, and to make some general pronouncements about violence, national security, customary law, national development, and unity.

On 15 February 1988, the Majene District Court found the owner of the primary roppong and seven members of his crew guilty of criminal acts of intentionally and willfully using violence against another person's property. The district court announced that the unrepentant owner and seven crew members who participated in severing the roppong's lines "showed no signs of acknowledging his wrongdoing." For the offense of "using violence against a person or a thing," the crew was sentenced to two months in jail.[35] The primary roppong owner and his entire crew of twenty-one were also found guilty of willful destruction of another person's property and fined under civil claims for damages resulting from that loss.

To establish its jurisdiction over these events at sea, the district court determined that the sea is a public (D. *openlijk*) place and that the allegedly criminal acts were committed in an open or public manner. To reach this determination, the court argued:

Considering that at this time, when science and technology are so so-phisticated that the sea as well as the heavens are no longer places that are closed, or that are not seen by the public, the sea is now a lively cross-roads [B.I. *lalu lintas*] where the public, the populace, or the masses can observe [events]. (PPNM 1988: 70–71)

That the high sea of the Makassar Strait, where rafts are moored like space stations in six thousand feet of water, rising, falling and occasionally snapped from their moorings by currents and violent storms, is a public place, would not come as a surprise to the raftsmen of Mandar. By 1989, the Makassar Strait had been colonized and populated by hundreds of roppong from the Sulawesi coast to the coast of Kalimantan.

Roppong crews bivouacked nightly on the seas, moored to their rafts, where they prayed, fished, and watchfully smoked the night away. In the early predawn hours, crews awoke, prepared their purse seine, got their engines going and, in an operation resembling a marine military drill, boat boss and net boss—the "commandos" barking and shouting orders in mid-ocean—would ring the roppong, haul in the net, and sail for shore while the fish were counted and sorted. As they returned, smaller, lighter, wind-driven, double-outrigger *sande'* would sail toward them, the occupants hoping to moor their craft to the mid-ocean roppong, where they would spend the day trolling or fishing from the platform and return before dusk.[36] The Makassar Strait, then, is almost continuously observed and inhabited by Mandar fish-ers and their roppong. In its decision, the district court explicitly invalidated the Mandar fishers' customary practice of permitting severance of an intrud-ing roppong's lines; the court stated that such practices must be "nullified" and "abolished" because they would "provide opportunities for individuals to play judges themselves, and, if this tendency is overlooked and continues to grow, it is not impossible that they [the practices] would threaten national stability" (PPNM 1988: 73–74).

Majene District Court Decision No. 11 of 1988 is also significant because it shifted the locus of authority over this "public" marine landscape from Mandar fishermen and their local practices and sensibilities to the jurisdic-tion of the district court. The decision asserted state authority in order to re-order relationships among men at sea, as it reconstructed and repositioned the meanings of cultural and legal practices that Mandar fishermen hold to be in accordance with community standards of justice and fair play. Customary law, in Nancy Peluso's phrase, had been "captured and criminalized."[37] In rhetoric that logically encompassed the themes of cultural difference and the status of culturally distinct customary laws, the decision warned that "Customary Law such as this," and other local legal practices in addition to the ones that had been "erased" by the court's decision, could be considered "threats" to "development," "ethnic unity," "national stability" and the national ideology of PANCASILA (PPNM 1988).[38] The Majene court decision thus interposed judges, prosecutors, expert witnesses, and legal clerks alongside boat owners, investors, and local fishermen, and thereby reconstructed the landscape of authority over the Makassar Strait and among these parties.

This decision stands for the proposition that the district court has established jurisdiction over acts it considers criminally tortious that are executed on the waters of the Makassar Strait. In invalidating the authority of local fishing communities to order relationships concerning property, permissions, and disputes among themselves, the district court enunciated its decision in the admonitory voice of an expansionist, developmentalist state seeking to assert its hegemony over the sea, its resources, and over relationships between local fishermen[39]:

> Customary Law such as this, if tolerated, in the judgement of the Chamber must be erased and not considered valid any longer, even more so during this period when the Government and the Indonesian People are in the process of increasing development in every field. . . . Custom like this, if tolerated, would become an obstacle [to] development and would also threaten the laws of unity [B.I. *peraturan persatuan*] and the unity of people [B.I. *kesatuan bangsa*]; . . . custom like this would give an open opportunity to a person to act as if he were himself a Judge [D. *Eigen richting*] and if [this possibility] were overlooked [and] continued to grow, it is not impossible [that] it would threaten National Stability [B.I. *Stabilitas Nasional*] . . . within the framework of National Law development and guidance which is based on PANCASILA and the Basic Laws of 1945, therefore Customary Law of the kind mentioned above must not be considered valid any longer. (PPNM 1988)

The use of potentially ominous political phrases like "threaten the laws of unity," "act as if he were himself a Judge," "National Stability," and "unity of the people" suggests that court officials took this marine dispute as an opportunity to broadcast several strong messages about the extent of state authority and the limits of customary law at sea. Even far from the courthouse, where men cannot be seen by the eye of the state, the conduct of local fishing groups would henceforth be judged and tried by federal courts. Alternative sources of authority, including community standards of justice and fair play, are characterized in the decision as destabilizing practices that threaten national security, ethnic unity, the rule of law, the quasireligious state ideology PANCASILA, and economic development.

By converting everyday fishermen into state witnesses, the governmental gaze is cast upon unseen ocean regions. By converting a property rights dispute between owners of fishing gear and ocean sites into a case about national unity and ethnic division, the federal district court dilates the pupil of state authority.[40] It configures a landscape in which local legal rules, claims, and practices are envisioned as political threats to national unity.

The images, tone, and cadence of the court's deliberations contrast sharply with Mandar fishing calls. A centralized, bureaucratic state with the legal and police power to regulate fishermen's conduct on the seas here begins to sound:

> Considering that the primary accusation, article 170 paragraph 1 KUHP [criminal code], sounds as the following: "Whoever openly and [in] joint effort us[es] violence to a person or to a thing is in danger of criminal incarceration for a maximum [of] five years and six months." (PPNM 1988)

Through this opinion, the court rationalized the extension of its authority to regulate social behavior in remote regions and over unseen events, to command witnesses to appear in court and to testify.[41] It rhetorically situated countervoices and arguments and cultural difference, with legal consequences, in an antigovernmental, antinational zone. The 1988 decision was unilinear, originating from a single center of power and committed to a vision of a strong state. Those aspects of local practice and culture that were construed as threatening national unity and development, including opening up local sections of the sea to regional investment, were invalidated.[42]

At the same moment that Mandar fishermen paused to announce their presence on the seas to Nabi Heder in the Makassar Strait, providing shares of food and respectful speech in exchange for his permission to fish without being considered thieves, the district court in Majene also demanded deference, scolding men for their failure to provide notice to the fisheries office, to ask for permission to install a roppong, and to pay the authorities' registration fees. The contrast in tone between the wild calls of flying fishermen and the somber bureaucratic cadences of the district court, recalling the names and numbers of legal chapters, is striking. The droning tone of the court decision constitutes a compelling and possibly intimidating voice and source of authority on the Mandar coast, the voice of the developmentalist state.[43] While ilongi were being sounded on Mandar seas, the text of the Majene ruling and a subsequent appeal were being written in Indonesian, itself an inscription of united state power and its language. Was anyone listening?[44]

No response was expected from Mandar fishermen other than compliance with the ruling. This judicial decision was not a conversation but rather an oracular pronouncement, a formalized publication in jural ritual speech addressed to a faceless, undifferentiated mass of Indonesian citizens. The fixed text of Decision No.11 is not the give and take of negotiation, shuttling between one speaker and another, but a monologue establishing state power and authority to universally articulate order among men in a relatively remote region of the marine environment.[45]

Resisting Voices: Tuna and Hot Hearts

During the summer of 1989, in a placid village several kilometers north of the Majene regency capital, fishermen on the north Mandar coast were telling stories of tuna, national development, and resistance in local waters. In August 1989, two pole-and-line tuna vessels, owned by non-Mandar capitalizers and operating from a base in Pare Pare, a port city about a hundred and thirty kilometers south of Majene, cruised into the waters off Pamboang village to begin tuna-capture operations.

Pole-and-line vessels depend upon the capture of live bait, which is kept in a tank, through which seawater is constantly pumped. The bait, thousands of tiny fish called chum, is obtained from stationary lift-net platforms (B.I. *bagan*) that are operated throughout the night in shallow, inshore waters. When dawn breaks, the pole-and-line vessel, its hold containing bait fish, takes off for deeper waters. The crew locates schools of tuna by following clusters of birds diving for the fish. As they near the school, the vessel master begins chumming—heaving scoopfuls of small fish overboard—to keep the school on the surface and to drive them into a feeding frenzy in which they will snap at anything that moves and flashes silver. As the school begins to bite, a score or more of young men, poised on the flat, snub-nosed bow with unbaited hooks, repeatedly flip their hooks into the chumming waters. At the glint of a steel hook, the tuna, already driven into an indiscriminate feeding frenzy, fail to distinguish between silvery bait fish and hook and they strike. With a single back-arm movement, the hooks are set and fish are flipped up and out of the sea and onto the deck. Within ten or twenty minutes, hundreds of skipjack tuna may be captured by a single pole-and-line vessel. As the tuna are gutted, the deck suggests a floating slaughterhouse of marine game—the heaped, silver carcasses of skipjack splashed with red and shining brightly.

In 1989, when pole-and-line vessels began operations for the first time in Mandar, taking on bait and fishing in the waters off Pamboang village, local fishers resisted. Here is how the story was told to me by a local fisherman in a village several kilometers south of Pamboang:

> Two boats from Pare Pare came into our area in August, taking on bait and capturing tuna. But we forbade them to fish in our waters using that equipment. It wasn't the local government who forbade them, it was us. If we wanted to take the problem on by ourselves, the local government said it was up to us. The local government told us to be patient and let them take the fish or build boats like theirs ourselves. We knew that they had permission and that they had all their letters.

When the pole-and-line vessels concluded an especially successful haul of tuna at sea, Pamboang fishermen sailed to their boats and demanded a share of the catch.

> People got angry and went out to the crew, pulled alongside, and asked for fish. The crew gave them some and they were still angry.[46]

Fearing that all fish in local waters would rapidly be exhausted, Pamboang fishers marched on the local government offices, demanding the boats be excluded from their area. When they found the governmental response inadequate, they took the problem of what they described as unfair levels of extraction into their own hands[47]:

> We spoke with them [the pole-and-liners], on land and on sea. We were angry because of their techniques. We shouted *cappu unalla*, com-

pletely finished, all the fish [in the area] are gone, captured. We thought to ourselves, "They will capture them all until the fish are finished. Finished!"[48]

For the fisherman who spoke these words, outsider fishing represented an intolerable instance of inequity engendered by the gross lack of proportionality between the catch of the outsiders' gear and the techniques and capacities of local fishermen[49]:

> It is not a question of rights, of us having the rights [B.I. *hak*] to the waters. Fish are free to roam, from here in Luoar to Pamboang and up to Mamuju. And fishermen are free to roam as well, following them. And so are outsiders. But what we found intolerable was the way in which they caught the fish. They took too many fish because their techniques were fantastic [B.I. *hebat*]. They caught two hundred fish in twenty minutes. For every one hundred fish they capture, we capture one. On top of this, once they get the fish to market, they sell them to consumers at prices lower than we fishers can afford to sell them! We were mad, we were jealous, and we conducted our own rebellion [B.I. *pemberontakan*].
>
> We had a meeting [B.I. *musyawarah*] in Pamboang and conducted a rebellion of our own to protect our needs. There were no leaders in this meeting. It was just the common people [B.I. *rakyat*]. After all, the outsiders [B.M. *to laen*] were taking care of their own needs, and so were we. We cut the nets of the *bagang* at night. The rebellion was successful. The proof is, they haven't come back to pole-and-line fish near Pamboang since last August. We opposed them.

A boat captain in Pamboang, whose son worked on one of the pole-and-line vessels that provoked the incidents, denied that bagang netcutting had taken place near Pamboang. He placed the scene of the events further north, where, he claimed, violence had been used to repel boats at sea when local fishermen threatened and fought the outsiders by brandishing knives:

> It was like this: for one week, the first week they arrived, we just watched the situation—how they took on bait fish at night from the bagang, how they went out and sprinkled the fish on the waters and captured fish. Our thoughts were: the fish are going to be finished off. We could foresee this result by witnessing the way they operated. We saw the proof. We

saw how they just throw out the bait. The fish go crazy [B.I. *mangamok*] on the surface and they don't stop fishing until a whole community [B.I. *lingkungan*] of fish is finished. Our hearts were hot [B.M. *lopai atena*]. We thought it is best to report them to the police and district officer.

In Pamboang, after meeting with ineffectual government responses, local fishermen experienced violent emotions, "hot hearts" and "wild hearts."[50] Ideas of rights and law, "our own law" in contrast to national law, as well as sources of law—permissions and letters—emerged for the first time in this version.

We marched to the district leader's office and told them that they [the outsiders] should be driven away from this area. It was our own law [B.I. *hukuman sendiri*], not national law. The government people, the harbormaster, the police, and the district head said: "We [the officials] are not daring enough to chase them away. They [the pole-and-line fishers] have all the letters of permission they need. What was their response? We can't do anything." The feelings of our group were: "We have no hopes from the government. If the [outside fishermen] continue to operate like this, after a while, we will not be able to capture any more fish. We went amok in our own hearts [B.I. *mangamok dalam hati sendiri*]. . . . We feel it is our area [B.I. *daerah*]. Every action must have a foundation [B.I. *dasar*]. If we didn't feel it was our territory [B.I. *wilayah*], then we wouldn't have acted. We did not affirm, we did not permit [B.I. *memberi izin*], we didn't approve of their operation in our area. It wasn't valid or true [B.I. *tidak dibenarkan*].[51]

In his impassioned account, ideas of territory, authority, permission, and outsiders, associated with local fishers' negotiations for access with local spirit guardians as well as Indonesian fisheries policy and law, are linked to discourses defending local livelihoods and territories. The "we" of these protests is not the national "we" of the district court, nor is it the incorporeal "we" of spirit guardians giving permission to enter their territory, but rather it is a populist, highly localized "we"—the *rakyat* or everyday society of the Pamboang area—refusing to give outsiders permission to conduct operations in their area. The distinction between "us" and "strangers," or *to laen*, moreover, has a basis in class distinctions between those outsiders, who have access to capital and strikingly efficient technologies, and the local, "everyday people," who can catch only one fish for every hundred fish caught by outsiders.

This fisherman's account configures the conflict as one between two different sources of rights, in which "our" law is opposed to national fisheries statutes. While local fishermen's authority originates from a foundation based on "our own law" over "our territory," the legitimacy of the outsiders' boat to enter local waters is based on permissions granted in remote Jakarta and embodied in "letters" of permission[52]:

> On what basis did we reject their operation? Because according to customary law this area is considered our waters. But according to the government, it is not our area. They [the outsiders] have rights because they have the letters. We [the Pamboang fishers and the pole-and-line fishers] were talking to each other with our backs turned toward each other. They wanted to fish and considered that they owned the whole area because they had letters of permission.

The arguments of the chief fisheries officer in Majene suggest the magnitude of the differences between a governmental optic on rights to resources and these emerging, volatile fishermen's views. In the account from the fisheries office that follows, local communities are positioned primarily as communities in need of development. Local ideas of access limitations to local waters are criticized as an impediment to economic development and democracy:

> Fishermen here think they have the authority [B.I. *wewenang*] to capture fish in these waters and control a territory [B.I. *wilayah*], but they don't. Perhaps these ideas came from the feudal times when rajas owned and controlled the rights to stone fish weirs, when their slaves worked these areas in the ocean and gave the fruits of their labor to the rajas. But now we are a democracy and these ideas are no longer valid.

This official derided local expressions of outrage and desires to control access to the resources and territories near one's community. He dislodges these expressions from their concrete context—a situation of conflict in the present—and attempts to merge them, through an act of creative insertion, with a devalued precolonial and colonial past. A strategy of delegitimization is attempted by associating an emerging expression of rights with social hierarchies emblematic of an undemocratic, pre-Independence social order:

But after Independence, these areas disappeared and the Nation now owns them. This older system of rights is no longer valid. It has been erased by the national laws [B.I. *undang undang*]. In the old days, fishermen didn't travel much, they tended to fish in their own local waters, in and around each kingdom [B.I. *kerajaan*]. Very few outsiders came to fish in local waters. Now fishermen [local] are astonishing [B.I. *hebat*] in the way they think they have rights to use all the [local] resources.

This official explicitly embraced the idea and ideal of open access—that any fishermen from anywhere can come and fish in local waters—as a democratic right of all Indonesian citizens: "The ocean is not divided and bounded the way land is, into governmental divisions like regency, village, etc. All Indonesian citizens have the same rights. If someone from Jakarta desires to fish in local waters, they have as much of a right to capture fish here as anyone else."

Not unlike the district court decision, this fisheries official situates talk of customary practice as backward-looking, reactionary discourse harking back to a "feudal" or colonial past. Rather than being viewed as eruptions of populist sentiment for economic justice and equity, local protests are pitted in opposition to Indonesian citizenship, democracy, and development.

This chapter has explored the poetics and politics of power over the living world of the Makassar Strait—its creatures, fishing sites, and claims of rights—in three recent moments of Mandar history. It has examined how conceptions of power and authority over the strait and its regions are configured and reconfigured, contested and renegotiated. Rather than discovering several seamless, culturally coherent visions or versions of power and Mandar marine nature in different cultural sites—an autochthonous version, a statist version, and a counter-state version—we found complicated versions of power and marine nature in Mandar that were often imbricated within one another, contradictory, and more kaleidoscopic than static. Each moment of flying-fishing, raft-fishing, and trolling for tuna involved active reworkings and deployments of a variety of available cultural materials.

In fishing for flying fish, for example, a diverse assortment of cultural styles and "works" were brought together, including Arabic words and phrases preceding non- or pre-Islamic prayers and poems. These materials and performances were deployed in a landscape inhabited and controlled by shape-shifting, place-based hierarchies of Muslim and non-Muslim presences. Among these spirit powers were a fractious family of siblings inhabiting particular named points and their adjacent waters.

Mandar flying fishermen, however, did not conceptualize the recent launching of a global telecommunications satellite as a postmodern technological rupture of their fragile, autochthonous cultural world. They handily incorporated the telecommunications satellite's existence within their already complicated and variable models of prayer, power, and communication. Despite the presence of numerous ancestral templates for action, moreover, Mandar flying fishermen seldom spoke about these diverse fishing practices as based on customary law or rights. Scenes of distress, or unequal power and conflict, may often catalyze the production of novel articulations between cultural practices and rights discourses.

In the second moment of Mandar fishing, when a mid-strait bamboo fishing raft was cut from its moorings and set adrift, the idea of custom or customary rights was prominently raised as a political issue by the government. The district court construed the practice of severing the intruding raft's anchor lines as a serious matter with implications for national stability, civil peace, and unity. The court constructed the case as a site in which questions about cultural differences, customary law, and the conditions for national political life were raised. For perhaps the first time in Mandar, a contemporary Indonesian court focused on local culture, scrutinized a particular portion of its legal culture, and invalidated it, labeling it a political threat to national life. In the context of widespread and widely publicized Indonesian national and regional competitions for local cultural distinctiveness in the visual and performing arts, it is interesting to note what aspects of cultural practice and performance the Indonesian government seized upon and criminalized: acts that involve property rights relations, control of access to resources and territory, and the use of force.[53]

Despite the contrasts—in form, tone, vocabulary, and audience—between the poems of flying fishers and the words of court justices, the ways in which authority is configured in the world of contemporary flying fishermen and the district court display marked similarities. The district court assumes a national space that is hierarchically and territorially divided into national, provincial, and district-level authorities. Ideally, behavior that is deferential and respectful permeates the relations of citizens to district, provincial, and national courts, as it underwrites successful behavior at district, province, and national political and administrative levels. Mandar flying fishers' ideas of local spirit jurisdictions, based in the waters around particular promontories and encompassed within overarching regions managed by Muslim and non-Muslim presences, are strikingly similar to the territorial divisions of the Indonesian government. Conceptions of politesse, politics, and perhaps the proffering of gifts or material offerings, are part and parcel of the landscapes of cultural authority over the seas assumed by the district court and by many Mandar fishermen.

In the off-the-record remarks of a few anonymous fishers in Pamboang village, remarks catalyzed by their personal observations of the unequal-access relations and technologies, the idea of custom is seized, albeit momentarily. In their conversations and off-the-record musings, talk of rights and custom, on the one hand, and of local historical relationships to particular marine landscapes and their resources, on the other, emerge as possible grounds on which to build defenses of community rights of access to local resources.[54] These kinds of talk and improvised protest about rights and custom are a form of desperate theorizing or countertheorizing. They are precipitated by perceived injustices and statist assertions of power and property rights over vast, unseen territories and valuable resources, mapped and monitored without reference to local communities, livelihoods, or historical claims of right (Lynch and Talbott 1995; Zerner 1992a; Moniaga 1993).[55]

At a moment of incredibly rapid industrial expansion and growth, talk about territorial and resource rights, custom, and indigenous communities' historical relationships to local landscapes is increasingly common throughout Indonesia. This discourse is a historically complex and increasingly transnational conversation implicating Dutch colonial strategies of codifying customary law, as well as unrecorded talk among small-scale fishers, forest farmers, and agriculturalists. It is also a conversation and a campaign that increasingly includes regional, national, and international environmental and socially progressive non-governmental and donor groups.[56]

Where, in this welter of voices, poems, texts, and contested visions, is the Mandar sea? Where, at the end of this complicated tale of erotic poems and legal opinions, of resource extractions and assertions of rights, of customary law invalidated and customary rights raised up, is marine nature in the Makassar Strait? It is at the water's edge, at the lip of the sea, haunted by a ner-

vous Mandar spirit. It is within the optic of the district court and its pronouncements. It is flying with the unseen *Manurun,* the mobile spirit of the
flying fish observing the acts and beholding the intentions of flying fishermen everywhere, even under the waters. It is within the unrecorded but remembered protests of isolated groups of poor Mandar fishermen, outraged
by the technological capacities of pole-and-line fishing gear. It is in the silent
prayers offered up to marine spirits as well as the ancient, yet improvised
erotic poems of South Sulawesi's flying fishermen. It surrounds a cluster of
flying-fish traps, floating hundreds of feet behind the *Rachmat,* bedecked
with an offering of "spirit bananas."

Raymond Williams has elegantly asserted that "the idea of nature contains, though often unnoticed, an extraordinary amount of human history"
(1982: 67). Although some conservationists would still have us believe in an
idea of nature wholly separate from the hubbub of human history and contention, it is difficult to imagine the nature of the Mandar marine world without tracing the evolution, dispersion, and interaction of overlapping worlds
of poetics, politics, prayer, and law in Mandar.[57] It is the kaleidoscopic motion of a variety of historically produced social templates and discourses, projected onto the Makassar Strait like a cluster of Bakhtinian ray words passing
on their way toward an object, that makes this sea sparkle.

Notes

This chapter is based on research conducted in the Mandar Regency of South Sulawesi Province (January–September 1989) with the support of a Fulbright–Hayes
research fellowship. I would like to thank the Center for Social and Cultural Research (Pusat Penelitian dan Pengembangan Kemasyarakatan dan Kebudayaan),
under the direction of Dr. A. B. Lapian, and the Indonesian Institute of Sciences
(LIPI) in Jakarta for sponsoring this work. In Sulawesi, I extend my thanks to the
Center for the Study of Coastal Societies (Pusat Penelitian Masyarakat Pantai)
at Hasanuddin University (Ujung Pandang), Sulawesi, under the direction of Dr.
Mukhlis, as well as the family of Dr. Darmawan Mas'ud and Haerani Mas'ud of
Majene. The Fisheries Research and Development Project (FRDP/USAID) affiliated
with the Central Marine Fisheries Research Institute (Pusat Penelitian dan
Pengembangan Perikanan), permitted two additional periods of research in South
Sulawesi and the Makassar Strait (October–November 1989 and January–April
1991), for which I am grateful. My thanks to Ali Poernomo, Brian Duncan,

Conner Bailey, Richard Pollnac, and Rudi Schmittou for bringing me on board and encouraging my penchant for concrete, field-based studies. The Rockefeller Brothers Fund and the Liz Claiborne–Art Ortenberg Foundation contributed support to the Natural Resources and Rights Program, making production of this essay possible.

I wish to express my appreciation for the generous companionship and support I found during my year as a fellow at the Woodrow Wilson International Center for Scholars, with special thanks to two former staff, Charles Blitzer, formerly the Wilson Center's Director, and Mary Bullock, the Asia Program Director during my tenure (1991–92). Special thanks are due to Jane Atkinson, who provided insightful comments on this chapter, as well as to Ken George, Elizabeth Coville, and Anna Tsing. Toby Alice Volkman, my wife and colleague, whose keen eyes and ears have seen and heard these pages, has substantially contributed to their clarity. The Rainforest Alliance has supported the research and educational goals of the Natural Resources and Rights Program, under whose auspices this essay was revised. All the usual disclaimers apply.

1   The trading ships of seafaring peoples, including the Javanese and Chinese, as well as of regional peoples, the Bugis and the Mandar, have plied the Strait of Makassar, carrying goods on interisland and international voyages. On historic patterns of maritime trade in Southeast Asia, see Reid (1988, 1993), Horridge (1985), and Manguin (1993). Fishing and the collection of marine commodities, however, has probably been a predominantly regional enterprise.

2   During the 1970s and 1980s, the terms *plasma* and *nucleus* were used by the Indonesian government to indicate "parastatal enterprises," in which the "nucleus" was conceptualized as a private sector/government-funded core, while the "plasma" was composed of individual peasant cultivators or fishing folk.

3   See Bailey, Dwiponggo, and Marahudin (1987) for discussion of key Indonesian fisheries laws. See also Zerner (1991a) for analysis of the status of community claims to local waters within the legal framework of Indonesian fisheries.

4   See Blaikie (1985) for a classic political-ecological analysis of soil erosion. See also Bryant (1992) and Harley (1989) for recent expositions of political ecology, and see Beinart (1989) for a political ecology of colonial conservation.

5   In exploring the Mandar marine imaginary, I often use the word *soundings*. This is not an indigenous term, but rather my gloss on the variety of ways through which Mandar fishers seek to establish contact with and control over the movements of fish, currents, winds and waters, their safety and fate at sea, and a good catch. Mandar fishers talk about how they link up with fish and draw them to the boat, and their practices, including singing, shouting, and calling, as well as quietly or silently praying, have suggested the use of the term. "Sounding" is intended to

evoke the physical production of sounds and the penetration of a medium such as water or air by acoustical performances. Many Mandar seek to exercise authority and power over marine creatures or spirits by deploying sound in performance —whether the abrupt, repetitive sound of shouting, the soft calls of ancient or improvised couplets, or the plaintive sounds of the *kacapai*—a Bugis stringed instrument that is bowed and whose sounds are wafted out over the Makassar Strait. When Mandar speak of these soundings, they often use communications metaphors or images and to explain them: "calling," "connecting," "seducing," "flattering," and "transmitting." The power to affect the spirits who control the sea is often linked to the capacity of the speaker to stimulate desire, to flatter and to please, and, occasionally, to goad local spirit authorities and fish into action.

6 On the aesthetics of sound and other kinds of ritual performances as an avenue into cultural dimensions of feeling, sensibility, and politics, see Feld (1990), Roseman (1991, this volume), and Schieffelin (1976). On the political economy of sound and its relations to various forms of political organization, see Attali (1989).

7 Even the above description suggests a kind of codified relationship between so-called pre-Islamic, purely autochthonous Mandar marine beliefs and practices and Muslim beliefs in which local spirits are classified as animist while all spirits prefixed with "Nabi" are identified as later Muslim elements. The variety of beliefs and practices that are present in contemporary Mandar, and the variation among individuals, defies this kind of neat before-and-after divide.

8 I am indebted to Jane Atkinson for this insight.

9 Throughout this essay, Mandar words will be indicated by the abbreviation B.M. (for "bahasa Mandar"), Indonesian words will be italicized and preceded by the abbreviation B.I. (for "bahasa Indonesia"), and Dutch expressions will be preceded by the abbreviation D.

10 Human rapport with the flying fish, and, in particular, the capacity to "call" the fish to boats, is sometimes explained on the basis of a kingdom at the bottom of the sea, structured like the former petty kingdoms of the Mandar coast, populated by a raja along with his palace guards, nobility, and advisers. According to the story, a lone Mandar boy, the son of a terrestrial raja, descended to the bottom of the sea, where he performed an operation on the marine raja, freeing him of the golden fishing hook he had swallowed. As a gift, the boy was granted anything he desired from the undersea kingdom. He chose to command the troops of the underwater raja's warriors, the *to barani,* and returned to the surface. That is why, when Mandar rajas walk along the seashore, it is said they are able to command schools of cavorting flying fish to come to them, calling them to their side by calling them *raja, lord,* or *daring ones.*

11 On commercial codes governing the shipment of goods, see Lopa (1982). See Reid (1988, 1993) for a broader geographical account of the history of maritime commerce in Southeast Asia.

12 The question of whether, and how, varied historical attempts at political, legal, and administrative control of the Makassar Strait—its peoples, goods, trading routes, and resources—were effective, and what the consequences of these initiatives were, poses an important theme beyond the scope of this essay.

13 Strategic reconfigurations of the meanings and uses of custom, culture, and customary law are being enacted throughout the Outer Islands of Indonesia; see Fried (this volume) and Zerner (1994a,b, 1996). See also Tsing (1999) and Li (1999, 2000, 2001) for explorations of the idea of articulation and the uses of adat, traditional society, and the "tribal slot" in Indonesia during and just after the Suharto era.

14 See Atkinson (1984) for an illuminating analysis of imagery and efficacy in Wana sayings and spells. See also Atkinson (1989) for insightful accounts of how shamanic power is created, maintained, and manipulated among the Wana people of Central Sulawesi.

15 See Basso (1984) for an insightful analysis of the ways in which an Apache community reads moral narratives into local landscapes and place-names. See also Tsing (this volume) and Hugh Brody (1982). I am indebted to Bernard Neitschmann for the insight that ritual practices may also constitute the basis of local claims to territories and rights (personal communication 1987).

16 The Arabic term *Nabi* means prophet. The attachment of the Arabic title Nabi to the names of locally powerful marine spirits, as well as the practice of commencing and ending prayers and magical spells with Arabic phrases, are poignant reminders of Islam's historic engagement and, until recently, accommodation with local religious practices and beliefs. See Bowen (1993: 77–101) for an elegant analysis of similar kinds of accommodations, and a variety of local interpretations and tensions concerning these practices, among the Gayo people of Sumatra. Islam's historic engagement with Mandar non-Islamic religious practices and conceptions of spiritual powers in the marine world, perhaps best described as an accommodation, contrasts with contemporary strictures of Islam, which have become more exacting in the last century. I am indebted to Jane Atkinson for this insight. Only one Mandar fisherman with whom I interacted was at pains to establish his distance from the Nabi. He explicitly stated that he made no requests to the Nabi, but rather, only prayed to Allah.

17 Conceptions of the distribution of power and authority in the marine environment are highly variable. The fisherman quoted in the passage that follows situated authority over fish under the jurisdiction of Nabi Heder and Nabi Nuh. At-

tempts to systematize or codify loose, changing, individualized articulations of marine authority immediately implicates the problems and politics of ethnographic codification.

18 The use of former Indonesian president Sukarno's nationalist trope, "from Sabang to Merauke," to describe the furthest reaches of Indonesia's territory suggests to these older fishermen the extensiveness of Nabi Heder's domain and the magnitude of his authority in powerful imagery.

19 Although they were not supposed to know or use them, women knew many of these calls. At sea, a family of circumlocutions or substitutes for nouns normally used to refer to animals living on land, the coast or estuaries, including dogs, goats, cats, chickens, and crocodiles was used. For references to similar lexical shifts in Malay fishing villages, see Coville (1979), Annandale (1903), and Firth (1946).

20 Shares of fish or cash profits from fishing or trading voyages are also allocated through *bare* calculations. The same word, *bare*, refers to shares of food offered to the spirits.

21 See Lopa (1982) for a summary of commercial share systems for trading voyages; see Zerner (1991b) and Kallo (1988, 1990) for historical accounts of raft fishery share systems.

22 Ideas of fairness and balanced exchange—remembering to provide something small, appropriate, and preferably sweet for the spirits, but not taking more than one's share—inform Mandar discourse and practices, not only between boat crews and the spirits, but also among crew members and between boat crews and their capitalizers. Crew members and boat bosses operating deep-sea fish-catching platforms known as *roppong* make secret redistributions of the catch before they reach land. These redistributions are made in order to fairly provide individual sailors with an equitable proportion of the catch. As the number of rafts has grown from ten to as many as three hundred within the past two decades, the scad fishery is apparently being overfished. Although formal crew shares have been proportionally enlarged to keep pace with the expanding number of shares each catch provides, the number of fish caught and distributed is decreasing. Raft crews multiply their formal shares by a factor of ten, before cutting out the share of the catch owed to the boat and engine owners as well as other capitalizers, in order to secure what they believe to be a fair share of the total. Such secret sharings are, in James Scott's well-turned phrase, a modest "weapon of the weak."

23 Pinang, or areca nut, is one of the ingredients of the *sirih quid*, which also consists of betel leaf, gambier, and lime. Sirih quid is commonly offered to guests, friends, and spirits.

24 See Zerner (1987) for a more complete technical description of the processes and

technologies of contemporary flying-fishing and the environmental effects of a rising global market for Sulawesian flying fish. See also Horridge (1985).

25 See Rosaldo (1975) for a vivid analysis of the role of metaphor in gardening and hunting spells in highland Philippines.

26 Compare Nuhung's explanations of the calls as analogous to telecommunications technologies with those given by Pak Abdul Paete, a Makassarese tourist guide to the Toraja highlands. Recalling his days fishing for flying fish off the Makassar coast, Paete contrasts Japanese high-tech versions of sounding by sonar and the "eastern" way of calling fish by "inviting them." Pak Paete casts his explanation in terms of an imagined eastern Other, exotic and close to nature:

> The Japanese catch flying fish in their own modern way, using sonar. But our way of catching them is by inviting them. How do our songs work? Through the art of invitation. Western scientists use modern signals to make female mosquitoes arrive, and we use songs. . . . We [Indonesians] know that things have blood, that if we cut them, they will be broken in two like a tree branch. . . . Fish have their own feelings and their own distinctive laws.

27 On the evocation of images of movement from political peripheries to centers, see Volkman and Zerner's (1988) analysis of a ritual poem chanted in the Toraja highlands, which links the movements of a swaying bamboo tree to the flow of goods. In this poem, all kinds of goods—fruits, cars, and cooking pots, among other things—are asked, through the mediation of a swaying bamboo trunk that is said to lean out over the landscape, to arrive at a remote village site, drawing these things back to the village where the ritual poem is being recited. See also Brenneis (this volume), Tsing (this volume), and Atkinson (1984) for analyses of charisma, charismatic claims, and sounded performances.

28 See Booth (1978) on the metaphoric yoking of meanings.

29 In 1987 Anna Tsing and I began our discussions about the poetics and politics of forests and seas. I am indebted to Anna for pointing out the sealike nature of forests, and conversely, the forestlike features of seas. See Tsing (1993) for a nuanced discussion of the disparity between Meratus perceptions of the forest landscape and forests as perceived and mapped by Indonesian Ministry of Forestry officials.

30 See Zerner (1997) for a more complete analysis of the history of roppong, including changing patterns of capitalization, technologies, and connections to global markets.

31 Until the mid-1970s, roppong operations were seasonally limited by the availability of labor, as well as by weather, waves, and currents. During the East Monsoon, crews of thirty or more fishers rowed heavy boats known as *bago'* to roppong anchored one to three kilometers from the coast. At dawn the bago' crews rowed around the roppong, ringing it with a large seine net. With luck, thousands of

scad were caught in the sweep, hauled aboard, and distributed according to predetermined systems of catch division. When the crew returned to the Majene area of Mandar, the catch was conveyed to fishermen's wives, who marketed it themselves or sold it to traders. For further details on roppong history, see Zerner (1991a, 1997).

32 The "first on site, first in right" rule is a venerable legal principle that is found in American jurisprudence as well as among practitioners of rotating agroforestry or swidden agriculture in Kalimantan (Dove 1983; Fried, this volume). In pre-Independence Mandar, rights to cultivate swidden gardens were established through cutting and burning areas of primary or secondary forest. These practices embody the Lockean notion that property rights are established through investment, particularly investment of one's labor (Rose 1994).

33 The density and number of roppong in the Majene area were even more limited in the early 1900s, when fewer than five roppong were in operation. By the mid-1970s, twenty roppong were operating in the Mandar area.

34 The precipitous rise in the density and absolute numbers of roppong in the Majene area was spurred by a conjunction of developments from 1970 through 1989, including motorization, the availability of polypropylene line, improved transport, and new sources of credit. Motorization dramatically enlarged the area in which roppong could be installed and reached within one day's time. With an inboard motor, bago' crews could easily move from roppong to roppong and fish on more than one roppong daily. The availability of more resilient polypropylene line, in conjunction with the use of increasingly powerful motors, stimulated the installation of a veritable flotilla of roppong anchored as far distant as thirty kilometers from the Mandar shore.

35 The jail sentence was suspended.

36 See Horridge (1985) for an excellent descriptive account of the construction and maritime virtues of the *sande'*, which are said to be the fastest wind-driven craft in all of Indonesia.

37 See Peluso (this volume) for an insightful account of the way in which state authorities politically recast and reposition customary access-limitation practices as criminal acts. See also Fried (this volume) and Dove (1983).

38 The word *pancasila* is a Sanskrit-derived expression meaning "five principles" and has been adopted as the Indonesian State Philosophy. Articulated in the post-Independence period, PANCASILA encompasses and encapsulates the essence of Indonesian national political, cultural, and religious life. The five basic principles of PANCASILA are: belief in god; nationalism; humanism; social justice; and representative government or democracy.

39 According to the senior judge of the panel issuing Decision No. 11, all local, cus-

tomary laws of the sea became invalid the moment Indonesia achieved independence in 1949, thirty-nine years before the decision in question was issued. While
Indonesia's Basic Agrarian Law of 1960 has provisions recognizing customary law
(B.I. *hukum adat*) and community territorial rights (B.I. *hak ulayat*), and procedures through which these customary rights may be realized as ownership rights,
there are no parallel provisions in the basic fisheries statute, Law 9 of the Government of Indonesia (1985). On the status of customary law and collective rights
under the Basic Forestry Law and the Basic Agrarian Law, see Zerner (1990a,
1992a). On the status of collective rights to coastal and marine resources, see
Zerner (1991a, 1997). See Lowe (2000) for an astute analysis of the political-
economic biases of Indonesian fisheries laws against small-scale fishers.

40 Did the decision raise any eyebrows in Majene? It is difficult to answer this question because local fishermen seemed reluctant or perhaps even fearful to comment on a decision of the government. One party claimed that the court was
bribed; another party—the man who severed the lines of the roppong—said the
court's decision was appropriate. His analysis was anchored in customary law: the
defendant (who had given him his orders) had not performed the customary
practice of conferring with the plaintiff before exercising his absolute right to cut
his cords. The defendant, who claims he acted in accordance with customary law,
has appealed both the federal and appellate court decisions. His case has been accepted for review by the Indonesian Supreme Court.

41 Compare the state's assertion of jurisdiction over unseen regions of sea, as well as
its capacity to command obedience as well as witnesses, with one fisherman's description of the power, mobility, and all-seeing power of the flying fishes' soul
guardian (B.M. *manurun*): "It is always on the move, ceaselessly wandering. Even
if the soul guardian was down in Ujung Pandang, while I was at sea, it could see
me fishing even if I was in Kalimantan waters. It always knows what is going on."
The state, in Jane Atkinson's felicitous phrase, "partakes of the same panoptical
powers as do Mandar soul guardians" (personal communication 1995).

42 Contemporary Indonesian government publications promote cultural difference
in the form of cultural performances, arts, dress—that is, the signs and appearance of difference. On governmental initiatives in promoting performative aspects of local cultures, see Acciaioli (1985) and Volkman (1984, 1990). On cultural
difference and rights to resources, see Fried (this volume), Zerner (1992a, 1994a),
Spyer (1996). On this linkage in the marine sphere, see Zerner (1994a, 1997),
Lowe (2000), and Bandjar and Zerner (1996).

43 While the dominion of Nabi Heder is vast and diffuse, and his location is uncertain, the site of this broadcast is fixed in the courtroom and as a text. While Nabi
Heder can cause the seas to swell and waves to rise, threatening boats and their

crews with death by drowning, the destruction of their gear, or the appearance of a shark, circling the crew and acting "abnormally interested" in them, the state's power to punish is the power to extract money from fishermen's pockets and hold men's bodies in prison.

44 Ilongi or their equivalent are not only used in Mandar. They are sounded throughout South Sulawesi, in local languages, by Makassarese, Bugis, and Bira peoples, during the flying-fish season. The decision also deploys a few key Dutch terms, such as *opnlijk*, as pivotal conceptual points. References to Dutch legal concepts and Indonesian-language discussion of these terms, augment the legal and linguistic authority of the opinion. Decision No. 11 was typewritten and the text was not published. Its pronouncements were communicated to those immediately concerned—the plaintiff, the defendants, and the twenty-one members of the defendants' crew—within the Majene courthouse. Its dissemination may have been quite limited.

45 On the problems and complexities of devolution of resource-management authority to local communities, the potentially problematic aspects of recognizing customary law, and the cultural differences linked to space and ethnicity, see Li (2001).

46 My sense of this demand for free fish is that it constitutes a category mistake in which ideas of a moral economy (Scott 1976) are mistakenly applied to a fishing economy that has been thoroughly commercialized. When local boats fortunate enough to capture an entire school of fish, and loaded beyond their capacity, reach shore, the excess catch is distributed freely to all comers who ask for a share. These distributions, common in the past, are expected between members of a face-to-face moral community. The pole-and-line vessels, home-based in distant ports and crewed for the most part by non-local fishermen, are not part of any such economy.

47 Conflicts do not only occur between locals and outsider-capitalized fishing gear. In the Bulukumba area of South Sulawesi, ongoing "rock wars" are waged by local roppong owners who are attempting to defend their territories and fish from capture by heavily capitalized, locally owned, motorized boats known as *pagai*. Wealthy insiders, with grossly disproportionate gear and access to central governmental power and permissions, even threaten members of their own families who still operate inexpensive roppong. One Bulukumba-based fisherman stated: "A fisherman's brother operating a roppong may be hurling rocks at a pagai owned by his government-employed sister, who works in the fisheries department. . . . She has a steady salary and can accumulate enough capital to invest in construction and operation of such an expensive vessel."

48 In most contexts, Mandar fishers consider marine resources to be infinite, despite

dwindling catches and significant variations in yearly catches obtained from a variety of technologies. For example, local imam have cited Koranic verses to stand for the proposition that resources have no limits other than those imposed upon them by Allah. Local fishers often evoke the powers of Nabi Heder, the "President of the Sea," as controlling the movements of fish, and particularly his capacity to direct the flow of fish to (or away from) individual fishers. The way in which Nabi Heder's powers are conceptualized, however, suggests the focus is on one's catch and on explaining variations in it as a function of one's relationship with Nabi Heder. See Ellen (1986) for discussions of local peoples' conceptions of environmental, particularly resource, limitations. See also Zerner (1994a,b) for discussions of Moluccan fishermen's conceptions of the dynamics and determinants of local trochus and fisheries stocks.

49 See Bailey (1988) for a historical account of Sumatran and Javanese fishers' tactics of resistance, including the use of Molotov cocktails, to the encroachment of Malaysian trawlers in local waters. See also Zerner (1992b) for an account of "rock wars" in a South Sulawesian fishery.

50 The Mandar expression *lopa ate,* literally translated as a "hot heart," evokes a state of intense anger, disturbance, agitation. It also implies a tendency to do something to get rid of the irritating stimulus. Hot hearts in Mandar are opposed to the cool hands (B.M. *ma'dingin limanta*) of good captains and leaders. "Cool hands" figuratively expresses the idea of *salama'* (B.I. *selamat*), a state of coolness and blessing (Darmawan Masud, personal communication 1985). Unsuccessful fishermen who are taunted by their peers for meager catches can be driven into a state of desperate, untenable shame. In such a dire state of agitation, they may be prompted to unleash their "hot knowledge" (B.M. *pa'issangan lopa'*), a form of magic that is said to result immediately in showers of short-term prosperity. Ultimately, however, the use of such "hot knowledge" is believed to bring misfortune. Thermal idioms of consciousness and fate also inform the trance rituals of the highland Toraja, a neighboring ethnic group. In the *maro* ritual, overheated ceremonial centers and worked-up souls and selves of trancers are cooled, like glowing ritual blades immersed in a bath of water, by being "showered" with ritual couplets containing images of wells, springs, and water sources (Zerner 1981; Volkman and Zerner 1988; Volkman 1984). Modest gains in fishing obtained by Mandar fishermen without the use of hot knowledge are said to "descend like tiny droplets of cool palm wine."

51 I translate the Indonesian expression *mangamok dalam hati sendiri* as "wild hearts." The verbal form, *mangamok,* evokes images of social disorder, chaos, wildness, the fury of a mob, or the individual chaos of a person entranced and moving out of control. There may never have been an actual social enactment of the disor-

der beyond the protest at the camat's office in Pamboang. Rather, the violence of the response to outside intrusions was experienced within, more like a riot deep in the heart, and hidden from the authorities' view.

52   The notion that conflicts over marine resources in relatively shallow, inshore waters between local fishermen and outsiders is recent was substantiated by this captain. Born in 1935, he believed that conflicts between outsiders and local fishermen over access to fishing territories and rights to resources were relatively recent. When he was young—"during the Dutch time," during the Japanese time, and during the period when the Dutch returned—"no outsiders entered our waters to fish. There were no problems like this."

53   On the criminalization of customary law, see Peluso (this volume).

54   See James Scott (1976, 1985, 1990) for imaginative explorations of the strategies and discourses of resistance.

55   On the rise of countermapping of customary territories as a form of lobbying for local rights and access to resources, see Peluso (1995).

56   See Peluso (1996), Riker (1994), Zerner (1994a).

57   See Cronon (1995a) for a collection of imaginative contributions to contemporary scholarship on the social and cultural invention of the idea of nature. See also Olwig (1995) and Cronon (1995b) for an analysis of Western cultural and religious history and their relationship to the idea of a pristine natural world. See Botkin (1990) on revisions of the idea of stable natural ecologies and ecological regions.

Singers of the Landscape: Song, History, and Property Rights in the Malaysian Rainforest

Marina Roseman

Into the Forest and History

A topographical watershed moment came for the Temiars of peninsular Malaysia in the 1930s, when British field ethnographer, curator of the Perak Museum at Taiping, and later, the first appointed Protector of Aborigines H. D. Noone published his "Reconnaissance Map of Parts of Upper Perak and Ulu Kelantan" (Noone 1936: 10). "During the last three years," Noone wrote, "it has been my privilege to traverse in many directions, and also to reside in one of the few remaining blanks on the map." Noone was intrigued by what Sir Hugh Clifford, British colonial Resident (1887–99) and later governor of the Straits Settlements (1927–29), had described as the last "untouched aboriginal block of Malayan territory" (Noone 1936: 10; Clifford 1904, 1929).

Centered on the central mountain range of peninsular Malaysia, the Perak/Kelantan watershed was refuge and homeland to a number of Orang Asli peoples, including Temiars. With Noone's map, the Temiars' last refuge entered the colonial record. Noone recognized that this represented a crucial period for the forest peoples and worked to institute protective legal and bureaucratic mechanisms for them. Nonetheless, the erosion of Temiar rights to land and livelihood followed the tracks of the mappers.

While "untouched" and "unmapped" by British colonial administrators, the region had long been mapped, in foot trails and songs, by Temiar hunter-gatherers and horticulturalists. Yet Temiar song maps have never entered the colonial or postcolonial discourse surrounding land ownership and property rights. In this chapter, I recuperate the song map as an ethnohistorical document comprising a new way of making claims to land.

Temiar rainforest dwellers of peninsular Malaysia sing their maps—theoretically, in their epistemology of song composition and performance; melodically, in contours of pitch and phrasing; textually, in place-names weighted with memory. They inscribe crucial forms of knowledge in song: medical, personal, social, historical, geographic. Occupying an inferior position in contemporary hierarchies of political power in the Malaysian nation-state, their carefully cultivated knowledge is devalued. Laborious processes of discovery, experimentation, and oral inscription in song and memory are usually dismissed as mere "trial and error," or as poetics without political consequence.

This knowledge rests on a particular inflection of the relationship among self, society, and cosmos that, in turn, is rooted in the way Temiars correlate environments psychological, social, historical, and physical. I trace here these interconnections, and propose that Temiar relationships between selves, communities, and their enspirited forest landscape are embodied in songs and ritual performances. A corollary of this proposition is that aesthetic forms and performances embody ways of constructing relationships to nature.

Second, I examine the slippage between the Temiar forest peoples' (sɛn?-ɔɔy sənrook)[1] way of being-in-the-world and that of what we might gloss as "out-foresters" (gɔb).[2] These include Malay peasant and court cultures of the precolonial period; the British colonial administration; and the contemporary Malaysian nation-state government. I investigate the disjuncture between Temiar ideas and language about societal relationships to the land, embedded in dreams, songs, dance, ritual, and social action, on the one hand, and the history of state ideology about and interest in forest resources, on the other. This slippage is manifest in the disjuncture between Temiar and state definitions of and approaches to land use, control, history, and ownership.

Contemporary discourses about authorizations of rights historically emerge in the gaps between divergent perspectives converging on the same "place." The position of Temiars and other Malaysian forest peoples (M. *Orang Asli,* "original people") vis-à-vis the present national government is the outcome of a long series of interactions among alternative ways of viewing land use and ownership. Throughout the course of these interactions, Orang Asli have had little chance to affect the choices, interpretations, or decisions made about who would live where and under what circumstances.

Are Temiar songs, which make cartographic claims in a form others might deem "entertainment," any less legitimate than written deeds or drawn maps? How does the designated form of a deed's inscription (written or oral, drawn or sung, "mythical/legendary" or "historic") interact with the status of the "author" of that form (indigenous peoples, demographic majority populations, colonial powers) to determine hierarchies of legitimacy and authority?

Sociological parameters traditionally investigated when studying the ne-gotiation of property rights—for example, networks of patronage, institu-tional organization, and methods of political persuasion—are conditioned by the modes of discourse through which they are conducted. What are the consequences of differences among claims staked through precolonial Malay land-clearing or Temiar fruit-tree planting; British colonial inscription of land deeds; royal decrees made by the Malay sultanates and/or British crown; Temiar enactment of dream-song and trance-dancing ceremonies; or postco-lonial Malaysian government legislation? What ramifications do differential British, Temiar, and Malay approaches to individual agency or group consen-sus hold for the discourse of rights? To explore these questions, I focus on Temiar meanings, messages, and relationships associated with the land artic-ulated in acoustical, linguistic, and kinetic modalities.

I did not set out to study land tenure or to be a rainforest rights activist, but over the decade I have now been studying with the Temiars, I have become involved with both. My draft call came through at least three venues. First, I recognized, as a scholar, the centrality of the tropical rainforest environment to Temiar conceptions of self and social groups. Second, I also recognized the historically unprecedented precipice on which this marvelously complex, intelligent and adaptable, hardy and yet fragile culture is suspended as we move into the twenty-first century. And third, the Temiars well illustrate the case for my longtime advocacy for aesthetics as pragmatics—for collapsing the polarities between political imaginations and realities. I take seriously the ways people imagine themselves in their arts, their oral and written liter-atures, public culture, press, or television commercials. Such imaginary acts, when publicly performed, are not "frills"; rather, they are crucial to ques-tions of legitimacy, identity, power, and authority—to the staking of claims whether by landed gentry or nomads. Whether networked through systems of newspaper readership and language distribution, or by the arboriculture of roving tree-planters and fruit harvesters, those anthropological entities we call societies and nations organize themselves into what Ben Anderson (1991) terms "imagined communities" through such material signs. Their modalities are as diverse as newsprint on wood pulp, fruit trees and the fruits they bear, or songs inspired by those trees.

About twelve thousand Temiar live in small settlements of 25 to 150 inhab-itants along rivers flowing east and west down peninsular Malaysia's central mountainous divide into the states of Kelantan and Perak. Dispersed in a low population density across 2,500 square miles of rainforest in the mid-1960s

(Benjamin 1967a: 4), Temiar settlements range from ten minutes' to several days' journey apart. From highland Temiar villages near the rivers' sources (altitude, 4,000 feet above sea level) to lowland villages downstream (altitude 1,000 feet above sea level), Temiar horticulturalists grow manioc tubers, hill rice, maize, millet, and other crops. They also hunt, fish, plant informal fruit orchards, and harvest jungle products for their own use and for exchange, as they have for centuries.

By the time that Noone began his reconnaissance into the forest interior, coastal and lowland riverbank areas had already been investigated and exhumed for mineral and agricultural use by Malays, Chinese, and British. The smaller upstream tributaries, areas away from the banks of major rivers, and the mountainous terrain, however, remained relatively unscrutinized by either lowland precolonial or European colonial gaze. An 1879 British mining engineer's map of the mining districts of Larut, near Taiping in Perak, is instructive here (see fig. 14). This series of primarily Chinese-worked tin mines in Larut generated Malay royal revenue; disturbances among Chinese mining-district leaders, and among the Chinese and the Malay Sultans and petty chiefs, endangered what were fast becoming strategic British colonial resources for international trade.[3] The violence was instrumental in legitimating British military intervention and economic intrusion in order to return mines to production.

Carefully wrought by a British mining engineer, the plan of Tupai, Assam Kumbeng, and Kamunting mining districts, in Larut, demonstrates how exploration followed the lines of colonial interest in economic resources, driven, in this case, by an upsurge in the global need for tin. The engineer's map and exegesis are intended to inspire capitalist investment; with British technological innovation, political control, and economic interest, he argues, Perak's tin mines would show increased production and greater profit. Larut's tin deposits, the engineer proposes, "exceed in richness those of any other tin-producing country in the East" (Doyle 1879: 1). While observing that the "Heathen-Chinee" has risen "superior to the difficulty" of mining by "bringing his proverbial ingenuity to the rescue" (17) with such innovations as the chain-pump, he surmises that, "if worked with British capital and enterprise, with appliances of modern machinery, [the Larut deposits] would surpass the production of any other part of the known world" (1).

Orang Asli areas lurk beyond the fringes on Doyle's map: note the "JUNGLE" enscripted in curves at the map's edges where detailed tin mines, gardens,

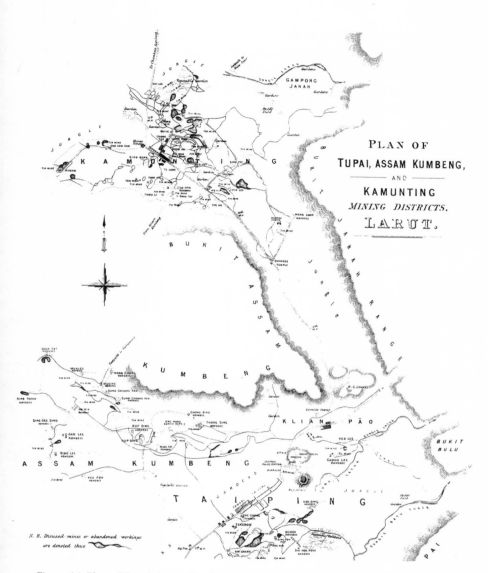

Figure 14. Plan of Tupai, Assam Kumbeng, and Kamunting Mining districts, Larut (northern portion, from Doyle 1879).

and footpaths peter out into the aboriginal absent presence. Just beyond the map's Chinese temples and Christian chapels, placed at forest's edge and mountain's feet to serve genealogically and cosmologically outlying spirits, short curved lines trace the mountains' perimeters. A quick glance at the map gives the impression that lowland areas are the positive ground, with jungle and mountain's edge the negative. The montane, upstream territory of the forest peoples looms like the ocean's edge of medieval and early renaissance maps: what strange beings lie in wait in the blank space at the crest of Bukit Assam Kumbeng (Assam Kumbeng Hill), bordered by the scalloped cartographic symbols so often used for coastlines?

By the mid-1930s, the area east of that delineated by Doyle's map—Clifford's "untouched aboriginal block of Malayan territory"—had been resculpted by colonial engineers, planters, and speculators. Noone writes:

> To-day the Gap road and its branches has cut across to Kuala Lipis in the south: the East Coast Railway now blazes a steel trail between the middle part of the main range and Gunong Tahan; whilst just to the south of the heart of the main range, the Batang Padang road cuts half across the mountains to reach the vortex of Cameron Highlands.
>
> Yet we may note that the northern half of Clifford's "Aboriginal Malaya," that which lies between Cameron Highlands and Gunong Noring, has remained undisturbed to this day. Small roads, like the roads to Lasah and Jalong from Sungei Siput, have, it is true, touched the fringes of this country on the west, but otherwise we face a territory of jungle hills nearly the size of the state of Selangor. (1936: 10)

With the publication of H. D. Noone's "Reconnaissance Map of Parts of Upper Perak and Ulu Kelantan," that northern half, an area of approximately eight thousand square miles, entered the colonial cartographic record. At the same time, during the 1920s and 1930s in the state of Perak, close to the Kelantan border around Jalong, the Kerbu, and the Kuah River, a new ceremonial genre arose. Temiar dream-song singer Datok Ngah Bintang received the first song of the genre cincɛm from the spirit of a marauding elephant invading his rice fields. Then his dead wife, reaching through dreams across the space of her husband's intense loss, gave him further cincɛm songs and dances. Ngah Bintang's cohorts and successors continue to receive cincɛm songs, primarily from the spirits of deceased human beings.[4]

In the genre cincɛm, singers bemoan their loss of land and cultural integrity through the spirit voices of loved ones lost: the genre incorporates "icons of crying" (Urban 1988) in the sob breaks of the singers' vocal delivery and in the song's descending melodic contour. Expressing their heightened sense of loss of territorial range in the poetic language of song texts (dɛhneeh pɛhnɔɔh), cincɛm singers metaphorically conjoin the term for graves with that for other constrained spaces they were now encountering. The term they used, in a slightly offhanded, jokingly poignant metaphor, is *opis kandang*. These dream-song singers and historians of the colonial incursion into one of the last as yet "unmapped" upland areas of peninsular Malaysia marked the extension of British imperial forms of power, knowledge, and representation into their upland forest homeland with a compound noun: *opis* (English, "office") *kandang* (Malay, *kandang* = "fenced-in enclosure"). The enclosed square offices of colonial bureaucrats, to them, were quite simply spaces of death.[5]

Ethnohistory: Indigenous Peoples and State-Formation

Speakers of an Austroasiatic, Mon-Khmer language with linguistic relations spreading up the Indochinese peninsula and over into West India, Temiars belong to what is known as the Senoi ethnic division of the aboriginal, or "Original Peoples" (Orang Asli), of peninsular Malaysia (see fig. 15).[6]

Within the contemporary Malaysian nation, the 105,000 Orang Asli of peninsular Malaysia comprise less than 1 percent of Malaysia's current population of nearly 23.2 million (2000 census). The balance includes 47 percent Malays, 24 percent Chinese, and 7 percent Tamil Indians (Malaysia, Department of Statistics 2000; Nicholas 1997). Orang Asli status within the nation of Malaysia, like that of many indigenous minorities in amalgamated nations, lies suspended amidst Malaysia's often-conflicting goals. These embrace, on the one hand, Malaysia's competition in the international economy, with subsequent demands upon rainforest land, timber, and hydraulic power, as well as the increasingly intense religious activities of the now Islamic Malay majority in states like Kelantan. On the other hand lies Malaysia's celebratory approach toward cultural difference in its expressive, performative dimensions, but its ambivalent posture toward cultural difference when this implicates rights to resources. These are subsumed in a governmental rhetoric of Orang Asli "integration," "sedentarization," and "development" overlaying an agenda of land and resource appropriation (Nicholas 1990; Gomes 1990).

Temiars rose to national consciousness during the post–World War II

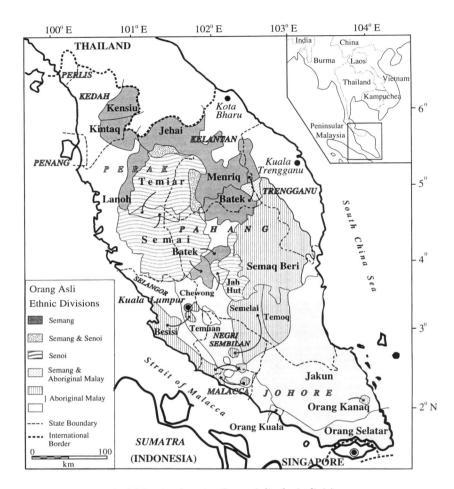

Figure 15. Peninsular Malaysia, showing Orang Asli ethnic divisions and regional locations.

"Emergency," when the British and then Malaysian government sought to counter communist insurgents taking refuge in the jungle.[7] Strategies of Orang Asli regroupment, ostensibly to remove them from sites of contention, resulted in widespread disease and death. These strategies were replaced by jungle forts: colonial outposts that courted Orang Asli with food, medicine, and supplies in order to influence them to remain pro-government.

Much subsequent national policy regarding Orang Asli has been guided, according to official rhetoric, by national security concerns. Yet, "national security" policies of aboriginal regroupment, sedentarization, and integration into the national economy (and the mainstream Malay population's Muslim religion) became easy foils for other agendas when the value of Orang Asli land and resources increased as Malaysia industrialized.

The position of Temiar and other Southeast Asian hill, forest, and coastal peoples as peripheral is a result of a long-term process of "indigenous" (but not autochthonous) state-formation by later-arriving Austronesian peoples practicing sedentary, irrigated agriculture. In Malaysia's national constitution and censuses, these *orang melayu,* or Malays, are now known as "indigenous" peoples and, along with Orang Asli, are legally designated *bumiputera,* or "natives of the country." Yet Malays are not original people from the vantage point of autochthonous groups such as the Temiars. Historically, *orang melayu* collapse into the taxonomic category "indigenous" from the perspective of later arrivals: Muslim traders arriving in the twelfth to fourteenth centuries, or European traders appearing by the sixteenth century. European colonialism furthered the aggregation of Malay "indigenous" (but not "original") royal kingdoms into states.

Indigenous lowland royal kingdoms "regionalized" their socioeconomic networks of trade and hierarchy, linking land and persons representing or responsible for that land; in Malaysia, these areas of royal authority spread upstream from coastal headwaters along river valleys and associated tributaries.[8] These domains were standardized as bounded land masses or "states" by the British colonial administration, then conjoined as the Federated States of Malaysia, which officially became a British colony in 1867. The eleven federated states of the peninsula, along with the states of Sabah and Sarawak on the island once known as Borneo, were later conjoined as the nation of Malaysia following World War II. Parallel independence movements throughout Southeast Asia subsequently transformed and "transliterated" the relationship between land, person, power, and knowledge.[9]

The forest has long been the eco-refuge for semisedentary Temiars who moved through specifically bounded territories—constrained by the presence of other upland forest and lowland peoples of the plains, on the one hand, and their own resource needs on the other (Dentan 1992). Temiars and other upland forest or "hill peoples" of Southeast Asia adjusted their range as colonial maps discovered their terrain. As children, Temiars learn that fear and flight, not aggression or hostility, are valued; indeed, the Senoi (including both Temiar and Semai) have become known as traditionally nonviolent peoples.[10]

Historical studies of the Muslim Malay enslavement of "pagan" Orang

Asli, a practice that extended into the late nineteenth century, indicate that Temiar socialization of fear and attendant strategies of flight may have been adaptive responses to encroaching Malay settlement and slave-raiding (Jones 1968: 289; Roseman 1980: 24; Roseman 1991: 180; Endicott 1983; Dentan 1992; Dentan et al. 1997: 55–59). Aboriginal slave-raiding was curtailed by British proclamation and court procedures in the late 1800s, though the practice continued through the 1920s, according to reports of Semai still living (Dentan, personal communication). However, other forms of coercion—including land and resource appropriation, pressures to Islamicize, and what we might term a "colonizing of the imagination"—continue.

Temiars demonstrated the depth and significance of their knowledge of the land when they worked as guides and members of special Jungle Patrol units (*Senoi Pra'aq*) during the Emergency following World War II (Leary 1995). Their topographic knowledge, and their caretaking—translated into "surveillance"—of the sites they inhabited, became pivotal, first for national security, and later for national development. Yet, like the World War II African-American veterans returning from their civic responsibilities in the European theater to disenfranchisement and racism at home in the United States, Orang Asli were not invited to engage in negotiations leading to the development of the Malaysian Constitution. Unlike the peninsular Malays—or even Austronesian peoples such as the Kenyan or Iban of Sabah and Sarawak, who constitute a majority within their state populations—the Orang Asli of peninsular Malaysia did not receive privileged treatment in these or subsequent federal and state documents. At present, Orang Asli human and property rights remain enmeshed in often contradictory constitutional legislation and subsequent acts and ordinances (Hooker 1991; Rachagan 1990).[11] Temiars and other Orang Asli are poised, if they are lucky, as "tenants-at-will" on "aboriginal areas" and "aboriginal reserves" or "regroupment projects," whose size and location, indeed, whose continued existence, remain at the discretion of the state and federal governments.

Moving through the Rainforest

As horticulturalists, hunters, and gatherers, Temiars have a peculiarly intimate relationship to their terrain. Moving through it daily, they gather information from subtle signs: leaves in motion; sounds that penetrate through a densely foliated, visually opaque rainforest; traces of footprints, feces,

Figure 16. Pandak Hibəl and banana plant. Photograph by Marina Roseman, 1982.

cracked twigs, chopped logs. The palpability of the land and its flora and fauna in Temiar experience is manifest in the way they think about and act toward it.

Temiar theories of self and society, cosmos and environment, are rooted in sensations that lead them to posit multiple, detachable, and permeable components of self in human and nonhuman entities. Temiar theories about the structure of existence and the person posit a collegial permeability between entities that post-Cartesian Western cosmopolitan philosophy, in contrast, hierarchically differentiates as "human" and "nonhuman."

Having moved through the forest with Temiars for over a decade, I find it easier to understand the homologies and resemblances they perceive between humans, with their head-souls and heart-souls, and trees, with their leaf souls and trunk or root souls. Everything in the Temiar universe is potentially bǝ-sɛnʔɔɔy, or capable of "having personhood." Attending to Temiar movements on the forest floor or up in the trees gathering fruit, we can partially comprehend how Austronesian maritime coastal peoples such as Malays, who gradually moved further inland and interacted with the Austroasiatic peoples of the forest, might later characterize the Orang Asli as *orang hutan* ("forest people"). When used by out-foresters, this appellation developed derogatory connotations: the Orang Asli were negatively characterized by Malay out-foresters as strange "people who live in trees."

Historically, forest peoples sometimes hid from Muslim slave raiders by building temporary dwellings in the trees; contemporary Temiars build off-the-ground shelters when traveling through areas where tigers are known to prowl. Yet, what was for Temiars a practical expression of their subsistence technology and sensuous intimacy as "peoples of the forest" became cause for negative typifications by peasants and coastal peoples, for whom the forest was more intimidating.[12] Thus is the Other typified.

Having Dreams, Receiving Songs, Naming the Land

Temiar practices of self-construction and resource appropriation elide in dream-song composition and ceremonial performance. Compositional agency is deflected from the human dreamer/singer onto the spirit source. The dreamer receives the song and conducts that song into the human realm during singing ceremonies. Boundaries between humans and their environment are obscured in the act of dream-song receipt and performance as the spirit's song moves through the medium's voice and body. Boundaries between self and society, while stated, are also sonically obscured during performance when the medium's initial phrase is diffused in the interactive group-choral response.

Dream-song recipients who have become mediums and healers blow the cool spiritual liquid kahyɛk (that flows from their spirit guides along with song) into the head- and heart-souls of patients and other participants. Temiars compare the human head-soul to a young plant shoot. Healers manipulate the area around the crown of the head, shaping it as they would when tending a young plant and singing into it (that is, "watering it"). From the plants and fruit trees that they sow, graft, and tend they receive many of their dream songs, contradicting out-forester notions of these hunter–horticulturalists as non-cultivators.

A medium from the settlement of Jɛlgək, near the source of the River Berok, recounts the receipt of a dream song from the spirit of a banana tree he had planted and tended (see fig. 17):

> The way of the Talĭn banana [L. *Musa paradisiaca*]. Down at the side of my house. I had already planted it, already tended it, shaping the ground around the young shoot. It emerged, this child of mine, as a boy child. Small, bending with the weight of ripe fruit, tiny! He was as small as the banana plant stem. The Talĭn banana's head-soul grew; becoming animated, he emerged, he sang, lah. He versed of Mount Raŋwɛ̃ɛ̃y, Mount Rɛnjiyɛs.
>
> It happened four months ago. I followed, repeating each phrase; if I didn't follow I'd remain ignorant. I flared to waking consciousness, pulling on my own true eyes—returning to my everyday way of seeing.
>
> He came that one time; after that, another month passed before he returned again. All he had to do was come that first time, and I'd already learned the song. (Pandak Hibəl, Jɛlgək, 22-vi-82, DN6)[13]

Singers of the Landscape

He versed of Mount Raŋwɛ̃ɛ̃y, Mount Rɛnjiyɛs.

Temiars map and mediate their relationships with the land and each other through song. Landforms traversed or cultivated become landmarks named and recorded in the songs Temiars receive from the souls of the landscape, its flora and fauna.[14] "I had already planted it, already tended it, shaping

Figure 17. Ading Kerah stands while singing, his head amid the cool, moist, fragrant leaves of the tənamuus?, while the chorus responds. Photograph by Marina Roseman, 1982.

the ground around the young shoot. It emerged, this child of mine, as a boy child. . . . The Talĩn banana's head-soul grew; becoming animated, he emerged, he sang, lah."

Temiar mediums are singers of the landscape, translating the rainforest environment—jungle, field, and settlement—into culture as inhabitant spirits emerge, identify themselves, and begin to sing in dreams, and later, in ritual performances. The forest becomes a social space when networks of association are established between humans and spirits, who then become parents with children, students with teachers, mediums with spirit guides.

Songs are termed "paths," a potent image for people living in dense rainforest. The disintegration of illness is metaphorically diagnosed as "soul loss," as a person's head-soul takes up permanent residence off in the forest with the spirits; healing involves singing the "paths" of spirits, who can fly above the dense forest of life and, from above the canopy, see far enough to locate and return the patient's lost head-soul. To counter the dislocation and fragmentation of the illness experience, mediums also sing "true names" of places that spirits have given in their dream-song texts.

In dreams, the spirit guide sings its path to the dreamer. Later, in nighttime ceremonies, the dreamer will become the initial singer with an interactive chorus. These ceremonies are held in the settlement, usually inside a house with a large enough central room to accommodate the singers, bamboo-tube percussion players and chorus members, and dancers. The room, decorated with jungle foliage, sets shy spirits at ease. These leaf ornaments visually, tactilely, olfactorily, and audibly link village (*deek*) and forest (*beek*), as well as person and environment (see fig. 18).

If the ceremony is being held specifically for curing purposes and the patient is too ill to be moved, the ceremony may be held in the patient's house, regardless of its size. For large ceremonies, such as the one held to mark the end of a period of mourning, or in communities where government planning efforts have encouraged smaller, nuclear-family dwellings, a separate structure houses the ceremony.

As the singer stands, vocalizing and dancing, his or her voice is now the voice of the spirit, singing of its visions as it flies above the forest canopy, alights upon mountain crests, scans the horizon, and finds and returns the dislocated souls of patients brought to be healed. Visiting the ceremonial room, the spirit comments in song on the flickering firelight and shadows of the dancers. Animated spirits of the environment sing about how much they enjoy the sounds of the dancer's rustling leaf whisks and dangling bracelets, or express their dismay over perceived insults. They sing about the sounds of the female chorus who vocally respond, returning each vocal line (or "mouthful") to the spirits like partners in a good reciprocal exchange, and, with their voices, as Temiars say, "following the path." Or, they may chide a tired, disheveled chorus to attend to their task as accompanists.

Mapping the Universe

What might sound like "merely a song" to a Malay precolonial peasant, British colonial speculator, or Malaysian postcolonial administrator is both map and history text to Temiar singers. So, too, what seems to be virgin, unmapped territories to lowland peoples and colonial explorers are well-traversed and productive homelands to upland hunters, gatherers, aboriculturalists, and horticulturalists.

The remapping of indigenous spaces by expanding metropoles and empires is nothing new.[15] But the ability of indigenous upland Asian populations to adjust to such incursions by taking refuge in so-called "unmapped territories" decreased dramatically as European exploration increased, innovations in communications proliferated, and technologies of industrialization penetrated Southeast Asia during the period from the 1870s through the 1940s. For people like the Temiars, there was nowhere left to go.

Hunter-gatherers and shifting cultivators often speak less about land *ownership* than the rights to range across and use, or *usufruct*. Charting a different history than the maps of colonial topographers, Temiar songs trace their experience and relationship with the land areas across which they historically ranged. This is one form in which they record their entitlement: their "title" or "deed" to land. Temiars recognize four types of property: territorial ranges, household plots (rice fields), garden plots (tapioca stands), and fruit trees. They distinguish categories and rights of property differently from precolonial lowland peoples, colonial administrators, and contemporary Malaysian government officials. Temiars do not speak of owning *land,* but do speak of *land areas* (sakaaʔ) that are historically theirs, on which they have proprietary rights to live, gather, plant, harvest, hunt, fish, and be buried.[16] These areas often include individuals' places of birth (tɛʔ jənom) or are otherwise associated genealogically with their places of origin (təmpad ʔasal kaneeʔ).

Despite the seeming fluidity of their semisedentary house and cultivation sites, village groups have historically maintained the territorial range, or sakaaʔ, encompassing their hunting, gathering, fishing, and swidden areas.

Figure 18. For those who can read the forest, a coconut tree from orchards associated with a past village site is visible amidst secondary forest. Temiars, who once lived here, and their descendants will return to collect from this and other fruit trees in the vicinity. Photograph by Marina Roseman, 1982.

Temiar villages are autonomous, or "segmentary," political entities. Village size changes as family groups or individuals join or leave a village; however, the village entity maintains stability through the continued presence of an amibilineal descent group, or *ramage,* related to a core group of siblings (see Benjamin 1966, 1967b). Sakaa? were respected by neighboring Temiar settlements, by other neighboring Orang Asli groups, and, to varying degrees, by precolonial Malay settlers.

Temiars do claim particular territories, then, but they concretize those claims in different ways than people of sedentary and literate societies, who stake their claims with wooden posts, written deeds, marked maps, or permanent house structures and cultivated fields. Furthermore, Temiar claims are not individual, but communal: village groups claim territorial ranges. Comfortable with the practice of joint ownership, Temiars have developed linguistic and musical genres that reinforce the positive ethical value placed upon group decision making and interaction.

Before the rice planting begins each year, Temiar village members jointly owning the use rights of a territorial range will gather together in semi-ritualized discussions termed bəcaraa?. During these discussions, members determine how they will divide cultivable areas surrounding the village into household plots (səlaay). Village members each contribute their opinions, which, like songs, are called "paths," or "routes" (nɔɲ), a potent image for these people of the dense forest. Once the land use for that year's rice fields has been mutually agreed upon, household plots will be cleared and planted. Household ownership rights are recognized in these plots or rice-field areas for the one or two years of their use. After this, the plots will be left fallow to reseed themselves from surrounding trees and plants, and will eventually revert to secondary forest. Household "ownership" rights are articulated in the form of control over production and distribution of rice. Household groups often organize villagewide labor groups to clear, plant, and harvest the crop; they also control the distribution of the produce, primarily hill rice, at harvest time.

Household rights are also recognized for garden plots, which are sometimes but not always geographically contiguous with rice fields. Garden plots are cleared, burned, and planted with tapioca tubers and other edible and ornamental plants by extended family households—relatives who share one "hearth"—or by nuclear-family units who share a sleeping-partition area. Garden plots give yields for a longer time than rice fields. Even more permanent in their geographic mark upon the land are fruit trees. These are either deliberately planted from the seeds of consumed fruits, or they are tended from seeds fortuitously cast aside by humans or other hungry mammals ("husbanded collection") (see Ellen 1988, quoted in Dentan 1991: 423).

Traces Upon the Land: Fruit Trees and Land Tenure

In the rainforest, where abandoned houses of wood, bamboo, and thatch quickly rotted, and cleared fields returned to jungle fecundity in a sustainable course of development, fruit trees became the most permanent manifestation of past residence for semisedentary Temiar, who traditionally moved their village sites every two to five years while enabling fallow land to refresh itself.

Fruit trees become associated with the persons who plant or tend them. Though groups go together to gather fruits, which are then distributed through a village, the planter/tender holds rights of determining when to gather and how to distribute the produce. When Temiars die, their names are no longer spoken, and they are often referred to by the village site that was being occupied at the time of the death. The death of a village member was often reason for moving the village. Yet siblings maintain rights to the trees of deceased parents; the trees thus enshrine historical records of social relations, both in terms of genealogies and of village-site histories (Benjamin 1966). Title genealogies to the fruit trees are not discussed by using the ancestor's name, which is linguistically tabooed after death, but by using the village-site names that replace them. Benjamin notes:

> Temiar genealogical knowledge beyond the parental generation is very limited, and when looking back in time they regard the fruit trees as the joint property in each generation of the sibling group associated with the one man who is regarded as its "guardian." So the titulary genealogy of groups of fruit trees takes the form of a single line of inheritors descending from the man whom succeeding generations regard as solely responsible for planting up the old orchards. This process of genealogical amnesia whereby the collateral parts are shed has, then, an important result: the genealogies of guardian-headmen, titulary rights in fruit trees and restatements of each group's history of land-attachment are automatically stated by one and the same genealogical recitation. (1966: 18)

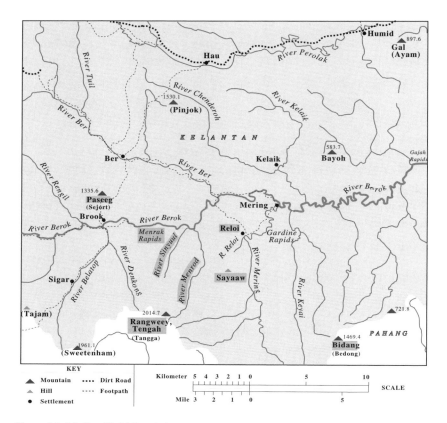

Figure 19. Mother Fluid Beauty's song map.

Dentan, building on the work of Benjamin, Kirk Endicott, and other Orang Aslists, notes that the ownership of fruit trees is basic to indigenous Malaysian (Orang Asli) notions of land tenure, and suggests that Orang Asli generally, "except for the Batek, assigned particular trees to particular individuals in a way that contravened the pervasive stress on sharing but kept people from simply felling trees to get the fruit" (1991: 422; see also Dentan and Chooi 1995).

This "ubiquitous arboricentricity" (Dentan 1991: 423) contravenes current national notions that so-called shifting cultivators do not have areas they historically claim. It also brings into question whether their relationships to those areas are entirely those of usufruct rather than ownership. Third, since jungle produce such as fruits and tree resins (Gianno 1990) were often used in exchange relations for salt, cloth, knife blades, and other market goods from non-rainforest peoples, it also refutes the notion that Orang Asli are "merely subsistence-oriented" and need to be "integrated" into the market economy (Gomes 1990).

The right to compensation for fruit trees lost to rainforest destruction or forced governmental relocation is one of the few Orang Asli rights of compensation in the revised Aboriginal Peoples Act of 1954 (Section 11) that is not listed as discretionary, though as Hooker (1991) notes, methods of establishing a claim to fruit or rubber trees, amount and method of payment, as well as responsibility for administration of compensation, are not clearly indicated in the ordinance. I have seen main and subsidiary logging roads bulldozed over fruit trees in the vicinity of Temiar villages. Nonetheless, the growing indigenous pan–Orang Asli political organization POASM (Persatuan Orang Asli Semenanjung Malaysia—Orang Asli Association of Peninsular Malaysia) urges Temiar communities to plant fruit trees in order to help stake their territorial claims.

Representations of the Real

Individual ownership of fruits while they remain in trees, as well as household ownership of rice fields and tapioca gardens, is obscured in typical Temiar fashion, which instead highlights egalitarian and sociocentric ideals. Groups of women from various households troop together through each other's gardens digging tapioca tubers, ostensibly sharing the produce of their gardens while still in the process of collection. Similarly, villagewide work groups harvest household rice plots in consecutive rotations, and the subsequent produce of each household's rice field is distributed through the village work group and beyond. Tendencies toward individual, or even nuclear-family ownership, then, are intentionally obscured even though they exist—in keeping with the dynamic tension Temiars maintain between celebrating the collective or sociocentric self and retaining the integrity of the individual or egocentric self. This dynamic tension drives what we might call, following Keil and Feld (1993), Temiar "muse-ecology": the conjoint musical practice and cultural ecology of this rainforest group.

Rights to geographic ranges, household plots, garden plots, and fruit trees were not claimed in writing or entered on pictorial maps. But they have been encoded in Temiars' ethnohistorical "recountings" (kerɛnwəəh), origin legends (cənal), and in the dream-song histories (nɔɲ, "way"; gənabag, "singing") that mark the areas people lived on, ranged across, and, in our terms, "claimed" as theirs. Temiar dream songs result not from abstract or generic gestalts of "tree" or "mountain," but record particular experiences with *this* tree, *that* river, *these* mountains intimately encountered or (if we recognize their personhood in Temiar fashion) "dwelled with" by village members.

A wealth of material on land tenure and migration is embedded in Temiar songs and associated dream narratives (see fig. 19). Upstream on the Berok River in the settlement Kelaik (Kɛlyɛt), the medium-singer Busu Alang received a song from the female spirit of the crest of Mount Gohaaʔ. Playing back a tape-recording of the song I had recorded during a singing and trance-dancing ceremony the preceding night, I elicited the dream narrative associated with that song. Busu Alang revealed that Mt. Gohaaʔ, farther upstream near the settlement of Bər, is his birthplace (tɛʔ jənom). The song text, naming the various mountains of that area, demarcates the "place of origin" (ʔasal kaneeʔ) for the core kinship group of Kelaik: "You heard about it at the point in the song where [the spirit of the mountain] versed all those names together. The group near Mt. Gohaaʔ, the group of Mt. Raɲyaal. Mah, up-river."

Not far from Busu Alang's settlement of Kelaik is the settlement Rəlɔɔy (M., Reloi), located on a tributary of the upper Berok River. Here, while living in his grandfather's wife's home village, Ading Kerah dreamt the young female head-soul of nearby Mount Raŋwɛ̃ɛ̃y. In Ading Kerah's dream, the male head-soul of Mount Galɛɲ took the female spirit downriver for two weeks and slept with her. After he brought her back, she appeared to Ading Kerah in a dream. She revealed her "true name," Mother Fluid Beauty, which she allowed him to give to his wife.

When the spirit of the landscape, Mother Fluid Beauty, sings through him during ceremonial performance, he names the rivers and mountains that constitute the territorial range of Rəlɔɔy in particular, and the upper Bərɔk River Temiars in general (see fig. 20). A segment of her song text, from a 1982 performance, translated here, illustrates this. The five verses each have three melodic phrases (-1,-2,-3) with jɛnhook phrases (-J) interspersed.

1–J Respectful greetings, Mother Fluid Beauty!
1–1 Mother, Mother Fluid Beauty of the Mɛnrod River,
1–2 Mother, Mother Fluid Beauty of the Siɲĩ̃l River,
1–3 Gathering kəwar-leaf bouquets.
2–1 Where has the kəwar soul strayed?
2–2 Circling up above,

Figure 20. Musical transcription of a verse of Mother Fluid Beauty's song.

2–3 And deep inside.

2-J Yəh, welcome to all!

3–1 I sing, forgetting, remembering,

3–2 I sing, bravely, fearfully,

3–3 Here in the ceremonial house.

4–1 I arrive, blowing like the wind,

4–2 Mothers, whirling around Mount Sayaaw,

4–3 Far across the land.

5–1 Circling wide the land,

5–2 Coming home, soaring,

5–3 Playing atop Mt. Bidaɲ.

As she encircles the land in song, she proceeds to name the Mɛnrod River; the Siɲĩ̃l River;[17] Mt. Sayaaw; Mt. Bidaɲ; the Mɛnrod River again; the Mendrak falls upstream on the Bərɔk River; Mt. Pasəg, a small hill on the other side of the Bərɔk River; and Mt. Tɛŋah, another name for Mt. Raŋwɛ̃ɛ̃y.[18] The place names she sings show her range, and his village's sakaaʔ (see fig. 19).

British-Malay deeds and titles to *real estate* are contracts between people, or between people and the state. The mutual recognition of sakaaʔ by neighboring Temiar and other Orang Asli settlements is indeed a contract between people. But Temiar song maps record their territorial range in a contract that gives voice to the landscape itself. Their "contracts" bind people with places, yet deflect agency to the *place*, whereas contemporary European and European-influenced jural systems foreground the *person*.

Temiar concepts about land range and use may not be directly translatable into national or international terms, but our task as ethnographers is to render them comprehensible across these diverse modes of discourse. Interactions of sedentary populations with hunting-gathering and shifting cultivators have historically been fraught with tension and incomprehension (Pearce [1953] 1988). Malay peasants who cleared permanent rice fields called their cultivated fields "live land" (*tanah hidup*) and the surrounding jungle, "dead land" (*tanah mati*) (Wan Hashim 1988). But for Temiars, the jungle is alive with imaginative *and* material resources.

When British colonialists introduced the Torrens system of land tenure in 1890 to replace the Malay system, their conception of land usage and ownership was incorporated with that of Malay peasants and sultans, excluding the Orang Asli. Permanently cultivated "live land" was registered, titled, and deeded (Wan Hashim 1988). So-called "nonalienated," or unregistered, lands reverted to the colonial powers and the Malay sultanate, and later, to the state and federal governments of Malaysia. Temiars were effectively disenfranchised and rendered landless, except as wards of the colonial and later the federal and state governments.

Understanding the aesthetics and pragmatics of Temiar song performance is crucial if we are to comprehend inflections of ownership across other cultural dimensions. Temiar concepts of song ownership are informative here: a song is most powerful when sung by the dreamer who received it directly, who claims it as his or her "own path" (noŋ rii?). There is, then, a recognition of "ownership"—legitimized in the embodied conduction of personal dream receipt and vocalization—that empowers and energizes a song in performance in a very special way. This performative definition of empowerment is cognate with Temiars' proprietal bias toward the processual. This is seen, as well, in their emphasis upon usufruct (land usage rights) rather than domain (ownership of place).

A song is most powerful when sung by the dream-song receiver, or "owner" (whom I have elsewhere termed the "interposer" rather than the "composer"), of that song. The power source of the song, however, is deflected to the agency of the spirit guide (that is, to the landscape). Furthermore, this power is actualized most thoroughly when it is sung not solo by the dream-song receiver, but with choral interaction (that is, when it is communalized, embedded in social relations).[19]

Temiars mediate their relationship with the forested landscape in song. So, too, Temiar dreamers incorporate new commodities that enter their society—for example, dreaming songs from parachutes and airplanes as they do from birds; from watches and perfumes as they do from pulsating insects or fragrant flowers; from the spirits of the British, Japanese, Malays, and visiting anthropologists as they do from members of their own communities, living or deceased. As long as things from "downstream," or the "market," were fewer than those from "upstream," or the "jungle," and could be absorbed economically, ideologically, and spiritually into their system without tipping the balance of their lifestyle, these dream-song appropriations represented their way of absorbing the power and prestige of outside incursions.

As the battle for rainforest land becomes ever more contentious, however, and as life for many of the lowland Temiar becomes confined to two acres per "nuclear family," itself a somewhat foreign concept, the power to maintain equity vis-à-vis the non-rainforest-dwelling "Other" through dream songs becomes less viable.[20] Yet these dream songs, which mark the relationship of particular people to particular landforms, mountains, river rapids, and fruit trees, may, like the fruit-tree genealogies that link these shifting cultivators to settlement sites of the past, provide a way for present-day Temiars to lay claim to land that is historically theirs.

Fruit Songs, Mountain Songs, and Land Tenure

Local discursive practices and resource-management practices of Temiars differ from state discourses, statutes, and interests. The differences revolve around the following issues: (1) usufruct or land-usage rights (rights to property with land as an agent) vs. property rights as ownership (with land as object); (2) land ownership by the communal entity (the Temiar settlement) vs. ownership by a political entity recognized by the state: the individual citizen or corporate entity; and (3) the marking of claims by "imaginary" (songs) or "material" markers (such as fruit trees) vs. claims marked through inscriptions written in the mode of those in political control of the state.

These issues of land ownership have their cognates in musical composition, performance, and affect: (1) emphasis on the performative enactment of a song, empowered by the agents of the landscape; (2) a performative value on community participation, manifest in the relationship between initial singer and interactive choral response; and (3) the valuation of seemingly immaterial resources such as songs. Aesthetics and aesthetic forms are fundamental, undervalued aspects of Temiar and, indeed, human experience. When we attend to performative and expressive cultural dimensions, we find novel uses for classic ethnographic evidence like songs, myths, and ritual enactments: as vehicles that articulate relationships to landscapes in general, as well as articulating relationships to specific sites, regions, and resources.

Recognizing Temiars as legitimate political entities—as citizens and corporate entities—with the right to own is an essential first step preceding the extension of land rights. The Malaysian government has extended corporate notions to communal village groups in their Malay Reserves. But Malay Muslims are constitutionally entitled to own land, whereas Orang Asli are considered to be wards of federal and state governments. Temiars are allowed to dwell but forced to move at the government's discretion.

Is it possible to inject Temiar ways of singing the landscape into the current discourse about land claims in Malaysia? As records of ownership, Temiar songs remain in the realm of the aural, a realm one step closer to the imaginary than writing. Perhaps we hesitate to endow Temiar songs with historical authenticity because we fear they might just "dream up" whatever songs are useful for contemporary land and resource negotiations. Literate societies are driven by the desire to fix the traces of memory, but even in writing, the trace is always shifting. The written word undergoes hermeneutic transformations when political contexts determining who controls the interpretation and enforcement of written laws and contracts change. For Temiars, experience in life transformed into knowledge from dreams, that is then recorded in songs and manifest in ceremonies, is very real indeed.

For those who need harder wood on which to knock, there are the fruit trees. The boundaries between what might otherwise be categorized as "material" or "immaterial" are problematized by Temiars, who mark their historical relationship with the land through a tree's relatively stable physical presence; its seasonally recurring flowers and edible fruits; its resins and latex; as well as its dreamable spirit.[21] Is it any coincidence that one of the primary Temiar musical genres originating in the upland areas of the western Malaysian state of Perak (nɔŋ pɛnhəəy, "the way of the Pərah tree") emerges from the spirit of the annually fruiting perah tree (L., *Elateriospermum tapos*)?

If there were Temiar divas, the perah tree would be one of them. The change to red-tipped leaves on this tree marks the beginning of the new year in the rainforest: after the rains and before the flowers of the fruit season. Its nutty fruit is mixed with tapioca and baked in bamboo tubes to produce a special form of the staple tapioca, a treat of the season. Perah is the subject of much poetry in song texts, and, in a dream, gave its special ceremonial names, pɛnhəəy and podɛɛw, to the genre's composer/interposer, Keranih Laloh of Grik. The genre emerged during the Japanese occupation of Malaysia during World War II, between 1942 and 1945.

Among Temiars dwelling in the upland areas in the east coast state of Kelantan, two other significant genres are also associated with fruit and latex-producing trees: nɔŋ tahun, "the way of the annual fruits," and nɔŋ doog, "the way of the Ipoh tree fluid" (L., *Antiaris toxicara*), the latex of which is used to produce blowpipe dart poison. The former was composed in the late 1960s by a Temiar medium born in Perak, who moved to Kelantan. When he composed the first annual fruits song, he was posted on the Aring River, a tributary of the Lebir, among the Batek Deh, an Orang Asli group of the Sem-

ang ethnic division for whom fruit trees are also central materially, spiritu-
ally, and aesthetically (Roseman 1991: 91–99; Endicott 1979a: 3–5, 55–57).
The latter, the way of the Ipoh tree fluid, is prominent among Temiars in the
Cameron Highlands, whose territory borders Semai areas.

To comprehend Temiar concepts of ownership, practices of use, and theories of social and environmental relations is one step. To find ways to respect
and empower them as they confront the concepts and practices of peoples
more powerful, and of population sectors whose imaginations of reality are
enforced as reality, is the true challenge of our transcultural and transnational times.[22] Such a course would enable Temiars to sustain their environments while charting their own course of development. Wan Zawawi
Ibrahim's recent compendium (1996b) of Temiar voices, *Kami Bukan Anti-
Pembangunan! Bicara Orang Asli Menuju Wawasan 2020* (We Aren't Against
Development! Voices of Orang Asli regarding Visions of the Year 2020), de-
lineates Temiars' ideas about how the goals of national development and
Temiar cultural-ecological integrity might be interwoven.

"Nowhere to Run, Nowhere to Hide"

In blues, rhythm and blues, and other African-American genres, singers
transform harrowing situations into masterfully transcendent poetic expression even as they document their tragedy. These song genres share certain
properties with Temiar dream songs. Both social groups strive for cultural
survival in oppressive conditions. Here, song's ability to crystallize experience personally and communicate it socially performs concomitant tasks:
the epic emotional transformation from downtrodden to heroic; and the
strengthening of subjective agency and group identity among imperiled,
marginalized segments of a population.

The erroneous assumption driving the disjuncture between traditional
Temiar approaches to land use and life goals, on the one hand, and contemporary national and international discourses surrounding property rights,
development, trade, and modernization, on the other, is that one way of con-
figuring the world is more "real" than another. Temiars emphasize individual
experiential and dream revelation in the construction of their cultural system; given this epistemological foundation, they also recognize the right of
Temiar groups living in other river valleys or settlements, as well as out-

foresters, to follow different religious practices. "We have all been given different tributaries, though they all flow from one river," a Temiar in Kuala Mu observed.

Yet recognition of the right to difference is balanced by respect for local custom. "One set of practices must be adhered to in the jungle, another in the cities," a Temiar in Belau commented about negative spirit retributions befalling out-foresters if they fail to practice Temiar customs of respect toward forest spirits when moving through the jungle. So, too, Temiars dwelling temporarily among Temiars in distant river valleys may be called upon to make restitution to offended spirits if they confuse their home practices with local customs.

Only the play of power makes one symbolic mode of engaging and articulating the world take precedence over another; bringing this dynamic to the fore has been Foucault's major contribution to social theory (1972, 1980c). In the colonial and postcolonial periods, Temiars have had increasingly less of this type of power. However, in the 1990 national elections, Kelantan Temiars wielded what has become, for them, a new form of power: electoral politics. They expressed their discouragement with the government party's (UMNO) land policy by voting as a bloc, and thereby provided the swing vote for the opposition to come into power in that state. This did not entirely obviate their difficulties, as the predominant opposition parties in Kelantan are organized around Islamic religious preferences, which denigrate as "pagan" Temiar cultural and religious practices. Ultimately, the Temiars are caught between the proverbial rock and a hard place, with nowhere to go.

Temiar lands are being rapidly deforested and converted into oil palm or rubber plantations. Temiar patterns of flight into deeper jungle continued to serve them into the 1960s, but no longer present a viable strategy. The network of logging roads that brings new settlers usually reverses rather than augments Temiar economic fortunes (Hood and Hasan Mat Nor 1984; Hood 1990; Gomes 1989, 1990). These "developments" are rendering them, under government supervision, equal to the poorest Malay peasants and small rubber landholders, a step down rather than a step up (Endicott 1979b).

So-called marginal peoples like the Temiars may once have been able to locate themselves on the fringes in what Dentan (1992: 223) calls "refuges": places where "refugees" (relatively powerless people) can find a relative degree of safety from supervision by invaders, or from such social predation as enslavement, massacre, genocide, or forced assimilation. In Dentan's paradigm, invaders and refugees refer to poles of a relationship that occurs across a frontier. This is a land area on the margin of an expanding invader population that is still occupied by weaker people with a relatively low population density.[23] While that margin exists, refugees can elaborate their way of being-in-the-world, even as they accommodate to interactions with invaders.

Temiars were never primeval forest dwellers living in a mythically complete harmony with their forest surroundings, and we should not romanticize them as such. Nor need we enshrine them like static museum relics of a prehistoric past. They have always been interacting and encountering, always changing. In earlier epochs, they had more luxury of space, demography, and forest resources with which to develop a relatively nonviolent, exquisitely poetic, yet utterly practical relationship with one another, their environment, and their cosmos. When pushed into a corner by scarce resources, they, too, for subsistence wages, guide loggers into their dream-song forest and hunting preserves to select trees for felling. Eco-philosophy, like nonviolence, is contingent upon circumstances.

Nonetheless, Temiars have much to teach to other societies who are trying to come to terms with modernization, even postmodernization, without losing their souls, their songs, their families, or their communities. When the land, its flora, and fauna are treated disrespectfully, Temiars note, the spirits are offended and may cause illness or misfortune. Such reasoning, formalized in the psychosocial, religious and philosophical stance of animism, is becoming more familiar in Western scientific theory and practice—in environmental toxicology and resource management, for example—as we experience how the environment "strikes back" when mistreated.

We are poised within a problematic moment in the charting of global and regional, legal and developmental policy pertaining to environmental resource management, governance, and the rights of indigenous peoples. Does any other social group have the right to take the Temiar dream world and forest habitat to build, instead, their own dream houses? or to build the socioeconomic power of a nation, like Malaysia, that must now compete for survival within an international economy? By learning to hear and value the history of ownership inscribed in a cartography of song, it may be possible to chart a route that respects Temiars' "songpaths" through the forest, and gives them the right to make deliberate and informed choices about their future.

Notes

An earlier version of this essay was presented at a conference, "Culture and the Question of Rights in Southeast Asian Environments: Forests, Coasts, and Seas," organized by Charles Zerner and sponsored by the Asia Program (Mary Brown Bullock, Director) of the Woodrow Wilson International Center for Scholars, Washington, D.C., on 3 June 1992. The essay has benefited from the insights of co-panelists Jane Monnig Atkinson, Don Brenneis, Nancy Peluso, Anna Tsing, and volume editor Charles Zerner; and from other readers, including Robert Dentan, Charles Keil, and Edward Schieffelin. A version of this essay appears in *American Anthropologist* (1998, vol. 100: 106–21); portions contained herein appear with the journal's permission, and the editorial contributions of Barbara Tedlock and Dennis Tedlock are gratefully acknowledged. Research assistants Elizabeth Blakesley and Ritu Jayakar assisted with bibliography and graphics, respectively.

Field research with the Temiars of Kelantan and Perak in 1981–82, 1991, 1992, and 1995 was conducted under the auspices of the Social Science Research Foundation, Asian Cultural Council, Wenner Gren Foundation for Anthropological Research (Grant No. 4064), National Science Foundation (BNS81–02784), and Research Foundation of the University of Pennsylvania, with additional travel funds provided by Universiti Sains Malaysia and Malaysian Air Lines (1991). Analysis and writing were furthered by a Guggenheim Foundation Fellowship (1996–97), Professional in Residence Fellowship from the Annenberg School for Communications at the University of Pennsylvania (1996–97), and the National Endowment of the Humanities (2000). My gratitude to these institutions: to my sponsors at Universiti Malaya, Cultural Centre; to the Universiti Kebangsaan Malaysia and the Muzium Negara (National Museum, Kuala Lumpur); and to the Orang Asli Broadcast Unit at Radio–TV Malaysia, Jabatan Hal Ehwal Orang Asli, and the Economic Planning Unit of the Prime Minister's Office, whose staff shared their extensive knowledge and services with me. Temiars and other Orang Asli from Kelantan and Perak to Gombak and Angkasapuri have been wise and patient teachers, hosts, and friends; so too, several Malaysian families have provided urban home bases.

1 Temiars use the term sɛnʔɔɔy sənrook, "people of the forest," to refer generally to the aboriginal peoples (M. *Orang Asli,* "original people") of the Malay peninsula.

2 The Temiar orthography used here combines aspects of the orthography used by Benjamin (1976, 1985) with those suggested by Diffloth (1975). Abbreviations identifying the language of other non-English terms include: M., Malay; L., Latin (for ethnobotanical and ethnobiological identifications); T., Temiar (used only when clarifying an identification in comparison with another language).

3 Patrick Doyle, mining and mechanical engineer, gives a short description of the disturbances (1879: 1–2).

4   From a series of interviews with Datok Ngah Bintang's son Alang Uda A/L Ngah Bintang in Kg. Kenang Baru, Jalong, Sg. Siput, 1995 (T95-OH2, T95-OD3). (Roseman archival collection: T = Temiar; FN = Field Notes; OR = Original DAT)

5   The term *kandang* encompasses a wide range of meanings—from the animal's pen to the tiger's cage to the witness stand, with its positive valuation associated with shelter (as in the water buffalo's byre), and its negative, with prison. See Wilkinson (1959: vol. 2, p. 505). Roseman (1995), track 3, provides an example of this phrase's use in cincɛm.

6   Temiar constitutes one dialect among sixteen linguistic groups or dialects spoken by the two-thirds of the Orang Asli who are Austroasiatic speakers. The remaining third are Austronesian speakers of roughly four Malay dialects collectively termed Aboriginal Malay (Diffloth 1975; Benjamin 1976; Wurm and Hattori 1983).

7   On this complex historical moment, see Jones (1968), Roseman (1980), Leary (1995), Dentan et al. (1997: 61ff).

8   Wolters (1967, 1982) discusses the riverine and maritime orientation of early Southeast Asian polities. On the relationship between the territorial range of multiple political centers (*mandalas*) and personage, he notes: "The importance of a *mandala* did not depend upon its geographical size but on networks of loyalties that could be mobilized to provide armed power to leaders whom I described as 'men of prowess'" (1982: 25). See also Kessler (1978: 38ff).

9   The Malaysian nation, constituted in 1963, included peninsular Malaysia (which attained independence in 1947), plus the formerly British Singapore, Sabah (North Borneo), and Sarawak (Northwest Borneo). Singapore separated in 1965, alleviating tensions between that city's Chinese majority and the Malays, who were in administrative control of the Malaysian government (Andaya and Andaya 1982).

10 See Dentan (1968, 1992) on Semai and Orang Asli nonviolence; Howell [1984] 1989a and 1989b on the Chewong. Dentan and Williams-Hunt (1999) present a powerful and disturbing narrative of violent responses to current conditions of underdevelopment and land loss in a Semai community.

11 Scholarship on Orang Asli historical and contemporary status vis-à-vis the nation-state has grown tremendously, with contributions by Malaysian, other Asian, and Euro-American authors (e.g., Rashid 1995; Ibrahim 1995, 1996a; Dentan et al. 1997; Edo 1998; Benjamin and Chou in press).

12 Hodgen (1964) describes how Christian monotheistic and evolutionary taxonomies sought to position "pagans" in relation to categories human, nonhuman, and superhuman.

13 Temiar 1981/82, FN1690. The song is recorded on Temiar 1981/82 OR88–1.

14 For further ethnographic examples of the mediation of land and person through song, see Schieffelin (1976, 1979) and Feld (2000) on Kalulis of Papua New

Guinea; Weiner (1991) on the Foi of Papua New Guinea; Parmentier (1987) on Ngeremlengui district, Belau; Harrison (1989) on Andean Quechua; and Roseman (2000) and Yamada (2000).

15 See, for example, Anderson (1991), Winichakul (1994); Frank (1998: 2, 64).

16 Etymologically related to the Malay *saka*. Wilkinson (1959: 1001) comments on the Malay *saka:* "Maternal heritage, in contrast to paternal (*baka*). Of family property, ancestral traits, etc. . . . In Minangkabau and Negri Sembilan *saka* is all-important: *nyiur nan saka* (inherited trees); *terbit pesaka kapada saka* (inheritance comes through the mother), Malay Saying." Of the related *pusaka* or *pesaka,* he writes: "Heirloom; family property. . . . In Malaya rather an indefinite word for any heirloom. . . . In Minangkabau and Negri Sembilan pusaka represents property of which the family enjoys only usufruct. This covers all inherited property in contrast to personal earnings (*harta pencharian*) which are the absolute property of the persons earning them during their lifetime and only become *harta pusaka* at death; . . . *Tanah pusaka:* inherited land that one cannot readily alienate" (894).

17 Malayanized spelling of Siɲĩ̃l, found on area maps, is Sinyuul.

18 Temiar 1981/82 FN1616–17, 1646–68; OR85, OR86 at 5 minutes 33 seconds in.

19 A song's power can be transmitted from dream-receiver to another person by singing or dancing the song together. While singing together, the dream-receiver also transmits to his or her "student" the cool liquid kahyɛk that flows with spirit-given songs. Once learned in this manner, the song can be transmitted to further recipients through replication of the same process. If received through such secondary transmission rather than direct dream receipt, the song constitutes a secondary repertoire. Such a song is not as powerful as a song received directly by a dreamer.

20 The attempt to separate extended family and even villagewide units of residence, production, and consumption into nuclear units is part of the government-sponsored transformative process that affects the very core of Temiar social and environmental relations. It is strangely at odds with contemporary trends in urban Singapore, where a family's position on the list for government housing is advanced if it includes more than two generations. Urbanized Singapore is encouraging extended-family households, while Malaysia truncates them—both, ostensibly, in the name of progress.

21 Laderman (1981) charts the interplay between the immaterial and material, or the symbolic and pragmatic, using the terms "symbolic" and "empirical" to discuss the multiple attributes of cultural items.

22 See Appadurai (1996) on transnationalism, the interface of the global and the local; Roseman (2001) on its impact on indigenous peoples.

23 See also Bellwood (1996).

Writing for Their Lives: Bentian Dayak Authors and Indonesian Development Discourse

Stephanie Gorson Fried

I am sick and tired of descriptions like "people of the weeping forest" . . . and writings about certain "Dayak" groups who use "palangs" in their penises. I am tired of seeing drawings of bare-chested women in rural longhouses. These have all become entertaining exhibitions . . . both here and overseas.—M. P. Lambut, Perlukah Mendayyak-kan Orang Dayak

If only our ancestors had gone to school and learned to write, then we would have a Book of Traditions, a sacred Book, just like the Christians except that our Book would be much thicker and so much older than theirs. If only our ancestors had written things down, we wouldn't have so much trouble.—Kaq Jeran, Bentian Dayak shaman at annual rice harvest ceremony, March 1992

Kalimantan Dayaks have long found themselves to be objects of scrutiny, interest, derision, hope, and fear.[1] For centuries, explorers, botanists, soldiers, sea-goers (including Joseph Conrad), missionaries, traders, anthropologists, government officials, and more recently, environmentalists, have written about the "Dayak" peoples of Kalimantan (see figs. 21, 22).[2] To many citizens of modern Indonesia and foreign visitors alike, the term "Dayak" still conjures up images of exotic headhunters and backward savages from distant jungles where the grasp of religion, modern government, and market forces are tenuous. "Dayak," however, simply means "upriver" in many Kalimantan languages. This implies that others, those who have named, written about, and otherwise publicly defined the Dayaks, have historically come from elsewhere, from downriver and beyond.

By the early 1990s, as the nation-state of Indonesia celebrated the forty-fifth anniversary of its declaration of independence from Dutch colonial rule, Kalimantan Dayaks were in the process of writing about themselves, their traditions, and their surroundings. This essay presents a contextual analysis of five documents produced between 1986 and 1992 by Bentian

Figure 21. Indonesia. Map by David Lindroth.

Dayak authors from the Kutai District of East Kalimantan, illustrating the process by which oral accounts of ethnic identity and customary rights to land and natural resources are now being expressed in a written form. The documents are drawn from a wider selection of Bentian newspaper and magazine articles, seminar papers, official proposals, letters, and unpublished manuscripts that represent attempts to "normalize" Bentian identities as modern, property-owning citizens of the Indonesian nation-state. The appearance of such documents on resource use and cultural identity reflects profound changes in the web of social relations linking Dayak communities to outsiders who value their forest resources.

Throughout most of Dutch rule, the trade in forest products was of vital importance to the Kalimantan economy (Peluso 1983; Linblad 1988). It linked Dayak communities, through familiar river intermediaries, to coastal Malay sultanates and then on to Dutch traders as well as ethnic Chinese and Arab entrepreneurs. During the first two decades following Indonesian independence, the forest-products trade continued much as it had under the Dutch, as Jakarta-based Indonesian and ethnic-Chinese entrepreneurs replaced their departed colonial counterparts. Once part of a system of rulers and the more-or-less ruled along a river network, articulated, yet not intimate with the Dutch colonial apparatus, Dayak villages in New Order Indonesia were now directly engaged with a much broader and more powerful series of national and transnational actors seeking access to Kalimantan forests.

Beginning in the late 1960s, as the New Order regime consolidated its power, new regulations and governmental policies brought about enormous changes in the exploitation of Kalimantan's natural resources. In 1970 control over Kalimantan forests and logging concessions was removed by law from provincial-level patronage systems and placed firmly in the hands of the national government. Innovations in transportation technology and shifts in the interests of the Indonesian nation-state, including the rise to prominence of a national discourse of development and the rapid expansion of natural-resource extraction activities, made the trees in East Kalimantan forests highly visible, highly valuable, and relatively accessible to outside investors. With increasing speed over the next two decades, these changes altered the social relations embedded in the Kalimantan forest-products trade that still formed the economic underpinning of many Dayak communities. By the 1980s and the 1990s, many East Kalimantan Dayak communities found their access to the natural resources upon which they depended and which they customarily managed, suddenly and severely limited as a result of decisions made in distant Jakarta.

Attempting to protect their rights of access to the natural resources vital to their survival, Dayak communities are engaging in efforts to recast their customary, or *adat*, land rights into the "national print-language"[3] of the modern Indonesian bureaucracy. As Dayak authors attempt to capture and redefine terms such as "development," "logic," "law," and "rights" (or to redefine themselves in relation to these terms), they become involved in the complex process of transforming orally transmitted and negotiable adat into the fixed, black-and-white starkness of the printed page. No longer able to secure their lands and livelihoods through warfare, avoidance of the state, or oral negotiations with provincial officials, Kalimantan Dayaks are representing themselves through written documents to the distant and highly literate audiences that now wield power in the Indonesian nation-state.

In order to understand the context in which Dayak-written documents have begun to appear, we must first explore relations between the modern Indonesian nation-state and its Dayak citizens, as well as the role of custom and customary law in modern Indonesia.

Figure 22. Kalimantan, Indonesia. Map by David Lindroth.

"Development" and the Modern Indonesian Nation-State

"Certainly Development does not encompass everything on earth at this time, but it has become one of the greatest foci of attention for the inhabitants of this planet. . . . Development . . . has become one of the . . . most important key-words [in the Indonesian language]. . . . President Soeharto is named the 'Father of Development.' The current administration has not only called itself the 'New Order' but also the 'Development Order.' All of the cabinets in the New Order administration have been called 'Development Cabinets.' . . . This key-word has become a focus of authority and legitimacy, and a departure point from which to re-interpret old facts and direct the future course of history" (Heryanto 1988).

Heryanto's statement reflects the enormous importance of the concept of "development" (*pembangunan*) and its concomitant, "modernization" (*modernizasi*), in Indonesian discourse.[4] This discourse of "development," interpreted or shaped by "special experts," underlies many of the activities of the modern Indonesian nation-state. The language of development, imbued as it is with technical jargon, statistical data, and theoretical posturing, is no mere byproduct of the process of development.[5] It is, as Heryanto indicates, an integral part of this process. "It is within language that Development operates. . . . Failure to understand the dynamics of language is just as fatal to our comprehension of Development, as failure to understand the rotational movements of the earth is to our perceptions of the universe" (Heryanto 1988: 24).

In modern Indonesia, rainforest-shifting cultivators, including the Dayaks of East Kalimantan have, as Tsing perceptively notes, quietly "become icons of the archaic disorder that represents the limit and test of state order and development" (1993: 28). Facing what Tsing calls "the dilemma of marginality," groups such as the Dayaks, "which, in official discourse are marginalized as tribal minorities, outside 'civilization,'" are in a sense thus positioned simultaneously inside and outside the state, and are seen as both a target of and a hindrance to development (Tsing 1993: 26; see also Dove 1986a; Weinstock 1989b).

It is within the context, then, of the Indonesian development discourse and the positioning of Dayaks as disorderly marginals by definition, that written documents on the identity, citizenship and adat of Dayak groups are being produced. Dayak communities, cognizant of the increasingly negative

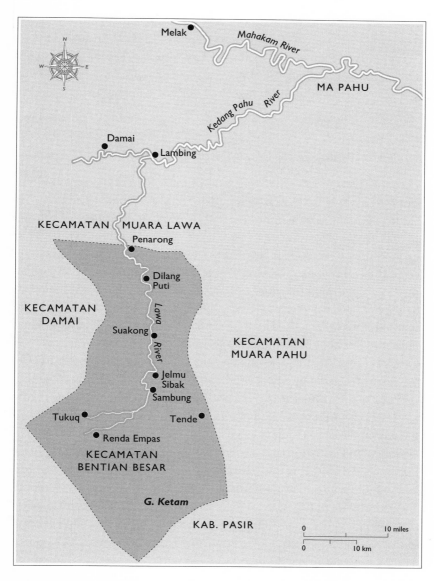

Figure 23. Bentian Besar district, East Kalimantan. Map by David Lindroth.

significance of their marginal status, are struggling to participate in what has become an immensely important process of defining both the terminology utilized in development and their own positions as actors in the development discourse. Without the ability to participate in definition-making, Dayak communities stand in danger of being written, and then developed, out of existence.

Swidden Cultivators in the Development Discourse

One of the characteristics that signals the primitiveness of Dayaks to government officials is what is seen as their irrational attachment to systems of swidden agriculture, sometimes referred to as "slash-and-burn" or shifting cultivation. In Kalimantan, as in other areas, dissimilar activities carried out by widely different groups of people are commonly labeled "shifting cultivation." These activities may range from the environmentally destructive mobile truck farming practiced near urban centers by immigrant, market-oriented farmers, to complex systems of sustainable cross-generational rotational agroforestry practiced by long-term Kalimantan inhabitants. There is a substantial scholarly literature on the latter systems that indicates their ecological suitability for areas of poor soils and low population density. The former are carried out by what Myers (1992) refers to as "shifted cultivators," that is, migrants, often unfamiliar with the nonvolcanic and thus highly fragile tropical forest soils of Kalimantan, who farm without apparent regard for environmental constraints.

Swidden and other forms of agriculture shape the Kalimantan landscape in complicated, and at times, counterintuitive ways, often producing misleading impressions. Official visitors to field sites where Dayak rotational agriculture exists side by side with the intensive vegetable cultivation of recent immigrants, see, in the immigrant farms, neat rows of carefully tended, familiar vegetables evenly spread across the bare soil.[6] Productivity, order, neatness and sanity are self-evident.

Moving on to Dayak fields, the visiting (often immigrant and urban) official eye is assaulted by a tumultuous and macabre vision—charred remnants of tree trunks are strewn disconcertingly all over the small field that has been hacked out of the surrounding forest. Destruction and disorder are the overwhelming impressions. Both recognizable and unrecognizable vegetables, fruits, medicinal plants, and ornamentals are planted, apparently at random, mixed in with the rice crop. Rattan shoots rise here and there from the uneven, fully covered ground. Simply walking through the field is a difficult undertaking, with dead branches underfoot, the soil obscured by a dense mat of plant life, both dead and living. Many officials voice their fear of hidden snakes or potentially fatal deer traps as reasons for not venturing into Dayak fields.

The dualities of non-Dayak fields/Dayak fields, order/disorder, safety/danger, reason/unreason that often arise from a single official site visit to "shifting/extensive" and "sedentary/intensive" cultivators of East Kalimantan are largely due to the snapshot vision produced by this single visit. Short-term observers are often unable to interpret these agricultural inscriptions on the landscape and reach erroneous conclusions about the destructive and irrational nature of shifting cultivation.[7] Meanwhile, national newspapers, quoting government officials, consistently feature articles such as "Shifting Cultivation is Suicide" (*Kompas,* 26 August 1986) and "240 Billion Rupiah Annual Loss Due to Shifting Cultivation" (*Kompas,* 18 September 1986). These articles focus on the forest destruction, soil loss, and Imperata grass infestation resulting from shifting cultivation. All forms of shifting cultivation, "called in some government reports, 'disorderly farming'" are assumed to be equally damaging (Tsing 1993: 156). "Irrational tradition" is blamed for the rotation of fields. For example, Tsing quotes a government official who proclaims that "a Dayak group in East Kalimantan even moves its fields if someone finds a centipede in the boat on the way to the field" (1993: 156).

Dove, in his research on agricultural policy in Indonesia, found that while swidden agriculture produces higher returns to labor than does intensive cultivation, it is "regarded by government planners not merely as less good than the systems of irrigated rice cultivation [which produce higher returns to land]; [it is] explicitly regarded as something bad—as irrational, destructive and uncontrollable" (Dove 1986a: 222). He found that returns to labor, which are maximized by swidden cultivators, generally tend "to be maximized by landless laborers and landowning workers, while [returns to land] are maximized by non-working landowners and extracting governments" (238).

Adat and Adat Law

One final topic that must be discussed prior to the analysis of the Bentian documents is the concept of *adat,* meaning "custom or tradition." In modern Indonesia, an archipelago of thousands of islands and hundreds of different

cultures, adat is a term of great significance. It is most often used in reference
to the customs and practices of Indonesia's myriad cultural groups. Each cultural group is said to have its own body of adat practices, which includes marriage, birth and death customs, methods for the determination of resource
ownership and utilization, of permitted and prohibited behaviors, and processes for conflict resolution, including sanctions for violations of adat. Local
methods of conflict resolution and processes for addressing adat violations
are often referred to as *hukum adat,* or adat law.

Under Dutch colonial rule, both national and customary (adat) law were
recognized and utilized in dispute resolution. The Dutch attempted to codify
the primarily oral and negotiative processes of many of the peoples under
their domain. Given the iterative, flexible, and precedent-based but negotiated and contested local nature of adat methods of conflict resolution,
the written codifications were, in many ways, pale reflections of essentially
robust community undertakings played out over time with many participants.[8] The Dutch versions of adat as written law often reflected Dutch assumptions of a static body of Dayak law and glossed over the complex emer-
gent nature of adat practices. These Dutch codifications of adat law provided
the basis for a dual system of administration of justice in the Indonesian archipelago.[9] With Indonesian independence, the uneasy bifurcation of the legal system into national and adat law continued.

Of particular relevance to Dayak communities at present are Indonesian
laws concerning forested lands. Article 33 of the Indonesian Constitution,
"the primary text which expresses state authority over all forests and forest
resources," states: "Land and water and the natural riches contained therein
shall be controlled by the state and be made use of for the greatest welfare of
the people" (Zerner 1992a: 24).

Basic Forestry Law No. 5 of 1967, which "constitutes the fundamental legal
structure and source of state authority for forestry planning," differentiates
between state forest—"a forest region or forest growing on a piece of land
not covered by any proprietary rights"—and proprietary ("titled") forest—
"a forest growing on a piece of land covered by proprietary rights" (Zerner
1992a: 24). Zerner further notes that the Basic Forestry Law appears to suggest that state forests, which constitute approximately 74 percent of the entire Indonesian land mass, are uninhabited and are completely unencum-
bered by customary legal rights (*hukum adat*) or regional community rights.

"The vast expanses of Indonesia's designated state forest lands are in fact inhabited or directly used by approximately 30 million people" (1992a: 25). The World Bank goes even further and estimates that as much as 60 percent of Indonesia's forests may be occupied and/or claimed by local communities, with up to sixty-five million people, many of whom are indigenous forest dwellers, directly dependent on forests for their livelihood (World Bank 1994).

The conflict between state and adat claims to forest land appears to be somewhat mitigated by the General Official Explanation of the Basic Forestry Law:

> In connection with the inclusion of forests which are under the control of customary law (*hukum adat*) communities within the designation State Forest, this does not annul the respective rights of the customary law community as well as its members to make use of or to obtain benefits from that forest as long as those rights, in reality, still exist. Their implementation must be concluded in such a way so that they do not disturb the accomplishments of the objectives stated in this [Basic Forestry] Law. (Zerner 1992a: 24)

With rapid changes in transportation, communication, and international markets making the trees in Kalimantan forests both desirable and accessible to those far removed from Bornean jungles and river networks, the complex and overlapping legacy of largely oral adat legal systems and written national law has proven to be of far-reaching significance to Dayak swidden farmers.

Such forest peoples are faced with the daunting question of how they can protect access to their lands, rivers, and forest resources as the private sector, backed by the governmental apparatus, increasingly engages in massively destructive resource extraction on their territories.

The Bentian of the Middle Mahakam Region: Rattan Cultivators, Forest Managers, and Authors

East Kalimantan is the site of great ethnic and cultural diversity. Since at least the sixteenth century, Islamic Malays have lived along the coasts and the lower reaches of major rivers, as have ethnic Chinese, who are largely concentrated in highly populated urban areas.[10] Dayak shifting cultivators have often inhabited the forested regions further upriver than either the Malays or the Chinese. This description of Bornean cultural geography, however, presents somewhat of an oversimplification because there are Malays in the interior, just as there are now Dayaks in the urban areas. Additionally, with Indonesian independence, increasing numbers of (predominantly Javanese) police and military officers, schoolteachers, and other Indonesian government officials now reside in the interior, as do entire settlements of logging and mining camp workers and Javanese transmigrants.[11] Nonetheless, in the minds of most East Kalimantan inhabitants, Dayaks are strongly associated with forested upriver regions and Malays are associated with downriver regions and coastal cities.

Although the Netherlands East Indies Company and, later, the Dutch colonial government occupied various parts of what is now Indonesia for over three hundred and fifty years, the island of Borneo received scant attention from the Dutch. Other islands were more accessible, so Borneo was largely ignored until the mid–nineteenth century (Peluso 1983; Rousseau 1990). The Middle Mahakam region of East Kalimantan is located at the fringes of former colonial territory, once ruled by the Dutch through the Malay Sultanate of Kutai. The Kutai Sultanate, based in the royal city of Tenggarong, approximately 275 kilometers downriver from the Middle Mahakam region, derived most of its substantial revenues from the trade in forest products collected by upriver Dayaks (Peluso 1983).[12] In response to Dutch demands for rattan in the 1800s, Kutai sultans placed a tax, to be paid in rattan shipments, on upriver Dayaks. In response, Middle Mahakam Dayak communities, including the Bentian, developed an innovative system of intensive rattan cultivation integrated with their swidden agriculture (Priasukmana and Amblani 1988; Fried 1992a,b). As a result, the region is now well known for its rattan production.

The Bentian and thirteen other groups identify themselves as belonging to the Lawangan Dayak family. Approximately 250,000 Lawangan occupy a territory of one-quarter million square kilometers from the middle section of the Barito River in Central Kalimantan to the Middle Mahakam River in East Kalimantan (Weinstock 1983b). Bentian historians and adat leaders trace the history of their departure from their Central Kalimantan homelands to an era twenty-four generations ago. The Lawangan ancestors of the group that would later be known as "Bentian" were defeated in battle. They left Central Kalimantan and migrated north, seeking remote, inaccessible, and therefore

safe locations in which to settle. These groups no longer identified themselves as Lawangan, but took on the names of their group leaders, or named
themselves after a salient feature of their landscape (Nasir 1991b). As they
moved north, they encountered the Tementa'ng people, who were also Lawangan from Central Kalimantan but who had migrated to the region earlier.
The Tementa'ng did not welcome the strangers to the area until they had fulfilled a *penyua,* or gift obligation, of one hundred Chinese urns, one hundred
water buffaloes, and a slave. The new groups, which eventually came to be
called "Bentian," presented the requested penyua goods and the slave to the
king and, in return, were granted the rights to an area called Nine Rivers.[13]
The penyua, then, represented the transaction that defined Bentian rights to
their forested adat territories.[14]

The Bentian, like other Lawangan groups, are swidden agriculturists who
practice a form of rotational agriculture suited to the poor and easily eroded
soils of the region. Clearing patches of old-growth secondary forest to plant
rice with dibble sticks, Bentian farmers, unlike most other swidden cultivators, also sow large quantities of rattan seeds and seedlings in their fields.
These seedlings mature after seven to ten years into productive rattan vines,
their weight supported by thick secondary forest regrowth in the fallowed
fields. The Bentian continue to harvest rattan for up to thirty years or more
after planting. Rattan is currently a staple commodity for the local inhabitants of the region, as it has been for well over a century.

Norwegian naturalist Carl Bock, during his 1879 visit to the Bentian region, noted that rattan,

> besides forming the chief article of trade in its raw state, . . . furnishes the
> material for the manufacture of an endless variety of useful objects. . . .
> Take away his rattan, and you deprive the Dayak of half the articles indis-
> pensable to his existence. What crochet-work is to the European lady,
> rattan plaiting is to the Dayak housewife. She is always manufacturing
> either sleeping-mats, sitting-mats, sirih boxes, baskets of all shapes and
> sizes, and for all kinds of uses, besides long pieces of plait to be used as
> cords, ropes, or threads, in dressmaking, house-building, raft construc-
> tion, and the hundred-and-one other purposes of daily life in the forest.
> (1985: 204)

Rattan gardens in the Bentian region function very much like bank accounts for their owners. When rattan prices are low or when farmers choose

not to sell for other reasons, the clumps of constantly growing rattan shoots may be left in the fields, growing longer and more valuable (adding interest) every day that the farmer does not sell the crop. In the case of a family emergency, a withdrawal may be made from the bank account. Even if rattan prices are still low, the harvest of a ton or two will cover hospitalization costs, school expenses, or other urgent needs. Additionally, small amounts of rattan are harvested every month, regardless of the market price, in order to provide the income necessary for the purchase of subsistence goods such as cooking oil, batteries, and soap.

The Bentian strategy of a diversified and flexible household economy, which involves rattan production for export markets as well as fruit, vegetable, and grain production for local consumption, has proven successful enough to see them through the first few years of a traumatic drop in the price of rattan.[15] This flexibility makes Bentian swidden agriculturalists easily competitive with the large, single-commodity-dependent commercial plantations currently favored by the Indonesian central government and by international financial institutions such as the World Bank and the Asian Development Bank. Such plantations, when exposed to severe price fluctuations, face a substantial likelihood of worker layoffs, social unrest, and bankruptcy.

To the untrained eye, Bentian rattan gardens often appear to be "natural" secondary forest filled with looping, spiny rattan vines. To the Bentian eye, rattan gardens are a sign of human presence and land ownership. The gardens are clearly demarcated by borders of fruit trees, small streams, hills, honey trees, or other obvious planted or natural features. In the Bentian region, land ownership claims are not usually documented on paper. Instead, these claims are validated by village members chosen to act as ownership witnesses, or *Saksi*. For each field owned by a Bentian farmer, at least one other villager (preferably an older one) acts as a witness (Saksi) to the ownership of that particular field. According to Nasir, a Bentian official:

> This Witness is ready to be called on at any occasion to testify about the truth of the ownership claim. . . . Before testifying, the Witness is sworn in first by the Tatau [Bentian adat leader] with the Ineq Rodot oath. Whosoever bears false witness . . . will die within at most one month, eaten by Ineq Rodot. Ineq Rodot is the name of the Tiger God. The Tiger God Oath is very honored and feared in the Bentian Besar [Region]. This

oath is still valid[16] and the apparatus for it is still cared for[17] by the Ta-
tau. . . . Because of the extraordinary power of this Oath, very rarely do
people want to bear false witness. Because of this, if the witnesses who
are called feel hesitant about the truth of their statements, they have the
right to refuse to be called as a witness before being sworn in with the Tiger Oath. (Nasir 1991b: 18)

Disputes about the ownership of property and land in the Bentian region,
then, are played out not through official land-ownership certificates and
written procedures but rather through complex adat processes involving living witnesses, sworn to tell the truth on the threat of painful death from supernatural causes.

The Bentian Besar Region under the New Order

By the late 1960s, remote areas of East Kalimantan had become more accessible than ever before as local motorboat construction soared, corresponding
to the flood of outboard motors into the province (Peluso 1983). A logging
boom, driven largely by local entrepreneurs and teams of Dayak loggers, occurred on the newly accessible riverbanks of the Mahakam and its tributaries
(Peluso 1983).[18] In 1968, State Regulation No. 6 was passed to allow provincial governments the power to grant logging concession rights. In 1970,
however, State Regulation No. 21 was passed, which removed the control of
forested areas from provincial governments and their patronage networks,
and placed the allocation of logging concession rights firmly in the hands of
the central government in distant Jakarta.

   With the 1970 ban on local small-scale logging operations and the shift in
decision-making power over access to timber away from provincial governments and local entrepreneurs to the national government and Jakarta-
based entrepreneurs, many upriver peoples of Kalimantan found themselves
severed from the web of social relations that had, in times past, connected
them with visitors to their lands. No longer would the process of forest-
resource extraction pass upriver from the national level (whether Dutch or
Indonesian), through the hands of the local sultanate (or after Independence, the provincial government), to Dayak adat leaders, and on to the indigenous, forest-dwelling communities. Instead, businessmen or their employees could now make their way directly from Jakarta to the hinterlands,

bypassing traditional downriver intermediaries and arriving unexpectedly upriver in speedboats, airplanes, and helicopters.

Until the introduction of relatively accessible motorized river and air transport to the area in the last thirty years, visits to upriver regions meant slow travel and frequent interaction with riverside communities, if not outright dependence upon their hospitality (often ensured by a show of force). The slow pace of river travel and the necessity of interaction with local people enabled word of new visitors and their plans to reach their upriver hosts. At the same time, word of upriver village traditions and adat law reached the ears of the visitors, somewhat lessening the shock of contact. For earlier travelers, including even the Kutai sultans, a working knowledge of the adat of upriver villages was prudent, if not essential.

In the late 1960s, however, men in Jakarta, speaking languages different from those of the upriver or downriver peoples of Kalimantan, yet claiming unity with them based on Indonesian nationhood, mapped out logging concessions, mining sites, and transmigration locations on what appeared to them to be vast tracts of empty and virgin forest. The rattan gardens, hunting grounds, and fields of the traditional farmers, known to Kalimantan villagers, river traders, and sultan's retinues alike, were neither known by nor visible to these mapmakers and officials, trained for the most part in city universities or by government bureaucracies on distant Java. The "Peoples of Adat Law," as various Dayak groups were to call themselves, and their adat forests and farmlands were not marked on these new representations of the Kalimantan jungles. In a sense, the upriver peoples of Kalimantan were invisible to the businessmen and planners now involved in the timber phase of Kalimantan's millennia-old forest-products trade.

The new resource maps of Kalimantan took on added significance as young and eager university graduates, civil servants, and employees of national and transnational timber and mining corporations made their way by airplane, helicopter, speed boat, and jeep into the Dayak upriver territories. With logging permits from the central government in hand, with their maps of "empty" and "virgin" forest, and with their beliefs in both the supernatural horrors lurking in the Kalimantan jungles and the savagery of the upriver headhunters, new visitors from the nation's capital arrived in Bentian territory. Most of these new arrivals were not aware that they were moving into regions traditionally claimed by the Bentian. Instead, they looked forward to challenging, relatively well-paid employment for a limited period of several years, even if it meant facing the perilous hardships of the Kalimantan jungles. Many of these newcomers were from families of modest means, hoping to make their fortunes through hard work in a dangerous post.

In the mid-1970s, as the first capital-intensive logging companies moved into the Middle Mahakam region, the shock of contact between the parties involved was considerable. Largely Muslim loggers and forestry professionals found "backward," non-Muslim (pork-eating) swidden cultivators on their logging-concession land, land that had been officially granted to them by the central government. Upriver villagers were suddenly confronted with newcomers to their adat territories who destroyed their rattan forest gardens (often not recognizing them as such) and knocked over ancestral grave markers to build "base camps," working for something called "development."

Bentian communities, shocked and confused by these events, reacted angrily to the desecration of grave sites and the destruction of productive rattan gardens. In 1985, Georgia Pacific, an American timber company that initiated one of the first large-scale logging operations on Bentian lands, paid a nominal sum as "compensation" to the affected Bentian communities (Triwahyudi et al. 1992). Even though this was essentially a token payment, the Bentian at that time still felt safe in the knowledge that, while some of their adat lands had been destroyed by logging operations, their territory was still large enough and their rattan gardens still extensive enough to provide a sufficient livelihood for themselves and their descendants. They had not yet seen the official resource maps of their region. By the late 1980s and early 1990s, logging operations had expanded, based on these official (and largely secret) maps. Governmental and private-sector plans for transmigration villages and plantations were also being implemented. The Bentian sense of security was to be deeply shaken.

The Bentian as Property-Owning Citizens: The First Rattan Proposal

In 1986, after the entry of Georgia Pacific into Bentian adat territory, a Bentian document appeared. Entitled "A Program for the Implementation of the Planting of Sega Rattan and an Environmental Information Analysis,"[19] it was written by members of the Bentian Family Group (BFG), an organization located in Samarinda, the provincial capital. The BFG was founded primarily by well-educated, urban Bentian, many of whom were civil servants. The initial goal of the BFG was to provide a supportive network for Bentian visitors to and residents of the capital city. Eventually, the BFG became interested in supporting Bentian social, religious, and economic activities in Bentian upriver territories as well as in the capital. By 1984, in response to a national government initiative, urban and rural BFG members established the "Semangat Membangun" ("Desire to Develop/Awaken/Build") Cooperative,[20] an official, government-sponsored cooperative (*Kooperasi Unit Desa*) designed to provide subsidized goods to villages in the Bentian district and to assist in the marketing of rattan. The name of the cooperative itself, "Desire to Develop/Awaken/Build," presented a clear reflection of governmental discourse and desires. The name not only indicated good citizenship on the part of its members but also indicated the Bentian recognition of their own marginal status as those who have not yet been "developed" or "awakened."

Two years after the establishment of the cooperative, the first BFG document was written, presenting a Bentian program for environmental preservation (*kelestarian lingkungan*). In the document, the Bentian request governmental guidance in securing and upgrading 30,000 hectares of upriver Bentian rattan forest plantations in the vicinity of eight Bentian villages. This document represents an attempt to demonstrate the proud Indonesian citizenship of Bentian farmers despite their current (and soon-to-be-eliminated) attachment to shifting cultivation. Recognizing the "unique personalities" of the Bentian, the document nonetheless makes a plea for the certification of Bentian rattan lands, thus ensuring the proof of land ownership for Bentian farmers as a mark of their full citizenship.

The proposal is written in a bureaucratic, "official" style of Indonesian, which represents at least two levels of translation: first, from the Bentian language—with its richness of forest terminology, its warrior heroes, gods, and history—to Indonesian, the nationalizing language, the language of commerce; and second, from Bentian adat ways of speaking and explanation—in general, geared to address crowds of onlookers engaged in an adat process, and filled with the potential to slide into supernatural threats fueled by past rivalries and mistrust—into categories of thought appropriate to the national development discourse that accepts the state as the final arbitrator of law and the promoter of "development," a goal toward which all must aspire.

Noting the "great interest and support of the [Bentian] people for Government programs especially those concerning environmental preservation," the authors position Bentian Dayaks as fully engaged actors in the national discourse of development: "We are aware that development is a responsibility [for us all] together, whether as a group or as individuals. Especially when the development under consideration is closely linked to the affairs of local people and to an increase in their standard of living, it is not necessary to simply wait for the Government to act" (Bentian Family Group 1986: 3). Reflecting governmental proclamations and requesting "leadership, improvement, and suggestions," the authors cite as their goal "the attain[ment] of a just and prosperous society with a healthy and preserved environment." They also explicitly indicate their support for government programs to eradicate shifting cultivation. "This proposal represents a statement from the Bentian people to ensure the success of the control of Shifting Cultivation and to become Sedentary Enterprise/Business Farmers, in a positive manner" (3).

Explaining and historicizing shifting cultivation, the authors state:

> Before the presence of logging corporations in this region, shifting cultivation was well adapted to the natural environment. [Bentian farmers] knew the terms "rotation" and "fallow." . . . Farming a plot of land for approximately two years and then leaving it [fallow] is one way to protect soil fertility. When a rice field is allowed to grow back into forest, after twenty or 30 years, that forest may be made into a rice field again and the soil fertility will be the same as it was originally. (25)

The authors, attempting to reinforce Bentian claims to "civilization" and "citizenship," strongly support the government's drive to eradicate shifting cultivation. Nonetheless, they are fully cognizant of the complex social and ecological relations embedded in Bentian rattan agroforestry systems, based, as they are, on shifting cultivation. As such, they caution that "spontaneously forbidding traditional farmers to clear the forest for [agricultural] fields represents a contradictory approach towards the unique personalities of the local people and their traditions. Seeking an alternative [to shifting cultivation] which can be accepted by the people, as a whole, is the best solution" (3).

The social relations and environmental constraints that mark the Bentian as marginal peoples are, here, gently and politely captured by the term "unique personalities," which attributes the marginalization of the Bentian to their individual, odd, and somehow special personal attributes. The BFG proposes, over a ten-year period, to draw Bentian shifting cultivators into a more intensive, and thus more sedentary, form of their current rattan cultivation, a plan designed to meet both governmental goals and Bentian realities. According to the authors, the first step in implementing their ambitious program of intensified rattan production in eight villages and the eradication of shifting cultivation is the issuance of certificates of land ownership to Bentian farmers. Tracing the history of rattan cultivation and its links to tenure claims and usufruct rights in the Bentian region, the authors state: "All of the village people (from the Bentian ethnic group) know that if they find sega rattan in the forest, not just anyone may [clear the forest to] make a field in that location. Long before sega rattan had an economic value, it was planted as a sign of land ownership" (25).

Adat lands, "inherited customary lands for which government land certificates have not yet been issued," are discussed. Citing the Basic Agrarian Law of 1960, where government-issued land certificates are to be made available free of charge to "weak economic groups," the authors request assistance for the land-titling efforts of Bentian adat lands.

The overall tone of the proposal indicates strong support for government programs and a desire both to provide the labor necessary for "development" and to share in its rewards. Making development a Bentian project and wholeheartedly accepting government programs to eradicate shifting cultivation, Bentian writers attempt to demonstrate, resoundingly, their identities as active, participating, and property-owning citizens of modern Indonesia. As such, they request that their farmlands and forest be shifted from adat law tenure to formally certified and nationally recognized proprietary status. The request for formal land ownership certificates reflects a clear awareness, on the part of the Bentian, of the practical necessity of backing up traditional land ownership rights with formal written proof of rattan garden and other land ownership.

Translation Struggles in the Press: A Bentian Example

In 1988 an article by Titus Pantir, a Bentian aristocrat and retired government official appeared in *Manuntung,* the largest East Kalimantan daily newspaper. It was written in the context of a widely publicized request by the minister for internal affairs, Rudini, for regional governments throughout Indonesia to act against people who neglected productive lands. It was also written in the general context of a continuous stream of articles in national and regional newspapers that equated shifting cultivation with environmental destruction, ignorance, primitiveness, and even "suicide." Titled "Abandoned Lands, Productive Lands, and Shifting Cultivation in East Kalimantan," the article appeared two years after the initial (and unheeded) Bentian request for governmental assistance in upgrading and certifying their rattan plantations. In his article, Pantir praises the goals of the minister for internal affairs, but warns that the minister's proclamation could have a "boomerang effect" if "the implementers of the decree are not able or not willing to translate the above terms wisely . . . If the term 'abandoned lands' is translated from only one viewpoint, that is, lands which are not continuously cultivated, this may bring great misfortune to swidden farmers who [as part of their management systems] leave their fields fallowed to revert back to forest."

Pantir's article represents a Bentian attempt to engage in the process of defining those terms that are crucial both to "development" and to the fate of swidden farmers like themselves. It reflects an awareness of the extreme importance of careful translation of the language utilized by government ministers to describe activities in remote provinces, as well as the importance of the translation of Bentian activities into governmental jargon. Any translation error, and specifically, in this case, one that might equate the shifting cultivators' fallowed fields with "abandoned, neglected" lands, could easily prove fatal for Dayak farmers since it would then allow the state to claim rights to Dayak-owned fallow fields. For this reason, it is desirable that lands that are fallowed and allowed to become forested by traditional farmers should not be included in the category of abandoned lands. This land is still "agricultural land" owned by the swidden farmer and used under a system of rotation. Attempting to redefine the identities of swidden agriculturalists, Pantir states, "Shifting cultivation . . . which is carried out by traditional farmers in Kalimantan is not the method of 'stupid' farmers, and also is not done in order to retain 'ethnic culture.' It is carried out to maintain the 'culture of agriculture' on dry fields . . . to ensure that agricultural lands, after a certain [fallow] period, can be reutilized and that productivity is maintained."

By placing Bentian land claims historically prior to the existence of the Indonesian nation-state, Pantir clarifies the fact that he is not writing about farmers "occupying new locations like those in resettlement villages, "those who moved as a result of urbanization, or spontaneous transmigrants . . . [but about] farmers in adat villages who have been there for centuries, well before the Basic Agrarian Law." He then analyzes the relationship of adat law to national agrarian law and defines adat land-ownership principles: "Adat ownership rights will not necessarily be recorded in administrative books and cannot necessarily be proven with certificates. What determines whether a parcel of land is in reality owned [under adat rights] is that the rights to it have already been valid for generations, there are signs of management/ownership, and the rights are respected by other people in the region." Pantir next grounds Bentian land claims firmly in the realm of "logic," thereby displacing objections to such claims to the realm of irrationality: "From the above analysis, whether based on regulations and legislation or adat law and reality, it would be bizarre, actually incomprehensible if land rights for inhabitants of traditional villages who have wrestled with the soil and with farming life since the time of their ancestors, were not recognized."

Contrasting the actual destruction caused by large-scale logging operations to the accusations of destruction continuously leveled at shifting cultivators, Pantir cites the results of a seminar held at the National University at Palangkaraya in Central Kalimantan: "The conclusion of the seminar was that for the last twenty years, the province of Central Kalimantan has already suffered a loss of 7.3 trillion rupiah as a result of waste in logging sites and timber processing. The income of the province during this period was far below this amount." The article ends with "the hope that swidden cultivators should not be viewed with excessive focus on their negative impacts."

The Second Bentian Rattan Proposal:
Industrial Forest Plantation Rights

Two years later, in 1990, having received no response to their first proposal, members of the Bentian Family Group decided to make another attempt to secure the rights to their adat lands and rattan gardens. By this time, logging operations and land clearing for plantations on Bentian adat territories had escalated. The Bentian were growing increasingly concerned and disturbed. They had been told by various government officials that their request would have more weight if it were made by a government body, such as an official village cooperative. Since membership in the Bentian Family Group largely overlapped with membership in the "Desire to Develop/Awaken/Build" Village Cooperative (KUD), it was decided that the cooperative would issue the next proposal. Cooperative members, "in the name of traditional farmers and cooperative members," requested from the Ministry of Forestry industrial forest plantation rights (*Hutan Tanaman Industri,* or HTI)[21] to 100,000 hectares of Bentian land that was then under cultivation. The request represented the second official written attempt to translate Bentian culture and aspirations into a form comprehensible to the Indonesian national elite in the context of the development discourse. The proposal is striking because it presents an imaginative and thorough response to the impact of the nation-state on traditional systems of export-crop production and on definitions of private property. In this document, the Bentian explicitly state their desire to participate actively (that is, to become "subjects") in the development discourse, as they struggle to appropriate national terms such as "citizen," "private property," and "industrial forest plantation." The earlier Bentian proposal was now expanded to include a total of eighteen Bentian villages and up to four thousand "shifting cultivators" and their surrounding secondary forest, filled with rattan and fruit trees "owned by the local people with the ownership status based on adat law."[22]

Cooperative members enclosed a cover letter to the Ministry of Forestry with their proposal, giving assurances that, unlike other projects, there would be no conflict with local people over the establishment of the HTI since it, in fact, represented their own wishes. Plunging into the discourse of aware/awakened/developed subjects and disorderly/unkempt marginals and their shifting fields, the authors stated:

This project is the manifestation of the awareness of the [Bentian] people to put themselves in order and change their traditional agricultural pattern to sedentary agricultural enterprise. . . . On the basis of their own awareness and consciousness, the farmers have already agreed to group together in a Village Cooperative (KUD) following the suggestions of the Government. Through the Cooperative it is hoped that the prosperity of the farmers will be increased and the dividing chasm between giant Businesses in the forestry sector and the farmers in forest areas will be narrowed. (1990: 5)

The proposal attempts to demonstrate that the concept of industrial forest plantations is actually a traditional Bentian idea and that Bentian agroforestry practices are consistent with the export-oriented objectives of the modern nation-state.

> Traditional farmers, since the time of their ancestors, have already carried out industrial forest plantations (HTI) in a traditional manner. This is signaled by the existence of rattan gardens and fruit trees spread throughout the forests that grew back in their fallowed fields. These plantations still exist. Not only do traditional farmers have a command of HTI technology, but their Mental attitude is also a great support. This Mental attitude includes, among other things, the custom of living in the forest, the habit of working in the forest and behavior which forms a unity with the forest. This represents Basic Investment Capital which cannot be separated from the development of the Industrial Forest Plantations. (1990: 5)

After translating Bentian forestry expertise into investment capital and reclaiming industrial forest plantations as a Bentian initiative, the authors cite the Indonesian constitution and national laws in order to reinforce Bentian claims of active citizenship, "This project . . . forms part of the mandate of Constitution, Article 3, to provide for a just and prosperous people based on Pancasila. Guided by Governmental Regulation No. 7, 1970 about Industrial Forest Plantation Rights/Concessions, the people in forest areas want to participate in the development of Industrial Forest Plantations" (1990: 5).

Citing academic authorities, including an anthropologist, "Prof.Dr.," and an agricultural economist, "Dr. Ir.,"[23] Bentian writers explicitly express their desire to be "subjects" rather than "objects" of development: "It is hoped that this project will place the farmers as 'Subjects,' so that there is no collision between the project and the farming people in the forest area" (1990: 5). The proposal's introduction closes with references to the Indonesian constitution, PANCASILA, God, and the "allegiance and awareness of the . . . [Bentian] people to participate in development while changing their traditional pattern of farming" (5).

Copies of the sixty-one-page proposal were sent to the minister of cooperatives, to three directorates under the Minister of Forestry, as well as to the governor of East Kalimantan, provincial-level forestry officials, cooperative officials, and the district head of Kutai Regency. The exceedingly formal structure of the proposal, familiar, no doubt, to the urban Bentian civil servants who had shaped the document, mirrored that of most current governmental documents. The proposal included a complex "organizational structure and duty chart" that detailed the relations between cooperative members, the governing board, "expert staff," and managers of the "industrial unit" and the "plantation unit." It also included a discussion of the legal basis for the HTI request (which cited ten national laws, presidential instructions, ministerial decrees, and the 1945 constitution) and a complete financial analysis of the proposed rattan-production system, including a series of calculations of internal rates of return based on Ministry of Forestry rattan-production data, as well as a discussion of rattan ecology and agroforestry.

The Kutai District Seminar
on the Traditions (Adat) of Dayak Peoples

In November 1990, five months after the HTI proposal had been submitted to government ministries, the Bentian had not yet received any official response to their request. That month, the government of Kutai Regency held an all-Kutai adat seminar on "The Traditions (Adat) of the Dayak Peoples of Kutai," in which the Bentian, along with all other Dayak groups in Kutai Regency, were invited to participate. Titus Pantir, a senior member of the Bentian Family Group wrote a document titled "Ownership Rights According to Adat Law as Viewed from [National] Basic Agrarian Law No. 5/1960." The author stood at the podium and read aloud the title and the following inscription on the cover of his document:

> Theme: Only with the ownership of sufficient and necessary agricultural land will the prosperity of village farmers increase.
> Subtheme: Human resources and natural resources represent the primary capital for village development. (Pantir 1990)

As the writer began to read further in his text, angry and apparently panic-stricken government members of the seminar organizing committee protested that the topics presented (adat law and Dayak land tenure) were irrelevant and detrimental to the "All-Kutai Seminar on Dayak Adat." The speaker was forced to step down from the podium, and the paper was never read aloud. The fact that the paper had been so publicly and rudely censored by government officials, however, led to increased interest in it on the part of the audience.

The thirty-six-page text that aroused so much official hostility was organized in seven sections titled "Ownership According to Adat Law," "Shifting Cultivation," "Ecosystems and Environmental Order," "Logging Concession Rights," "Development Concepts for Villages of the Interior," "Cultivator's Rights," and "Conclusions and Suggestions for the Provincial Government." As its bibliography indicates, the text is based on government laws and regulations; on speeches made by the president of Indonesia, government ministers, and members of the Peoples' Representative Assembly (Dewan Perwakilan Rakyat—the national legislative body); and on the 1945 Constitution; various encyclopedias; books on environmental preservation; newspaper clippings; and the Bible. The paper was written as "raw material, still rough, hopefully useful for seminar attendees; to be distributed to 'the people in the villages who do not know about [national] law.' . . . Not only for the farming peoples of adat law, however, but also for the provincial and National Government" (1990: 1).

Thus, the document represented both an attempt to explain "national" law to Bentian villagers and Bentian adat law to the provincial and national governments. The paper starts with a history of agrarian law and discusses early Dutch colonial law, which was based on the political-legal needs of oppression and thus did not guarantee legal certainty to the Indonesian people (1990: 3). The author then quotes a former minister of agrarian affairs, who said, "[With the nation] facing [the] take-off [stage of development], the pure Basic Agrarian Law must be carried out consistently, honestly and full of a feeling of service to citizens and the country. If not, poverty will increase in the villages" (4).

The author decries the fact the Basic Agrarian Law is not obeyed or enforced, which "tends to work against the owner of rights, especially the people of the villages who do not understand national law. . . . With the appearance of a new type of brutality over land, the farming people and other common people may be under the impression that the Basic Agrarian Law is not enough to protect their rights. In fact, the Basic Agrarian Law is there to protect the weaker groups, especially the small farmer. That is why adat law ownership rights are given a special place [in this Law]" (1990: 10).

Reclaiming the Basic Agrarian Law for the Bentian and other adat peoples, he states, "The Basic Agrarian Law is based on adat law. This is recognized in Article 5: 'The Agrarian law which applies to the earth, water, and air space is Adat Law as far as it is not in conflict with National and State interests based on the unity of the nation.'" (1990: 5) Identifying standard practices, the author continues:

> Adat law certainly has a special place in the Basic Agrarian Law. . . . This understanding and meaning will only be accepted by those who truly comprehend the 1945 Constitution and Pancasila with the goal of developing the Indonesian nation. . . . The weapons which are used by certain officials, including [land] speculators, to deceive the [common] people who do not understand the laws are: [land] certificates and State land [claims]. Land without a certification is then said to be State land. Truly tragic! . . . There is not a single article of the Basic Agrarian Law stating that ownership "will only be recognized upon presentation of a certificate." (1990: 10–11)

Reclaiming "logic/rationality" for the Bentian, the author reminds his readers of the fact that free land certification to "weaker economic groups" is guaranteed under the Basic Agrarian Law and has never been provided for the Bentian: "In a rational manner, there is no person who would refuse if they were given free certificat[ion] of [their] land" (1990: 11).

Historicizing the shifting cultivation debate, the author quotes research that indicates that the Dutch, who prioritized large, private-sector plantations and wished to control forest inhabitants, attacked swidden cultivators as "destroyers of the forests." He quotes an "Australian professor" as finding that "the destruction caused by the practice of shifting cultivation is minimal and usually does not influence the entire forest like that caused by timber industries all over the world" (1990: 23).

In modern Indonesia, however, "it is as if shifting cultivation is an enemy of the people, and an enemy of development. How truly unfortunate, the fate of traditional farmers. They have become a victim of advertising. In fact, what actually occurs in the field is not as bad as what they have been accused of. Since the stone age, our ancestors have been cutting trees to prepare their [fields for] agriculture. In the Bible (Genesis 4:2), Cain, the son of Adam and Eve, was a swidden farmer" (1990: 18).

Moving from biblical sources of authority to those of the modern nation-state itself, the author quotes Indonesian Ministry of Forestry research on Bentian agroforestry systems that clearly demonstrates the sustainability and viability of Bentian farming practices (Priasukmana and Amblani 1988). Discussing forestry law, he continues:

> Logging concession permits extend only to forest and not to other types of land, village land, agricultural lands, gardens, [or] fallow agroforestry fields. According to Presidential Instruction No. 1, 1976, if parts of the area used by a Logging Concession are actually for other goals [such as those above] . . . that area should immediately be released from the Concession area without waiting until the end of the Concession contract. . . . In reality [Logging Concession] areas have included entire villages and the agricultural lands of the inhabitants from the beginning, and to date [these areas] are still held. (Pantir 1990: 25–26)

The document reflects the now-pervasive Bentian fear that since villages and their adat properties are not accurately represented on logging concession and other new resource maps, local inhabitants will soon stand accused of trespassing on their own adat lands, newly recategorized as logging concession or plantation territories. This will occur if proof of land ownership through adat witnesses is replaced not by land certificates issued to Bentian farmers, but by concession rights issued to entrepreneurs in distant Jakarta.

> This will be much worse later with the next generation where history can only be read on the [official] maps, while the children and grandchildren of the traditional farmers have no authentic data [that is, proof of their adat land ownership]. . . .
>
> If we examine the Ministry of Forestry's programs such as the Industrial Forest Plantation (HTI) . . . [we ask] will traditional farmers own agricultural lands or not? If we look at the requirements and *tatacara* requests for HTI's . . . it is certain that traditional farmers will not be able to fulfill the requirements and will only be able to become laborers. This will remind us of the eighteenth and nineteenth centuries where the colonial government seized the agricultural lands of the inhabitants of Java for plantations of tea, coffee, sugarcane, teak, etc. . . . The grandchildren of those farmers are now beggars. (1990: 26, 30)

The paper continues with a discussion of "the concept of the development of villages in the interior" and poses the question, "Who must be responsible for the development of villages in the interior? None other than the sons and daughters of the interior themselves. The [East Kalimantan] Governor's Olah Bebaya concept provides a strong basis for this" (1990: 26).

The final pages consist of a discussion of land-management rights, the role of cooperatives in development, detailed suggestions for the provincial government and a call for "the recognition . . . of traditional agricultural systems [of swidden cultivation] as valid farm enterprises and a recognition of forests as traditional agricultural sites" (1990: 35).

This article reflects, in some ways, a shift in Bentian self-representations. While continuing to reiterate Bentian claims to citizenship and Bentian desires to be recognized as active participants in "development," the article moves away from identifying the "unique personalities" of the Bentian as the sole reason for their increasing marginalization. It also repudiates the "illogical and backwards" characteristics ascribed by governmental discourse to shifting cultivation.

The Bentian Adat Lands Crisis in Writing

In February 1991, five years after the first Bentian request for official recognition of their traditional rattan cultivation lands, eight months after their second Bentian rattan request, and three months after the traumatic All-Kutai Dayak Adat Seminar, Bentian representatives received a letter from the provincial office of the Ministry of Forestry, noting that, unfortunately, 84,000 hectares of the 100,000 hectares of requested Bentian lands had already been allocated to eight logging concessions and commercial (non-rattan, non-Dayak) industrial forest plantations. The remaining 16,000 hectares had been planned as the location of a transmigration project in the 1970s that had never been implemented. The Bentian were advised to utilize this region of 16,000 hectares for all of their proposed plans.[24]

By this time, a non-Dayak rubber company that had been granted industrial forest plantation rights in the region requested by the Bentian had moved into Bentian territory. The first phase of "land clearing" by the company destroyed 1,000 hectares of mature rattan gardens. This was the equivalent of emptying, without permission or advance warning, the bank accounts containing the life savings of the local rattan farmers. The Bentian and their Benuaq Dayak neighbors found out about the project when they heard the whine of chainsaws in their rattan gardens. The plantation manager, citing permission from "Jakarta," threatened to bring charges of subversion (serious charges, potentially leading to lengthy imprisonment) against anyone who objected to company operations. Bribes were paid to the village head and to a few other prominent villagers, effectively silencing them. The adat leader refused his bribe and started a round of letter-writing to government officials. The company hired the entire district governmental police force to act as a private security unit for the plantation. As of 1992, more than 20,000 hectares of rattan gardens were slated to be clear-cut by the company. Despair set in throughout the region, as the future of the adat lands that form the backbone of Bentian culture and agriculture came into question.

At this time, two logging companies announced their plans (in accordance with newly activated governmental decrees) to clear-cut large amounts of Bentian rattan gardens to make way for thousands of transmigrant families from Java who would be put to work as laborers on non-rattan industrial forest plantations that were scheduled to be carved out of tens of thousands of hectares of additional Bentian rattan lands. The proposed clear-cutting of Bentian rattan gardens and forests would clearly lead to substantial economic losses to the region and the nation, in terms of rattan income and local food self-sufficiency, as well as to irreversible environmental destruction and soil erosion. Transmigrant farmers would find it difficult, if not impossible to grow agricultural crops on their allotted two hectares of bare and eroded land.[25]

It was in the context of the announcement of logging company plans in 1992 that an additional, most unusual Bentian document appeared, titled "The Forest and Land Crisis Which Is Occurring in the Bentian [Region] as a Result of the Logging Industry." Unlike the earlier documents, this was written by a member of the Bentian aristocracy who is a rattan forest farmer actually residing upriver in the area affected by the logging concessions and the rubber plantation. In many ways, the document has the feel of a presentation made to an adat court during a conflict between two feuding parties, Bentian farmers and logging concession/rubber plantation managers, in front of a large audience. The author addresses "you, the traditional farmer," as well as those who accuse swidden agriculturalists of environmental destruction and those who listen to the accusers.

The forty emotionally charged pages cover Bentian history, Bentian methods of "environmental protection," and Bentian adat, focusing on adat law for land utilization, borrowing, and ownership, and ending with a discussion of the problems faced by the Bentian and suggested solutions. The document is somewhat formally structured, containing a "Table of Contents" and chapters with chapter headings. The writings of other Bentian authors are freely quoted (often without citation) throughout the text. In contrast to the earlier, rather sedate and official-sounding Bentian documents, however, this document reads like a cry of pain and rage. The polite facades and carefully inoffensive wording of earlier Bentian documents have been replaced by direct talk and stark, clear descriptions. The beginning of the manuscript reads:

> Traditional Bentian farmers reject the accusation that they are destroyers of the forest. Accusations like this are baseless. For generations the Bentian people have possessed a culture and traditions which are useful for preserving natural resources and the environment.
>
> Traditional Bentian farmers welcome Industrial Forest Plantations. However, they do not want the Plantations to be developed on land owned by the [Bentian] people, destroying growing plants and rattan gardens which provide the main income of the Bentian people. Rattan income has already made a substantial contribution to the 4,000 Bentian people. They school their children with rattan money, they build houses with rattan money, they buy food and many other goods with rattan money. Because of this it is logical for the [Bentian] people to reject Forest Industrial Plantations if they are to be developed on land owned by farmers. The goal of development itself is to increase the standard of living of the people, not to destroy it and certainly not to destroy the commodities, like rattan gardens and land, which in reality make a large contribution to the [welfare of] the people. ("Forest Crisis and Land Crisis" 1992: 1)

Moving on to a brief description of Bentian history, the author states:

> Originally, the ancestors [of the Bentian] did not acquire this region simply by taking it. They received it from the Tementa'ng race by paying an

expensive *penyua*. The *penyua* which was requested and which was given to the [Tementa'ng] at that time consisted of one hundred large ceramic vases (*antang*), one hundred water buffaloes and one human slave. . . .

Since this Bentian Besar area was obtained by our ancestors with an expensive, if not priceless, sacrifice, it is logical for the [Bentian] people to defend and maintain it. [It is also logical for them] not to be pleased with logging concessions [and their plantations] which only come to destroy and take the land. This is because there is not a single person in the world who would allow other people to destroy their property which they have purchased at a high price. (5)

Placing the Bentian firmly in the position of "the civilized," the author states:

This author does not mean to defend swidden farmers. The author means to bring to the fore the above facts for no other reason than to straighten out the mistaken opinion that always discriminates against swidden farmers as the only cause of forest destruction. . . . If we want to understand truly, traditional swidden farmers who have, for generations, been civilized and responsible for the care of natural resources which form their livelihood and place of living. It is not logical that traditional farmers would destroy their own living places. (7–8)

Historicizing forest destruction, the author continues:

The effect of tree felling and burning by traditional Bentian farmers for the past 1300 years is much smaller compared to the impact of forest clearing by Kalhold Utama, Roda Mas, Gunung Putih Indah, and Dayak Besar [logging and plantation companies]. Their forest destruction in the last ten years is much greater and much worse. In the ten years since the entry of logging industries [into the Bentian region, our] rivers have become shallow because of large scale erosion and mud filling the river bottom. Because of the shallow rivers, water traffic is no longer easy and the Bentian people thus face many economic hardships. Before the presence of logging concessions our river water was clear and water traffic was not problematic. From this, it can be seen that the people near logging concessions suffer far greater damages than profits from the concessions. (8)

The document identifies and describes Bentian "adat institutions," leadership practices, land law, and "Bentian democracy." Adat is not simply described, however. It is demonstrated to the reader by a series of adat cases (that is, "If Farmer A does this to Farmer B's land, then . . ."). These cases unfold in the context of the document much in the same way as such precedents would unfold during an adat "hearing." Bentian guidelines for the utilization (borrowing) of lands by newcomers, including (non-Bentian) foreigners are described. "Democracy" is identified as a Bentian practice.

> For generations in the Bentian Besar [District] there have been Adat regulations for foreigners/newcomers who would like to utilize land in the vicinity of a village. . . . If the owner of the requested location refuses the . . . [potential borrower's] request, the Adat Leader/Village Head does not have the authority to force [compliance with the request] since an Adat Leader/Village Leader who uses force/is coercive to the people can be removed from his position. Thus the democratic principles of the Bentian people have existed for centuries, strongly implemented and are still maintained and defended. (21)

Turning to the activities of logging concessions and plantations on Bentian lands, the author continues:

> Based on [adat] land law which is valid in [the] Bentian region, logging concessions which enter the lands of the [Bentian] people, conduct surveys and destroy growing plants without permission fall into the category of violators of Adat law. Up to now, the logging concessions have not held consensus meetings [musyawarah, mufakat] with the people of the village or the Village Head, instead they carry out timber surveys and logging on villagers land. If we pay attention to Regulation Number 5, 1979 Concerning Village Government, we can see that the activities of the logging concessions in the field not only do not recognize adat law, but they also violate Governmental Regulations. (21)

Logging concessions in the Bentian Besar area are often abusive, assuming the authority of governmental regulations in order to influence the common people. This is very strange to hear, since, as far as the author knows, logging concessions themselves do not own the regulations but must obey them.

Next, the author clarifies the purpose of adat fines levied against violators of customary law, and differentiates them from the "modern" notion of compensation for land:

> Attention must be drawn to the fact that Adat fines are not the same thing as compensation. For the Bentian people, the term "fine" is that which is paid to someone who has been wronged because the payer of the fine has destroyed that person's property, whether property in the house or that outside of the house such as land, rattan plants, fruit trees, etc. The location or place where the destruction occurred is still owned by the original property owner. For example: A destroys one rattan clump owned by B. According to the Adat decision A is fined five antique ceramic urns [*antang*] for his wrongs. The location of the rattan clump is still owned by B. (23)

Analyzing the activities of logging concessions and plantations in the Bentian area in light of adat law, the author states:

> In the Bentian Besar District there are several logging concessions which have destroyed the ownership rights/property of the people, such as the PT. Kalhold Utama Company which has already killed thousands of productive rattan clumps at its Anan River Basecamp location. This is true of the Gunung Putih Indah plantation and the Roda Mas logging concession.[26] According to Bentian Adat, the small amount of money which has been received by the people who own the locations where rattan and other growing plants have been destroyed by these three companies, represents actually just the payment of adat fines. These locations still belong to the people. Nonetheless what has happened is that the companies have not even paid enough fines to cover the destruction of the peoples' property. And that is not all. They have also seized the people's land. Where is justice in this? (23)

Returning to the definition of development, the author continues:

> The goal of Development and the equitable sharing of the results achieved is not meant to be enjoyed only by the businessmen, even ordinary/powerless people must receive a suitable portion according to the Constitution, Article 33 Clause 3. Because of this, the presence of logging concessions in the field must absolutely be re-evaluated by respon-

sible parties. The personnel of logging concessions who invert the concept of Development, as has occurred in the Bentian [region], should be retrained in government ideology (*P-4*). (23)

Reiterating and historicizing Bentian citizenship claims that predate the Indonesian nation-state, the author, under the heading "The Obedience of Adat Land Owners to the Government" states, "The Bentian people, in connection with the lands which they own, have already paid taxes which were required by the Government . . . since the times of our ancestors. Before the term "tax" appeared this was called Balasteng/Head Money [by the Dutch]" (25).

Identifying the Bentian role in development, the author continues:

The government itself has already proclaimed rattan to be a commodity with an important share in non-petroleum earnings for the country. The Bentian Besar District is the largest source of sega rattan in East Kalimantan. . . . This means that sega rattan represents a large share in paying for development. If we look we will see that the biggest producers of rattan in this [nation of] Indonesia who produce foreign exchange for the country are traditional swidden farmers. Why are they said to be destroyers of the forest when in fact they make a large contribution to the Nation? What a tragic fate for traditional farmers. (36)

The author concludes by stating that "even the price of all of the wood in the world will not be enough to pay for the health of the people, or to rehabilitate the lands which have been destroyed, or to make the rivers, which have been contaminated by the logging industry, clear again" (39).

In this essay, we began with an examination of common images of Dayaks held by others. We explored the Indonesian development discourse and the role assigned, by default, to Dayak shifting cultivators in the context of this discourse. The Bentian documents presented above reflect the attempts of a marginalized people to position themselves firmly as actors in the development discourse of Indonesia, a discourse that shapes and colors their lives, even as it appears to be oblivious to their existence. The Bentian seem to be, in Tsing's words (1993), among those who "cannot escape citizenship in a modernizing nation-state, yet who are never assured of becoming full citizens."

A range of Bentian authors have attempted to represent their farming traditions and oral adat law in the national language and in a written form that they imagine will make sense to other citizens of Indonesia, especially to those in the modern Indonesian bureaucracy. This is a process of making visible to the "outside" world (to those downriver and beyond, across the Java Sea, in the nation's capital), existing Kalimantan agroforestry systems and the social relations embedded in them. These documents represent the attempts of a people, long classified by others as, perhaps, the ultimate Other, the legendary "headhunters of Borneo," to define, publicly, their identities as property-owning citizens of the Indonesian nation-state.

There is a discernible transformation in the content and tone of the Bentian documents over time. In all documents, concerted attempts are made to reclaim "development" as an activity in which the Bentian are full actors. All of the documents call for the enforcement of the Basic Agrarian Law that provides for free land titling for "weaker economic groups." The Bentian understand that without nationally recognized land certificates, adat law will no longer be sufficient to protect their ancestral rattan gardens, their economic livelihood, or their environment. From the earliest documents on, rattan is identified as an indicator of land ownership. Earlier documents, however, written in the modulated tones of politeness and compliance, accept almost at face value the governmental campaign to eradicate shifting cultivation. Later, as the situation grows more threatening and as a wide range of authors appear, Bentian writings move away from the complete endorsement of governmental policies aimed at the eradication of shifting cultivation. The later documents historicize shifting cultivation and identify it as a logical response to environmental constraints. The damage caused by Dayak farming is compared, favorably, to the damage caused by logging concessions. When over a five-year period no governmental response has been forthcoming to Bentian requests and pleas, politeness and indirect language give way to the direct expression of fear and anger.

Most of the Bentian authors whose works we have examined are engaged in the process of "translation." They have attempted to translate national law into terms familiar to Bentian farmers; Bentian adat law into terms familiar to national and provincial governments; Bentian activities into "citizenship" and "development"; and "development" and "citizenship" into Bentian activities. These translations, however, do not represent a simple literary exercise. The Bentian, like other Dayak authors, are writing for their lives. Attempting to fit themselves into the mold of "citizen," following the ritual motions required by the governmental apparatus—filling out forms, writing proposals, calculating internal rates of return—the Bentian still find themselves unable to achieve the goals they recognize as being easily achieved by other, less marginalized citizens of the Indonesian nation-state. They have engaged in years of fruitless letter-writing to governmental bodies in an attempt to have their needs, including their petitions for a rattan industrial forest plantation, addressed through official channels. For highly capitalized logging concessions and plantations, however, these same official channels have provided easy access to Bentian lands through the rapid issuance of logging concession licenses and industrial forest plantation rights.

In 1993, as subcontractors for P. T. Kalhold Utama (a member of the Kalimanis Group/Kiani Lestari conglomerate owned by Haji Mohamad "Bob" Hasan), surrounded by armed guards, began to bulldoze and burn Bentian rattan forests, agricultural lands, and grave sites in preparation for their planned industrial forest plantation and transmigration settlement, the Bentian launched their case in the press.

After Jakarta newspapers began to publicize the seizure and destruction of their lands, Bentian leaders were granted meetings with the ministers of transmigration and environment. The minister of transmigration, Siswono Yudohusodo, was disturbed by their accounts and declared that the government would, at the very least, not go ahead with its plan to move three hundred families of transmigrants onto Bentian territories as part of the Kalhold Utama Company's industrial forest plantation. The 19 June 1994 *Jakarta Post* headline read "Government settles dispute with Dayak tribes" and quoted the minister of transmigration's declaration

> that the plots belonging to the local people will be preserved in the 5,000 hectare concession area, while the resettlement area which covers 80,000 hectares, would be located somewhere outside the [Bentian] location. . . . He added, "We apologize to the people if the projects have caused anxiety." Siswono said that the government would never disrupt the lives of the Dayak tribes. "The government respects the customary rights of the Bentian tribes," he said. Siswono explained that the plots in the concession area—[upon] which the local people depend for their livelihood—would remain intact.

In the spring of 1995, however, despite the statements of the minister of transmigration, the Kalhold Utama Company moved two hundred families of transmigrants into tiny huts that had been hastily built in the newly bull-dozed Bentian rattan forests and graveyards. A brigadier general of the armed forces stated, on condition of anonymity, that the logging concession owner, a close associate of General Suharto, was simply more powerful than the minister of transmigration, the minister of forestry, and the entire Indonesian legal system. It remains to be seen, however, how long the impoverished transmigrant families can survive the climate of hostility and terror as they attempt to live in their tiny huts on the bulldozed, eroded, and forcefully seized Bentian lands.

In February 1996 the minister of forestry met with Bentian leaders. They presented him with detailed maps of their rattan forest lands. The minister then declared to them that he would excise their traditional territories from the logging concession areas. The Bentian are still waiting for the provincial government of East Kalimantan to fulfill the minister's promise.

Notes

Institutional support for this research and analysis was provided by the Research and Development Institute of the Indonesian Ministry of Forestry, the Indonesian Institute of Sciences (LIPI), Cornell University, the East-West Center, the Ford Foundation, and Mulawarman University in Samarinda. Much of this essay was completed while the author was at Cornell University's Department of Rural Sociology. The research was funded by a Fulbright–Hayes Dissertation Fellowship, with additional assistance from the GTZ Forestry Project at Mulawarman University.

Many individuals have contributed to the thought processes and data gathering leading to this essay. I cannot name them all here for various reasons, including, on the part of some, their wish to maintain their privacy. I owe a great debt of thanks to my Bentian hosts and friends for their ideas, their patience, and their contributions to my research efforts. I owe thanks also to the founding members of the PLASMA and UNMUL students; Ministry of Forestry officials, including Dr. Johannes S. H., Dr. Priasukmana, Dr. Tantra, Dr. Kosasi, Mr. Amblani, Mr. Endang, and the rest of Litbang Kehutanan Samarinda staff; and to Nancy Peluso, Chris Barr, Martijn van Beek, Joe Weinstock, M. Scharai-Rad at GTZ, Samarinda, and Michael Dove for critical comments and suggestions. I also thank Charles Zerner for providing substantial editorial input and significant insights into theoretical aspects of my data. I am grateful to my employer, Environmental Defense, for the consistent support of sustainable, community-based forestry efforts in Kalimantan and elsewhere, and for providing a stimulating working environment that yielded additional insights into the materials presented in this essay. The standard disclaimer holds true here: the views expressed in this article—as well as any errors that may have occurred—are my own and are not intended to reflect the views or policies of any of the above individuals or institutions.

1   The term *Dayak* has, at times, had derogatory connotations. Currently, however, members of groups labeled by outsiders as "Dayak," such as the Bentian, the Benuaq, and the Tonyoi, refer to themselves as Dayak out of a sense of pride and unity. It is in this spirit that the term is utilized here.

2   Borneo, like other islands of the "South Seas," has excited the imaginations of foreign writers for centuries. Adventurers, missionaries, and traders drawn to Borneo jungles recorded in great detail their impressions of their Dayak hosts, companions, and neighbors. Their descriptions, not surprisingly, revealed as much about their own opinions, prejudices, and plans as they did about the Dayaks. Reece, in his introduction to the reprint of *The Headhunters of Borneo* (Bock [1881]1985), cites the "veritable flood of travel literature on Borneo, most of it exploiting the perennial popular appeal of headhunters, bare-breasted women, orang utans, and other exotica. . . . Hardly a year has gone by without at least one book describing the adventures of some indefatigable traveller braving the Borneo jungle as if no one had ever done it before."

When Norwegian naturalist Carl Bock, the author of *The Headhunters of Borneo*, traveled throughout the Middle Mahakam region in the 1870s as a guest of the sultan of Kutai, he recorded his impressions of the Bornean people he encountered:

In mental capacity the Dyaks [*sic*] are on a footing with the Malays, but are not so slovenly and lazy as the latter, and have more inclination for work. They are not so reserved as the Malays, being fond of talking and amusements, though calm and not easily excited. Like all savages, they are very inquisitive and superstitious.

As regards morality, I am bound to give the Dyaks a high place in the scale of civilization. The question may be put, how can morality be attributed to a Head-Hunter? I am going to point out their good qualities first, and shall later deal with the Head-hunting customs. . . . The divine command "Thou shalt not steal" is strictly observed by the Dyaks; robberies and theft are entirely unknown among them. They would never touch any of my articles, however trifling, without first asking permission. . . . They are also very truthful. I wish I could say as much for the Malays and Boegis, who, from the crowned head downwards to the humblest soul, are reputed tellers of falsehoods.

The barbarous practice of Head-Hunting, as carried on by all the Dyak tribes . . . is part and parcel of their religious rites. . . . Head-Hunting is . . . the most difficult feature in the relationship of the subject races to their white masters, and the most delicate problem which civilization has to solve in the future administration of the as yet independent tribes of the interior of Borneo. (209, 215)

In 1891 the island of Borneo was divided into Dutch and British colonial regions. The British retained the northern portion of the island, which eventually became the states of Sabah and Sarawak in Malaysia, and the independent country of Brunei. The Dutch administered the southern portion of the island, which became, with Indonesian independence, the four Indonesian provinces of Central, South, East, and West Kalimantan (Peluso 1983).

3   See Anderson's *Imagined Communities* (1991) for an exploration of the links between the written (printed) word and nationalist claims.

4   According to Heryanto (1988: 14), *bangun,* the root word of pem-bangun-an, meaning "development," is associated with two clusters of meaning. The first includes "meanings which are related to the activity of constructing buildings/houses/bridges/roads." The second includes "meanings which are related to the activity of changing some[one] . . . from a state of sleeping/lying down/unconsciousness to becoming awakened/upright/conscious." A mother might say, "Bangun!," (Wake up! Arise!) to her sleeping child.

5   See, for example, Heryanto (1988: 23): "Like cooking which has too much MSG, Indonesian is thick with technocratic terms: engineering, proposal, target, scope, input, impact, obstacle, transfer, interact, standard, random , monitor, coverage, sophisticated, relevant, valid, labor-intensive, rationale, or take-off."

6   Officials are often foresters or agronomists trained in Java.

7   In addition to a perusal of the large volume of scientific research which demonstrates that shifting cultivation is often environmentally sustainable under conditions of low population densities, repeated visits to the same area over a period of years by interested officials would greatly help to clarify matters. In this case, the visiting observer might note that, after three to four years, the productive "sedentary" vegetable farmers have exhausted and abandoned their earlier plots, the thin, exposed soils now infested with tenacious *alang-alang* grass. With the money earned from vegetable sales, perhaps they have purchased the well-preserved lands of their Dayak neighbors, beginning the cycle of intensive vegetable production, soil exhaustion, Imperata dominance, and land abandonment again (see Dove 1983, 1985b, 1986a, for more details). The visitor might observe that the earlier, disorderly-looking Dayak fields have begun to grow back into forest and forested rattan gardens, still producing foods and medicines for human

consumption and providing habitats for wildlife. Closer inspection might lead to the discovery that the "forest" itself, from which Dayak fields had been cleared initially, is actually old regrowth from generations of Dayak fields. Only over time do the intergenerational land use and conservation strategies of Dayak swidden farmers become apparent. Only over time does the link between old-growth forests and former swidden fields become visible. Only over time does the cycle of high productivity, soil degradation, and site abandonment associated with migrant farmers come into focus.

8   See Tsing (1993) for a richly detailed exploration of the complex texture of adat processes.

9   See Zerner (1992a) and Lev (1976) for more information on Indonesian law. Zerner (1996) also notes that, more recently, adat processes have been utilized as part of attempts to "democratize the political culture of Indonesia in ways which recognize and respect minority cultures and agro-ecological practices."

10   Following Rousseau's usage (1990: 12), a Malay is defined as "a Moslem who speaks a Malay dialect."

11   Transmigrants are usually impoverished farmers who have been resettled in remote areas by the central government.

12   See Peluso (1983) for information on the history of Kalimantan trade.

13   The name "Bentian" appears to be a rather recent appellation. Carl Bock, a Norwegian naturalist, in his 1879 visit to what would now be called Bentian villages, never uses the term and refers instead to "Dyaks of village X." The Bentian say that they were named by a Kutai sultan during one of the annual pilgrimages made by Dayak leaders to pay their respects to the sultan in the royal city of Tenggarong (Nasir 1991b). Leaders of the Lempenai, Teriek, and Jorent groups, who were descendants of those who had participated in the *penyua* with the Temanta'ng king, visited the sultan to report, as requested, on "the conditions of life and the livelihood of the people under their leadership." They reported that their rice fields had all been attacked by ricebirds ("bentian" birds) from a nearby cave. The sultan declared that if this was so, "then from now on the name of your group will be Bentian since your place of residence is in the bentian cave area. Little by little the groups which were originally called Lempenai, Teriek, and Jorent, all became known as the Bentian people" (Nasir 1991b).

14   The current administrative district of Bentian Besar is located on a portion of the Nine Rivers land.

15   In 1989 the Indonesian government banned the export of raw and semi-processed rattan in an attempt to stimulate the national rattan-processing industrial capacity and to capture more of the value added to rattan by processing it within the country. As a result of the ban, rattan prices plummeted. Many river

traders went bankrupt and most of those remaining switched from rattan to other commodities. As of 1992, after three years of extremely depressed rattan prices, Bentian farmers, while experiencing economic hardship, did not face immediate bankruptcy or starvation since they still had access to their swidden fields, hunting grounds, and streams, which provided food and some cash income for their families. In addition, despite low prices, rattan could still be sold on the market.

16 "Still valid," that is, still utilized even though the area is nominally Christian. North American–funded missionaries insist that conversion to Christianity requires the Bentian to burn all "pagan" idols, charms, and magical oils. In addition, the missionaries forbid the use of supernatural oaths (*sumpah*).

17 "Cared for," or *dipelihara,* probably refers to the fact that the magically charged apparatus, in this case possibly consisting of a sacred tiger-tooth necklace and other magically endowed items, must be regularly "fed" offerings such as a few grains of cooked rice, tiny cigarettes, and blood, usually of sacrificial animals (although in former times human blood from a freshly killed victim was a requirement for the "feeding" of certain items).

18 This unmechanized logging boom, called *banjir kap,* occurred as urban entrepreneurs, usually ethnic Chinese or Malays, hired teams of Dayaks to fell trees lying close to the banks of rivers. Felling was done largely by axe and sometimes by chainsaw, where available. The trees were then dragged by the felling teams to the water's edge and were floated downstream. Due to a lack of heavy machinery, only trees close to riverbanks could be felled. Manual logging did not result in the severe soil compaction and erosion associated with mechanized logging. Economic benefits to local communities from this logging boom were substantial, and Dayak loggers were often able to purchase outboard motors or chainsaws from their savings.

19 *Sega* is the Indonesian name for *Calamus caesius,* the most commonly cultivated type of rattan.

20 *Semangat* means "enthusiasm, desire, or spirit" (as in "spirited"). *Membangun,* from the root word *bangun,* means "awaken, build, or develop."

21 Industrial forest plantations (*Hutan Tanaman Industri,* HTI), designed for the production of export-oriented tree crops including rubber, palm oil, rattan, and timber, are a major component of current Indonesian forestry and development policy. The establishment of large-scale tree plantations by both private-sector and government agencies is a vigorously pursued goal of administrators in several ministries including Forestry, Agriculture, Trade, and Transmigration. Official village cooperatives are considered to be governmental actors and are thus eligible to apply for HTI permits.

22 The request for 100,000 hectares of rattan land was based on Bentian calculations

that, given the low Bentian birthrate and a substantial amount of Bentian migration to urban areas, this portion of the Bentian ancestral homelands, already the site of individually owned rattan plantations, would be sufficient to ensure the continued viability of the Bentian population and their rattan production. The Bentian modeled their HTI request on the World Bank–supported nucleus-estate system of plantation development. The usual nucleus-estate arrangement reserves between 20 and 40 percent of plantation lands for private-sector plantations and a factory site, leaving the remainder for smallholders, who are allotted one two-hectare site per household. The Bentian plan, however, reserved 80 percent of the lands for smallholders, 1 percent for the "Desire to Awaken/Develop/ Build Cooperative," and the remaining 19 percent, or 19,000 hectares, for "public and village Government use," including land for village expansion, grazing areas, cemeteries, and rattan nurseries.

23 "Ir." is the abbreviation for Insinyur, an (originally Dutch) academic title indicating the completion of a technical university degree.

24 To understand what this offer of 16,000 hectares represented, it may be useful to recall Bentian calculations that, for eighteen villages, 19,000 hectares were needed simply for village territory and non-rattan agricultural land. Much of the remaining 81,000 hectares consisted of currently productive, individually owned rattan gardens. The existing eighteen Bentian villages did not all lie in the location selected by the government. The offer of 16,000 hectares in a single location was incomprehensible and insulting to the Bentian.

25 As of 1994, however, these facts appeared to make no impression on logging concession officials, who, in order to maintain their logging permits, were eager to appear to comply with governmental regulations regarding transmigration and industrial forest plantations, even if only in an unsuccessful, damaging, and pro forma manner.

26 Translations of Kalimantan logging company names are often revealing of their owners' desires for great wealth or their development-speak posturing. P. T. Kalhold Utama—the Ultimate Borneohold Company—is a part of the Sweet River (Kalimanis) group owned by timber tycoon and Suharto associate Bob Hasan. P. T. Timber Dana—the Timber Fund Company—and other subcontractors, P. T. Hutan Maligai—the Forest Palace Co.—and P. T. Adil Makmur—the Just and Prosperous Co. (a "just and prosperous nation" is one of Indonesia's stated development goals)—carry out logging plantation establishment operations (clear-cutting) for Ultimate Borneohold on seized Bentian lands. Golden Wheel (Roda Mas) and Scenic White Mountain (Gunung Putih Indah) also log and/or clear-cut for plantation establishment in seized Bentian adat forests.

Fruit Trees and Family Trees in an Anthropogenic Forest: Property Zones, Resource Access, and Environmental Change in Indonesia

Nancy Lee Peluso

Landscapes are culture before they are nature; constructs of the imagination projected onto wood and water and rock. . . . But once a certain idea of landscape, a myth, a vision, establishes itself in an actual place, it has a peculiar way of muddling categories, of making metaphors more real than their referents; of becoming, in fact, part of the scenery.—Simon Schama, *Landscape and Memory*

Setipa Mountain rises behind Bagak Sahwa, on the south side of the paved trunk road between the city of Singkawang and the town of Bengkayang. On the other side of the road, a wide strip of irrigated rice fields meanders along a river that stretches north to meet the Selakau River. Bagak, a hamlet of more than a hundred single-family houses, is laid out on a line lazily perpendicular to the trunk road, aiming toward Setipa's peak. The mountain and the hamlet are buffeted by a mile-wide strip of forest that winds around all the mountain's associated foothills. The village forest consists of tropical trees in mixed stands, scattered bamboo clusters, tangling vines slithering forth from the edges of cleared footpaths. The forest is dotted with only an occasional swidden patch of hill rice or a broad-leafed cluster of banana clumps. After the first half mile, the tangles and thorns are left behind; the forest takes on a parklike quality. Open expanses under a layered canopy of tall trees make it easy and relatively cool to walk from one giant fruit tree to the next.

Wrapping around the hillside, the park-forest contains hundreds of three-, four-, and five-generation durian trees, many of them triple-armspreads around, the emergents in the tightly closed canopy. Because their planters have passed on, they are remembered now by the planters' names: Nek Bantang, Nek Limo, Nek Suhotn, Nek Rawoh, Nek Garakng. Beside some of them are the trees planted by their living children and grandchildren: Si Anyap, Si Sulam. Other trees called "Si" were planted by men or women who died young—before having the honor of being called "Nek," or grandparent.[1] Some trees are named for the peculiar shape or taste of their fruit: Si Jongkup is named for its bottle-shaped fruits. A level below them in the multistoried canopy are the progeny of fruit trees planted at the same time as the durian: tangy *langsat*, creamy *angkaham*, sweet mangosteen. Up and down the slopes of Setipa's mountainside and the slopes of adjacent hills, these trees planted by Bagak hamlet's Salako ancestors have stood as witness to and subjects of the village's history.[2]

In this essay I examine the transformation of property and access conventions in an anthropogenic forest in West Kalimantan, a province in Indonesian Borneo. Both property rights and landscape are treated as processes that may transform one another but can not be unilinearly linked. The case illustrates the unpredictability of local social and environmental changes resulting from state and market interventions that change property rights and landscape composition. It also illustrates how property rights may be constitutive of places, but that alone, they do not create a place. Recognizing that nature/culture separations are more heuristically useful than real, I look at two convergent themes that examine the construction of this landscape: the anthropogenic forest and social relations in the forest.

The anthropogenic forest is examined in two aspects. One is the creation and management of forest landscapes by forest-dwelling peoples. I show how forest-dependent people not only deforest but also afforest or reforest spontaneously, that is, without government "sponsorship." This is perceptible only by looking at landscape change over a relatively long period—in this case, about a hundred years. Examining only a "moment" in a landscape process—such as the burning of a forest patch to make a swidden or extracting products from the forest—obscures the larger management processes in which local people play key roles. A second aspect of the anthropogenic forest is the notion that "nature" reserves created by government decree can interrupt local forest-management schemes. Such interruptions and their ignorance of local management processes may cause local people to alter the species composition of those spaces claimed by the government, as a means of symbolically contesting their appropriation.

Another set of themes more self-consciously addressing social relations in these forests is focused on property rights and access to forest resources. One theme is the way politics and discourses can alter the practices possible within a landscape and the means of accessing the landscape's resources. To untangle these processes of change, I examine the ways certain resources have represented or generated power, wealth, and meaning to those who control or have access to them (Shipton and Goheen 1992; Peters 1992; Berry 2000). In particular, I look at how fluctuating power relations, production relations, and the social meanings of resources have generated different landscape relations among land and trees through multiple generations of people occupying and re-creating the forest. A second theme is the fluctuation across space and through time between individual and corporate (group) property relations in various resources, notably long-living trees. I call these fluctuations "temporal and spatial zones" of access rights and landscape management.

These landscapes and property relations are not unique artifacts of a single village's history and experience. The managed forests of West Kalimantan and their relationships to swidden and wet-rice production systems have only recently gained the attention of researchers (Ex 1992; Salafsky et al. 1993; Padoch 1994; Peluso and Padoch 1996). In many ways, they resemble the anthropogenic forests of East and South Kalimantan, which are dominated by cultivated rattan, rattan and rubber mixes, and other recently reported agroforestry strategies (see, e.g., Tsing 1993: 167–70; Padoch and Peters 1993; Padoch 1994; Colfer and Soedjito 1995; Lahjie and Seibert 1988; Potter 1987a; Colfer and Dudley 1993; Leaman et al. 1991; Peluso 1992c). Moreover, the anthropogenic forests being created by these villagers have correlates in local-level forest management in other parts of Indonesia and the tropics in general (Michon et al. 2000; Alcorn 1981; Posey 1985; Hecht, Anderson, and May 1988; Balee 1994; Denevan and Padoch 1987; Fairhead and Leach 1996; Schama 1995; Brosius 1997).

I focus much of my discussion of resource tenure and meaning on durian (*Durio zibethanus*), examining this fruit tree in the context of villagers' management of other fruits. Durian's value and demand all over the island of Borneo—throughout Southeast Asia in fact—guarantees sales wherever there are roads or rivers to transport it. As discussed below, durian is both king and queen of fruits, an important component of both the social fabric and the physical landscape. The trees' biological characteristics of longevity and productivity influence the property relations and the physical configuration of land through many generations, illustrating the importance of temporal as well as spatial zones in the study of environmental change.

Subsequent sections describe Bagak's past and present landscapes. The following section explores resource tenure and concepts of temporal and spatial zoning. The historical discussion elaborates changes in the regional political ecology that have constituted and been constituted by local resource-management practices, including property rights and resource-access mechanisms. I then discuss in detail intergenerational property rights in fruit, contextualizing durian and its social relations within this particular landscape. How and why rights, access, and discursive strategies are changing are discussed in the following section. Finally, I discuss the several ways that this case confounds some of the accepted wisdom of resource management, landscape formation, and property relations.

Resource Tenure, Zoning, and Environmental Change

How resource control affects and is affected by power, wealth, and meaning will also affect that resource's management (Peters 1994). Property relations in agrarian resources, as with any social relations, are constantly shifting (Moore 1986; Berry 2000). The explanation of environmental change is complicated by the interactions of multiple aspects of property relations: (1) conflicting sources of legitimate authority, such as customary and formal legal systems (Moore 1986; Bromley 1991; Fortmann 1990; Peluso 1992c, 1993; Berry 2000); (2) negotiated systems of meaning (Dove 1986b; Posey 1989; Peluso 1992a; Shipton and Goheen 1992; Peters 1992; Brosius 1999a); and (3) an individual's position in different social networks (Berry 1989; Blaikie 1985; Okoth-Ogendo 1989; Brosius 1999b). Political-economic processes that influence access to resources such as markets, government institutions, and regulatory policies also play crucial roles in the ways that resources are used and managed (Moore 1986; Berry 1989; Bromley 1989, 1991; Vandergeest 1996).

A dynamic view of property impels a focus on "process," rather than simply on the institutions, social structures, or bundles of rights and responsibilities that are particular outcomes of processes and negotiations. The study of "property as process" requires multiscaled analysis, as has been the practice in political ecology. That is, one needs to study both local histories, the layered political-economic influences that affect local practice, and the ways that various actors have interpreted and negotiated change (Smith 1984;

Blaikie 1985; Blaikie and Brookfield 1987; Neumann 1992; Peluso 1992b; Bryant and Bailey 1997; Berry 2000).

In tropical forests, the complications of studying property relations and farmer decision-making are confounded by the sheer number of species. Even if we limit our discussion to species that have economic, medicinal, or ritual value, the range and diversity of agroforestry products is immense, as are the tenure arrangements pertaining to them. To take a single example, there are many ways to carve up the bundle of rights to a tree, as Louise Fortmann (1985) has so aptly shown. The largest bundles of rights include rights to own or inherit, to plant, to use, and to dispose of a tree. Each of these rights in turn can be subdivided; many of them interact with other factors. For example, tree tenure may determine or be determined by land tenure; or the two may be independent. Rights to use different parts of the tree may be allocated to different claimants; these multiple uses may not always be mutually compatible. Land rights and tree rights may be held by different claimants; change in one often, though not always, leads to change in the other. Whether or not a tree was planted or self-sown can make a difference in the types of claims of rights holders; whether it is used for subsistence or commercial use can also make a difference not only in claims but in the justification of such claims and the resources' meanings (Fortmann 1985; Fortmann and Bruce 1988; Peluso 1992b).

A tree's biological characteristics also influence tree-tenure bundles, including the length of time it grows and produces fruit, nuts, or other products; its reproductive capacity; whether the fruit is harvested or left to rot in the forest; and intensity of management (Peters 1994). These factors influence people's ability to cultivate or manage a self-sown tree and the tree's productive life span. Biological characteristics can also play important roles in inheritance patterns, the value placed on the tree, and the meanings of access to it.

Long-living trees also teach lessons in spatio-temporal zoning. Zoning is not only a spatial category, in which spaces are set aside for crop production, reserve forests, economic forests, urban areas, or other types of management. Zoning has important temporal dimensions, which can be illustrated by changes in rights to long-living fruit and nut-producing trees or to self-propagating species. Mixed-age stands of trees and other flora and fauna—a forest—can encompass several temporal zones of rights at one time. Though blurred, differences between the zones can be expressed by changes in the rights or means of access to individual forest components with each generation's passing. Over time, as the composition of a landscape shifts, zones of production and reproduction shift as well.

In sum, landscape and property are processes that respond to conjunctures of political economy, nature, culture, and politics. Changes are reflected in landscape composition and in the means of allocating access to resources whose value, meaning, and accessibility change over time and vary for the many people who use and control them.

Bagak's Landscape Today

Bagak is one of the two hamlets in Bagak Sahwa village. The hamlet is located entirely on the south side of the main road, flush against the hillside forest that borders the Gunung Raya Pasi Nature Reserve. In 1990 the entire village had a population of approximately 1,096 people in 258 households; 114 of these fell within Bagak's jurisdiction. The hamlet is located in subdistrict Tujuhbelas, in Sambas District, on a well-paved road running from the coastal city of Singkawang inland toward Bengkayang and beyond. This road was widened and hardened in the 1920s and 1930s by the Dutch colonial government and paved by the Indonesian government in 1963, but began as a footpath in the late eighteenth century when the area was claimed by the sultan of Sambas. The path led a few kilometers past Bagak to the sultan's gold mines in Montrado from the then small coastal settlement of Singkawang.

Over the past eighty years this hamlet of people, most of whom primarily identify themselves as Salako Dayaks, has been informally sedentarized[3] by the encroachment of other land users on their borders and the fixing of these borders by actions taken by successive colonial and national governments. The administrative village territory is bounded to the south by the relatively small (3,000-hectare) nature reserve, gazetted by the Dutch in 1932 as a watershed protection area for Singkawang. To the east of the village lie the agricultural lands of adjacent villages and special transmigration settlements for retired police and air force officers established in 1968 after the Confrontation with Malaysia and subsequent regional unrest associated with Suharto's New Order government.[4] To the west of the village is a Franciscan Catholic mission and K–12 school, established in 1916. To the north are extensive rubber-plantation lands established on the administrative village lands of Maya Sopa, which since 1980 have been worked by Salako villagers and some 4,000 Javanese transmigrants settled there.

Bagak Sahwa today consists of some 2,700 hectares of land, according to official village statistics. One-third (900 hectares) of this land is formally under the jurisdiction of the nature reserve, as part of the Ministry of Forestry's Department of Forest Protection and Nature Conservation, but was once heavily managed—farmed and occupied—by the ancestors of Bagak villagers. Today, the law requires villagers to acquire permits from the Department of Nature Conservancy (PHPA) to enter the reserve. This law is neither recognized by local people nor enforced by foresters. Foresters try to restrict certain forest uses such as swidden cultivation and hunting, which, although rare, still occur. Foresters are lenient, however, about people collecting fruit and rubber from trees planted within the reserve's boundaries for reasons discussed below.

In addition to some recent farming of irrigated rice fields located in Sahwa, Bagak villagers practice a complex, long-rotation form of land management: a kind of cyclic swidden-fallow agroforestry (see Denevan and Padoch 1987; Padoch and Peters 1993; Peluso and Padoch 1996). After the harvest of swidden field crops—rice, corn, cassava, and vegetables—and perhaps a second or third year's crop of peanuts or cassava, a swidden fallow is generally planted in rubber, fruit, or rubber and fruit mixtures. Such forest gardens are managed subsequently for both the planted tree species and the self-sown trees that sprout in the interstices and are selectively protected during slash weeding (see also Padoch and Peters 1993). Thus, because of the long productive periods of the trees, the swidden fallows become managed forests. Some swidden fallows are purposely left alone, without planting economic trees, allowing them to revert to successional forest specifically to save them for future field-crop cultivation. Other fallows are planted in low-management but high-production crops such as banana. Each crop, while often occupying the same spatial zones, creates temporal zones of access which differ significantly from one another. As discussed below, each household manages numerous plots under different types of vegetative cover for consumption or sale (fig. 24).

In addition, mature forests not used for swiddens or forest gardens were tapped for timber, resins, and other subsistence and commercial products.

Figure 24. A durian "forest"; tree to the right is a seventh- or eighth-generation grandparent tree. Photograph by Nancy Lee Peluso.

Rice self-sufficiency was crucial to local people when markets were few and food supply local; numerous large swiddens provided the family's food and dominated the landscape.[5] Today, only a third of the villagers planted swidden fields at all, the average size of these a meager one-third hectare. Economic trees—rubber and fruit in particular—dominate the landscape. "Rubber," in the words of one local woman, "has become our daily rice," and windfall profits accrue in good years to those with fruit to sell.

Bagak's Landscape Yesterday: A Short History

In former days . . . it was not the land that was important, but trees and their fruit. It was quite common for people to have [what is now called] "a garden" together, Mr. A with Mr. B, because they liked to plant their trees next to each other.—Nek Manap, *kepala adat* [village chief of custom], Bagak Sahwa)

The ancestors of the Bagak Dayaks lived in longhouses near the upper slopes of Setipa Mountain just outside what is today the Gunung Raya Pasi Nature

Reserve, in an area called Bagak Atas, or Upper Bagak. Living on the upper slopes of the hillsides allowed them to diversify their production while also defending themselves from their enemies.

While the Dayaks practiced swidden cultivation in the dry hills, the swampy lowlands to the north were farmed by Hakka-speaking Chinese agriculturalists. Their settlement/village was called Sahwa and may have been established as early as the late eighteenth century, soon after Chinese began mining gold for the sultan of Sambas at nearby Montrado (see Chew 1990). The Chinese cut the lowland forest and dug canals to drain the swamps and plant rice. Dutch colonial agrarian policy passed in 1870 prohibited Chinese and other "non-native" peoples from owning land. The Dutch ignored the fact that local Chinese had converted this forest to productive irrigated agriculture, and thus ignored their own criteria for recognizing land rights—that is, continuous cultivation and conversion of "unproductive forest" to more productive crops and long-term agriculture. Instead, they differentiated access to land by racial categories, denying the Chinese both "native" status and the stronger land rights that accompanied that status. Chinese could acquire usufruct rights to the land through agreements that were effectively long-term leases.[6] Although they did not formally own the land, the Chinese continued to alter it, improve it, and make it more productive. Chinese planters also leased rights from the Dutch colonial government to the hill lands between the wet-rice fields and the mountaintops, a settlement called Patengahan.[7] There they built houses and eventually planted fruit and rubber. They were the first non-Europeans in the area to grow rubber, a crop with solely commercial value.

The Bagak Salako generally maintained control of their forest and land resources, except for occasional tribute payments to the Malay Sultan of Sambas. The community sold or bartered agroforestry products with Malay traders who came to the longhouses seeking them; they sold fish, illipe nuts (used then for cooking oil), savory-preserved durian (*tempuyak*), sweet durian cakes (*lempok*), and fresh fruit. Some longhouse dwellers walked to Singkawang, bypassing the Malays and selling directly to urban Chinese for higher prices.

In 1920 the Dutch initiated plans to turn the upper slopes of the Gunung Raya Pasi complex, including Setipa Mountain, into a watershed protection area. The initial line for the reserve border was drawn where a water catchment device was to be constructed, encompassing all of the village's current and former living sites—the sites of their ancestral forests and lands. The longhouse occupants had to move off the mountain and forfeit these ancestral rights. Not surprisingly, people of Bagak Atas were not happy with the colonial government's new plans. Dutch officials worked with local leaders to convince people that they had no choice but to move from Setipa to the lower slopes of Patengahan, near the areas that Chinese had planted rubber and fruit. Eventually, people moved out of longhouses into single-family dwellings they built that were large enough to accommodate extended families.

The villagers' unhappiness with the new spatial arrangements caused some families to remain on the mountain (inside the reserve) until approximately 1940, eight years after the nature reserve was officially established and mapped. These families moved only because the controlleur threatened to jail them if they refused to leave or if they continued to make swiddens above the reserve boundaries. According to local sources, the head of the new village continued to negotiate with the Dutch to change the reserve boundaries to recognize the rights of local people who had planted trees or converted land there. Though it is not clear in exactly what year, the Dutch eventually moved the reserve boundary above the old longhouse sites, restoring a good deal of the people's territory, and constituting a victory for the local people.

The villagers have continued to "push back" the border in less organized, informal ways. Villagers harvest rubber, durian, langsat, rambutan, angkaham, cempedak, and other fruits planted by their parents and other ancestors within the border. During the Japanese occupation (1942–45), the Indonesian revolution, and the early years of Indonesian independence, villagers made swiddens within the reserve boundaries and planted rubber and fruit in the fallows. Government surveillance of state forests was practically nonexistent at that time. By planting productive tree crops, people were also staking their claims in the control of the hillside's upper slopes, negotiating new forms of old territorial and resource claims. The border continues to be blurred as people still plant fruit and rubber trees within the reserve, creating an informal buffer zone between the reserve forest and Bagak village forest. They also hunt the occasional deer and collect the products of various self-sown species such as bamboo shoots, candlenut, and rattan from within the borders of the reserve.

The intervention of the colonial state in the arrangement of the village's social and productive space did more than superimpose a new set of rules about land and forest use. Real and imaginary boundaries were imposed for the first time on the villagers' landscapes, affecting their access to the lands and land uses they had always preferred.[8] Current and past events were converging to create pressures for a new working landscape comprised of different zones of protection, production, and control.

The change in spatial arrangements helped spark Dayak interest in planting rubber. After people were denied legal access to the extensive tracts of reserve and secondary old growth on the mountain, it became difficult for everyone to find enough swidden land to produce their family's food. A few Dayaks experimented with planting irrigated rice near the Chinese but gave up—the time and labor demands of wet-rice production interfered too much with their other productive activities. Rubber was much less labor-intensive. By the 1930s, they could exchange rubber for government-issued coupons to buy food and other supplies as they needed them. Two additional factors helped increase their interest in planting rubber: moving out of the area that became the reserve and thus losing access to land for agricultural production, and the rising prices of rubber. Rubber's biological characteristics also made it an attractive crop: latex could be collected and marketed in virtually all seasons except the rainiest weeks. Uncollected latex did no harm to the tree's productivity. Until the Confrontation, it could be carried—without spoilage—to Malaysia and sold or exchanged for goods there. Or it could be sold along the road to Singkawang, widened by the Dutch in the 1930s. Rubber trees increased the value of their land and increased a household's diversity of economic options. When the first Dayaks moved down from Setipa, none planted rubber yet. Gradually, it became popular, and today, 85 percent of the villagers own productive rubber trees.[9] As late as the mid-1960s, however, Chinese were producing most of the one tonne of rubber exported daily from Bagak (interview with former village head, Bagak, 1992).

As the village's extensive resource territory was shrunk, the relative intensity of land use became increasingly important. Because of the combined impacts of the loss of land for expansion and the response to market opportunities in rubber planting, by the mid-1960s many people were no longer able to produce their year's supply of rice on their own land; they had to buy rice. Rubber and fruit gardens began filling up swidden fallows. To feed their families, then, the marketing of forest and agroforestry products assumed a more important role in people's subsistence strategies (fig. 25).

Figure 25. Swidden agroforestry. Rice in front half of photograph, mixed-fruit forest gardens (planted in swidden fallows). Photograph by Nancy Lee Peluso.

Important changes in the landscape and the redistribution of land began to emerge at this time—once again, largely because of the ways the state intervened in the allocation, formalization, and enforcement of property rights. In 1968 local Dayaks worked with the Indonesian army to violently force rural Chinese to move to urban areas such as Singkawang and Pontianak.[10] Approximately 150 hectares of paddy lands, productive rubber, and fruit gardens were left behind by the evicted Chinese. The stresses on land and changes in production discussed earlier perhaps contributed to local people's willingness to participate in the eviction of the Chinese from the lands they and their ancestors had transformed and managed—in spite of their own views that labor invested in land management and forest conversion generally imparted inheritable rights to land or trees.

When it became clear that the government would not allow the Chinese to return and reclaim their land, an ad hoc land distribution "council" divided the paddy fields and fruit and rubber gardens amongst local Dayaks. The council was organized by civil and military officials from the subdistrict and included the village head, the head of customary law, and a few informal village leaders. Some people had moved onto the land left behind to claim it before the meeting was held; the council formalized the claims of some, negated others. Other people refused to take any of this land, feeling that, as one villager put it, "the land was filled with tears." Although nearly impossible to retrace these at the time of the research, conflicts over some of these plots of land did apparently take place, according to some local people. Recognized claims were made official at the agrarian office, where people paid nominal registration fees for their land certificates. The second formal change was that the territories of Patengahan and Sahwa were combined into a single administrative village called Bagak Sahwa, based on the administrative village act of 1979. The village's symbolic borders were secured even tighter in practice, when transmigration (resettlement) areas for retired police and air force personnel were established on the eastern border of the village.[11] Besides rewarding these military men for their service to the country, the national state's desire to enforce permanent settlement was symbolized by the presence of ex-military families. Even more ominously, some of these former soldiers had served in the area during the Chinese evictions. The violent arm of the Indonesian state was thus represented in a very real way in the Sambas landscape.

In addition to the changes brought on by rubber, the move away from primarily swidden field-crop production also entailed an expansion of land-use categories and a change in the types of places fruit trees are planted. Easy access to the urban markets of Singkawang and Pontianak, facilitated by the paving of the road in the 1960s and the entry of Japanese vehicles (motorcycles and vans) in the 1970s, added additional incentives for tree-planting. Durian is no longer found only in former living sites; durian trees are literally taking over swidden fallows and displacing rubber gardens (which were themselves planted in swidden fallows). Some 97 percent of sample households have planted durian trees in swidden fallows; at least 41 percent have planted durian in or just next to their rubber gardens. Durian stems occupy 71 percent of the old and medium-aged fruit forests' total basal area (Charles Peters, personal communication 1994).[12]

At the same time that the ecological and economic importance of trees has been increasing within the landscape, forest garden land has taken on new meanings because of the trees that stay planted there for much longer periods than field crops. Fruit trees had long been either an individual's or a descent group's property; clearing forest for swiddens always gave the clearer's household rights to that land in perpetuity.[13] But the notion of a garden (*kabotn*) consisting of a relatively large unit of land where fruit trees were planted for commercial purposes is a new concept, although it was not uncommon in the past for someone to plant a cluster of three to six fruit trees (*kompokng*) and so claim or occupy a small piece of land. A garden was more frequently viewed as a short-term land use; one had a peanut garden or a banana garden. Multigenerational gardens dominated by fruit and rubber trees changed the temporal and spatial patterns of land use.

In sum, the relationships between land, trees, and the systems of tenure around them have been revolutionized by major changes in the political ecology of the region. In Bagak these have included: the formalization of borders by the government; the fluctuating enforcement of the nature reserve's borders and with it the fluctuating access of local people to the land and forest resources within those borders since 1932; the eviction of the Chinese and local Dayak's appropriation of some 150 hectares of paddy land, now used for wet-rice production; and the booming market for fruit brought on by political-economic change and the improvement and expansion of transport facilities. Each of these changes either constrained villagers' access to resources or expanded the markets for local products. The outcome of change was reflected in the landscape at different historical moments in shifting spatial and temporal zones of forests, fields, and rights or means of access to these. The changes also altered the ways some people valued the mix of resources and led to new types of property relations in many of them.

Fruit Trees and Family Trees

The previous section described the ways particular historical events of local, regional, national, and international importance converged with local practice to shape the current landscape in Bagak. Thinking of zoning as having both spatial and temporal dimensions, we have observed how forest became fields and then new forest again through various landscape processes. We have also seen how property rights and access to the various resources created in those zones were shifted, pushed, and pulled by actors with varying degrees of power at different points in time.

Let me now turn to the themes of zoning and resource access as these are experienced in different people's lives and embedded in their treatment of particular resources. Here, the differences in the biological characteristics of specific trees and field crops play an important role in the extent, intensity, or duration of spatiotemporal zoning—in short, in the kinds of territorialization—thus illustrating how ecological and sociological processes interact within the landscape.

Inheritance Ethics and Practice

For resident villagers in Bagak, land and trees still provide the most important sources of household income. Rights of resource access and control are recognized by the community on at least two bases that I discuss here: (1) kinship—the bilateral inheritance of rights to various resources, and (2) the investment of labor in resource production or management.[14] In the case of some fruits and forest products, participation in the harvest is both a right (by inheritance) and a conveyor of rights (by labor investment). Some examples of the ways that labor imparts preferred rights to one member of a descent group include clearing fruit or rubber gardens for a swidden, planting a tree on a piece of commonly held land, or clearing the brush from around a fruit or rubber tree to facilitate harvest of the tree's products.

In principle, both male and female children share equal rights to inherit their parents' resources, although primary rights to a household's resources remain within the household unit. The household, or the husband-wife pair plus resident children and elderly parents, manages a set of land-based resources in addition to any cash savings and movable property acquired by household members working outside the village or outside of agriculture. The cluster of household resources includes inherited lands under cultivation and in fallow, inherited durian and other fruit trees, rubber gardens, and lands cleared or trees planted by the parents during their lifetimes. When people lived in longhouses, the household unit was defined as an apartment (bi'ik) within the longhouse. As children married, they generally moved out of the apartment and built their own on to the parents' longhouse or another house in the same general settlement area. Whichever child remained within the apartment to care for the parents in their old age would inherit primary rights to the household's total resources. This child's spouse would move into the apartment and, after having children, the pair would eventually take over as co-heads of household.[15] The same pattern generally held when people moved to smaller dwellings.

The second point about resource distribution is that part of inheritance practice imparts greater rights to one of the children in a household—usually the one who continues the household and cares for aging parents. This individual gains the right to manage the household's productive resources. This task may be interpreted by rotating access to fruiting trees or it may involve dividing up the rights to particular trees among living siblings. This presents some disparities between principles and practices. Customs of intergenerational inheritance generally enable a relatively egalitarian mode of allocating resource access. In practice, however, having one member of a descent group in charge of the tree, even though this person will change through the generations, often gives him or her greater power over the resource and a greater control over everyone's access. On occasion, while custom dictates that grandparent trees have a different inheritance status than the trees planted by parents (see below), the primary rights to grandparent trees are taken by the person in each generation who continues the parents' household; they do not always return to the sibling group.

Other social mechanisms exist to prevent the monopolization of inherited resources by a single heir. For example, although the child who cares for aging parents in principle has primary rights to the household's land-based resources, parents sometimes divide up the trees before they die in order to prevent discord among the siblings, or to ensure that a favored grandchild or even a niece or nephew gets a specific share. In some cases, the children agree to maintain equal access to the trees and share relatively equally in the trees' management and fruit harvest. In other cases, some children of the tree planter are effectively eliminated from their inherited shares, either by sibling discord, as a result of having moved so far away that travel to collect fruit or cultivate a swidden is impractical, or by a sibling withdrawing from the co-heirs' pool.

Zoning, Temporal and Spatial

Fruit is the most complicated of the three landscape components, and is becoming increasingly so as regional political ecology and property relations change. Many fruit trees produce fruit through three to five generations. Durian may produce through seven generations. As explained repeatedly by nearly all the local people I spoke with, "rules" of access change in each generation and so do the temporal zones of proprietary authority. As the generations pass, more and more people have recognizable claims on the fruit of the tree. People insisted that moving residence does not necessarily eliminate one's rights of access to ancestral fruit trees; it is not uncommon for children or grandchildren to return to the village during durian season to share fruit with their siblings or other kin (cf. Appell 1970). Sometimes co-heirs living in one village will seek out a particular grandfather tree located in another "village," asking permission of the person in charge but rarely being refused access for a few days' or nights' harvest rights. These kinds of journeys, however, seem to be relatively rare, and more a matter of curiosity about ancestry than an occasion to demand a share of the harvest.

Temporal or intergenerational zoning of rights is generally interpreted as follows: while he or she is alive, the tree planter has exclusive rights to the fruit, although fruit is usually consumed with other household members, with family members in other households, and with guests. Profits from the sale of any fruit belong to the household or the planter. After one spouse passes away, the other is in charge of allocating access to the fruit, again generally sharing the annual harvest with other members of the household and sometimes the immediate family.

After tree planter and spouse have passed away, all male and female children inherit rights of access to the tree's fruit. However, as mentioned above, the child who "continues" the household usually retains primary rights, in that he or she makes the final decision as to who will have access to the fruit harvest among the siblings. In the third generation, after all the children of the planter have passed away, all grandchildren of the planter—a co-heir's group of cousins—have equal rights in principle. Once tree rights pass to the third generation, the tree is called a *panene'an* (grandparent tree), and the claims of the total group of descendants allegedly supersede the claims of the person in charge of the tree. Many local informants insisted that rights to the fruit of panene'an trees are not to be monopolized by an individual. The same rule holds true for successive generations—the fourth, fifth, or sixth generations of tree holders. One reason for the difference between the children's generation and the subsequent grandchildren's generations is that the "debts" of labor investment in parental care have been settled by favored resource access in the children's generation.

Each villager is in various temporal zones of resource control at any point in time. Tree planters (and their spouses) are exclusive owners; the children of the tree planters are small group owners (co-heirs); grandchildren and great-grandchildren constitute larger co-heir groups as the generations pass. At different life-cycle stages, a person's access to resources tends to be dominated by different zones of use-rights. As individuals or young married couples, they still depend on the efforts of parents and grandparents, in some cases inheriting their parents' productions, in many cases having some access to grandparent trees. When they still live with their parents, they share the parents' share. As people grow older, they tend to harvest primarily the trees they planted themselves.

This last point illustrates one aspect of the meaning of tree planting. Many villagers said that each generation has a responsibility to its younger and future generations, that is, to plant enough trees to enable them to first relinquish their *use* of the grandparent trees (but not their *rights* in them) and then to create the grandparent trees of the future. As noted earlier, even if they have pulled themselves out of the descent group pool, people may still join in the harvest of favorite trees: to enjoy a particularly delicious fruit, to sample a variety of durian "flavors" in a season, or simply for the fun of gathering with one's cousins. How well one's ancestors fulfilled their planting obligations is reflected in current resource tenure, landscape composition, and the number of trees or sites to which an individual can claim access rights.

The number of trees a descent group holds also affects the allocation of access and whether or not spatial or temporal zoning of access is important. One woman explained her observation that when an ancestor planted only a few trees, the descendants are likely to rotate access rights, in a system called *baboros*. Baboros has diverse forms: interested rights-holders may each take turns waiting for a few days, they may divide the waiting time between days for some and nights for others, they may take turns over different seasons, or they may all wait together and divide the day's or night's take of fallen fruits equally among themselves. Baboros is a short-term, temporal zoning strategy. Each claimant also has the right to send a proxy: a child, a nephew or niece, or a person with whom they agree to split their share. However, when an ancestor planted many trees in many places, it is more likely that the children or grandchildren will divide up access rights to the fruit by trees or clusters, using a more spatial zoning strategy, as it were. Especially when trees were planted far from each other, it may be physically impossible for the whole group to jointly harvest all the falling fruit together. Temporal and spatial zoning strategies may be combined by a family's agreeing to allocate exclusive access to trees to individuals for several years or the duration of the generation.

How access is divided among co-heirs also differs according to the species, the tree's natural characteristics (especially those related to productivity), its value, and the decisions of family members. Some fruits, such as rambutan, mangosteen, or rambai, are freely picked and eaten by village children.[16] The fruit from trees which must be climbed, and for which there is a good market, is generally divided equally among all claimants and only sometimes with an extra share for the tree climber. This is the case for rambutan, langsat, angka-ham, and coconut. For some families, these picked fruits may be distributed among the co-heirs whether or not they come to the harvest; others require a physical presence when the tree is climbed. Co-heirs who had moved out of the village might or might not be notified of a picking date and take part in the harvest; or they might have relinquished their claims. Again, this varies across families.

The Case of Durian

Durian is a special case, again, partly because of its physical characteristics and partly because of its social meanings and current economic value. When durian reaches its peak of flavor, it drops from the tree. At that point, it must be eaten, processed, or sold, because as the days pass, it rapidly loses flavor, quality, and value—all indicated largely by the intensity of the fruit's "fragrance." The fruits of a single tree do not drop all at once, but fall over a period of approximately seven to twenty-one days. Nor do all trees ripen at once. Durian season in a village may last two months or more. In Bagak, as in many other villages, durian fruits are never plucked from the trees. The customary head (*kepala adat*) in Bagak said that fines used to be charged people who plucked their durian to sell it, as this would affect the whole village, tarnishing the reputation of Bagak durian in the marketplaces of Singkawang, Pontianak, and elsewhere.

The uncertainty of a tree's production schedule, the necessity for immediate harvest, and the trees' longevity have led to a number of interesting harvesting rules that seemed generally applicable to the co-heirs' groups I interviewed. First and most important, to exercise a claim to inherited durian, a co-heir *must* be present at the harvest, that is, when the fruit drops from the tree. This entails building a temporary shelter to wait in for several weeks and carrying the fruit by the basketful down the hillside or selling fruits to carriers who make daily rounds through the forest gardens. Before the durian harvest, co-heirs may have participated in other forms of labor, sealing a claim to a harvest share, usually by clearing brush from the base of the tree where the fruits will drop.[17] Physical presence is a way of both restricting access and ensuring it.

Durian has special meanings. Unlike rubber, durian is an ancient crop. Although it has long been naturalized and is distributed throughout Borneo, some scientists believe it is not native (Ashton, personal communication; Padoch and Peters 1993).[18] Durian trees have special meanings and are markers of human settlement; where durian trees are found in the forest, there were settlements at one time or another (Padoch and Peters 1993; Sather 1993; Brosius 1999a). The history of a village's movements is marked in the landscape by the location of durian trees.[19]

Village social history is inscribed in the landscape through its old durian trees in other ways (see fig. 26). Unlike other trees, durians are named after the planter, after the flavor or texture qualities of the durian itself, or after an unusual geological feature of the landscape near the durian tree. As one farmer said, "We couldn't write their names down in a book so we remember them by the trees they planted." Frequently, the tree is named after an event that occurred near the durian tree. A durian tree where two brothers fought over the division of the fruits, one throwing his share down the hill in disgust, is named for this event. Whether or not villagers have inherited rights in particular trees, they share a collective interest in them—a claim to the history represented by the durians' presence in the landscape.

An interesting aspect of the naming process is that a tree can be named *only after it has begun fruiting*. This emphasis on the bearing of fruit mirrors other customary practices—for example, that a person is not fully considered a person until he or she has children and that a child and his/her spouse can become a head of the continuing household only after having children of their own.[20] When a person has passed on, the tree or cluster of trees he or she has planted are named after them, but with different honorifics attached depending on the planter's status as a parent or not when he or she died. The

Figure 26. Two durian giants. Photograph by Nancy Lee Peluso.

term "Nek" refers to a parent or grandparent, whereas "Si" is used for someone who died young without having children.

For the descendants of the planter, the durian harvest is a time during which one recognizes one's family. Because the ripening characteristics of durian require the harvesters to wait for the fruits to fall, and because the harvest experience is a representation and recognition of family ties, these trees are more enduring representations of kinship than other inherited resources.[21] All relevant family members have a recognized claim to co-owned fruit; to refuse a sibling or a cousin access for consumption is considered very bad form, and likely bad luck (some say the trees might not fruit ever again). Groups of siblings and cousins, or whole single-family households wait together to share the fallen fruits on the spot or divide them up to sell. Even though a great deal of durian is sold today, much is consumed when and where it is best: at the moment and in the setting where it drops. Any durian opened for consumption will be joyfully shared by all present, including passersby and guests of the co-heirs, all of whom feel free to comment critically on the texture, taste, or quality of the fruit. As falling durian know no time of day, waiting in the *pondok* (temporary shelter) at night has its own special thrills. The oldest trees are located in old longhouse sites, and harvesters often see or hear spirits in the forest while they wait. The hillsides are noisily occupied during the months of durian season.

The oldest durian trees in Bagak, apparently planted by another Salako group before the ancestors of the current residents came to the site, grow in the vicinity of the warriors' burial grounds. Each one of these trees bears a name, but villagers cannot explain their meanings because the stories disappeared with the people whose ancestors planted them. These trees, people say, are both owned by the whole village and owned by no one person. When their ancestors first occupied this territory, the durian trees were already there; someone else's labor thus provided them with fruit. The fruits of these trees have been slated ever since for residents or visitors who had none— either because their trees were not fruiting that year, or because they were newcomers, or because they were just passing through, or for other reasons. The trees were part of the village's common heritage. So strong are the feelings about the role of these trees in the village's social history that even those trees that stopped producing and fell or were cut down are still talked about in the present tense.

Under specific circumstances, durian are an open-access resource. For example, anyone can eat another's unguarded durian that happens to fall just at the moment he or she is passing by, whether or not the lucky person has inheritance rights to it. Similarly, a group of co-heirs waiting for their durian always invites a passerby to share in fruit that falls while the latter is passing. Not accepting such an offer or failing to follow ritual procedure for refusing can lead to fatal accidents, especially poisonous snake bites, cutting oneself with a bush knife, or falling out of fruit trees.[22]

Because of durian's longevity and its complicated inheritance patterns, creating durian "gardens" in swidden fallows imposes new constraints on farmers' land-use decisions and becomes a means of changing the distribution of village resources in land. Land under trees that live for four to six generations is taken out of field-crop production for a significant period—a century or more. Some not-so-obvious benefits derive from this situation. First, converting land under rubber or rice to durian may redistribute benefits (after at least a generation) amongst many people who share in the fruit yield rather than benefiting an individual or a single household who harvests rubber or rice. These more common rights in the resource and the land it occupies can extend through many years, creating a significant temporal zone. Moreover, even though the rights to some grandfather durian trees have been individualized and thus benefit individuals or single households, and the ethic of access changes somewhat if the durian fruit is to be sold rather than consumed (see below), the notion that descent-group members retain consumption rights to their ancestral fruit remains strong among village families. For this reason, cutting a productive tree that an ancestor had planted for "all my children and grandchildren" and disrupting the descent group's temporal management zone simply would not be right.[23]

Yields can be sporadic but highly profitable. A good durian harvest can earn the tree owner hundreds of thousands of rupiah in one or two months' time.[24] In 1991 a bumper crop of durian and other fruit was produced; on one day (10 February) at the end of the season, I counted some 10,000 fruits being sold out of the hamlet (Peluso and Padoch 1996). The following two years were generally poor or mediocre production years, although some individuals with widely scattered fruit holdings did moderately well. Of those in the 1991 sample who would venture estimates of the income from durian they sold, the average income was Rp. 338,200, with one person reporting Rp.

1,000,000 in cash income alone. (Hulled rice cost approximately Rp. 700 per kilogram in the marketplace at the time, compared to a village [farm–gate] price of Rp. 300–500 for a single durian.) For some families, these windfalls accounted for as much as one-half the year's cash income.[25] Moreover, these sales figures do not account for durian consumed or given away, nor for the durian made into *tempuyak,* a kind of preserved, salted durian. In good durian harvest years, such as 1994, many people reported selling ten or more kilograms of tempuyak at about Rp. 1,000 per kilogram (fig. 27).

In sum, managed forests of economic trees have been gradually taking over the swidden fallows of Bagak for some sixty years. Not all the species have equal significance in the economy or the social fabric. I have focused on the most important species in the discussion above. Durian, the most valued and valuable of the fruits, lasts five to seven generations, is locally consumed as well as sold, and has deep social meaning to individuals, to direct descendants of the planter, and to the community as a whole: it is perhaps the most important visible evidence of the community's settlement history. Both durian trees and fruit engender profound attachments, by the village, by families, and by individuals.

Commodification and the Individualization of Rights in Durian

Selling your durian trees is like selling your own grandmother.
—Pak Po'on, Bagak Sahwa

When market demand is as great as it is for durian, when it must be sold immediately after it falls, and when market access is easy, all members of a descent group are concerned that little fruit is wasted.[26] The market boom in fruit has led to two major changes in durian management. First, some families have permanently allocated panene'an (grandparent) trees to individuals. Second, people are opening up tracts of land—old fallows, old rubber gardens, and sometimes, the edges of the nature reserve—specifically to plant durian and other fruit gardens and thereby claim the land for subsequent generations of their own descendants—in other words, creating new spatio-temporal zones. Nevertheless, the trend toward individualization of durian rights is not absolute. Households and extended families vary in the types of

Figure 27. Men carrying durian fruits down the hill from their forest gardens.
Photograph by Nancy Lee Peluso.

tree-tenure arrangements they maintain, and some village trees are still managed for general access.

As mentioned above, social and ecological factors determine the distribution of access to descent-group trees. By consensus or by default, descent groups and the person in charge of their common trees determine what particular combinations of inheritance rights and labor investments will govern the allocation of panene'an trees they hold together. Four main considerations seem to weigh heavily on this decision: first, the number of trees the descent group holds; second, the relative yields of various trees; third, the productivity of each heir's allocated trees in previous years; and fourth, the other resources to which each of the co-heirs has access. As before, various interpretations of rights and histories of family practices mediate the allocation decisions.

Families who use relatively structured means of allocating access (for instance, by meeting at the beginning of a season) face ecological as well as social obstacles to their decision-making. At the time of year when access rights are discussed, many trees' potential yields are unknown. Durian yields fluctuate each year, although some trees produce nearly every year. Usually, older trees with many branches produce a great deal of fruit. Some years nearly the whole village has highly productive harvests; others produce nothing for anyone. Even within the same section of village forest, variation is common. Adjacent trees may differ significantly in productivity, depending both on the site's characteristics and the owners' management. Despite family attempts to balance their members' access to fruit, some villagers find they are out of luck and have no access to productive inherited trees in some years, although they may be able to lease them.

Recent changes in durian management have affected both temporal and spatial zoning patterns. Temporal changes in intergenerational rights to durian are most evident in the distribution of third-generation or older trees, for it is in the third generation that rights are first held by a large descent group—cousins. More than one-third of sample families had individualized harvest rights to panene'an trees, citing reasons such as grandparents and parents wanting to avoid disputes among children and grandchildren. I had many discussions with villagers not in this sample and also mapped the generational property rights in trees that fell within five transects of the village forest. All these data confirmed that individualization of panene'an trees had taken place among about a third of the village families.

Individualization of rights has also affected spatial zoning and created a land market, but value in a garden territory is a function of the number, productivity, and value of the trees planted there. Long-living trees planted in swidden fallows tie up the land for much longer than the average "unimproved" fallow. Increasingly, people clear fallows intending to plant some kind of forest garden immediately after the rice crop. Rubber, with its numerous stems planted in proximity to facilitate latex collection, has always tied up spatial zones for an individual or a household. Durian, planted intermittently next to other people's trees in the tembawang, traditionally tied up small spaces for multiple generations of descendants—a much longer-term temporal zoning. However, as durian trees begin to be planted in places they were never planted before, in larger garden clusters and in swidden fallows, spatial zoning or territorial strategies have become more common in the landscape.

Individualization of descent-group rights to durian trees occurs most commonly in one of three ways: the descent group may agree to distribute its commonly held trees among individual members, a grandparent may designate specific trees or clusters of trees to individual grandchildren, or an individual usurps the descent group's authority by simply assuming possession of a grandfather tree. They usually do so by planting young trees around panene'an trees or by building a shelter there without consulting the group. By planting trees around a panene'an tree, once the younger trees come into production, the individual collects the fruit that drops from those trees as well as from the panene'an trees. This is essentially a territorialization strategy—a squatting by one individual or branch of the family on the common, temporal rights of the larger descent group. The usurpation of rights takes place with the descent group's implicit consent, since all the tree planter's descendants have rightful claims to the tree's fruit. In several cases where this had happened, other family members explained their failure to assert their collective claims as an effort to avoid public discord. It may also be seen as a symbol of the trend toward individualization and territorialization.

Individualization of descent-group rights is by no means universal. Some families insist that the grandchildren and great-grandchildren of a tree planter are violating important customary practices in privatizing access to grandparent trees (Peluso and Padoch 1996). Indeed, when I first started asking about the privatization of panene'an trees, some of my village friends insisted I was wrong. They refused to believe it until they heard it themselves from other villagers. This sparked a great deal of discussion amongst those who felt it was not appropriate. Whether or not families have individualized the rights to their grandparent trees, nearly all villagers express the feeling that individually controlled trees are easier to manage and potential disputes are avoided, while the fruits of descent-group trees serve to support those in the family whose own trees do not yet produce.

Panene'an had served two types of redistributive purposes in the past, and among the families following the old practices, they still do. The first type is a redistribution of village resources between age groups. Young couples always depended on panene'an until their parents' or their own durian fruited, at which time many of them stopped participating in the harvest of panene'an trees. The second type is a redistribution that aids the weaker, less diligent, or less clever farmers, who benefit from continued access to the trees and fruit of their ancestors with little effort. Most villagers regard long-term dependence on the trees planted by one's forebears as both a sign of laziness and a handicap to one's children and grandchildren. Unless today's farmer plants fruit trees, his or her children will suffer, and their descendants will not be able to prosper from the land.

What aspects of commodification have most changed the landscape and the rights to durian, one of its key components? Durian has long been a commodity and has long been sold by Bagak villagers: commodification of durian did not begin with either the paving of the road or the growth of nearby cities. Though not detailed here (see Peluso and Padoch 1996), rubber began the major landscape transformation from one dominated by rice fields and fallows and fruit forests. Durian harvests were limited to one time of the year and the fruit could not be stored except as tempuyak—a much lower value product. The ecology and biology of rubber—particularly its capacity to produce year-round for a market that had fluctuating prices but was nonetheless available—gave it an edge over durian as a means of simple reproduction when sedentarization and other political-economic changes resulted in rice's declining viability as a subsistence crop. Once rubber had provided a strong subsistence base for virtually the whole village, other changes in the regional political ecology—especially the paved road and greater urban demand—spurred the spread of durian and its transformation to a commercial crop with multiple meanings and values. Now the burgeoning urban markets for fruit, the transportation infrastructure to which the village has direct access, the durian planted in village gardens and the nature reserve, and the perseverance (and luck) of the village leaders who refused to contract village land to plantations on their borders have put Bagak durian at a premium. People now plant it in many previously unfamiliar places (fig. 28).

In this essay I have examined changes in the landscape of a West Kalimantan village and the interactions of environmental change with resource-tenure patterns. The case is instructive on several points. First, in terms of understanding landscape processes, the experience of Bagak confounds the stereotypical understanding of tropical peoples' forest transformation and agricultural intensification—that is, that it is predicated on an evolutionary model that "starts" with what is assumed to be "natural" forest and moves "toward" the production of field crops for food. In such cases, intensification of agricultural production may involve increasing labor or capital inputs per unit of land and an emphasis on commercial or subsistence field agriculture, usually in concert with increases in population growth and sedentarization (e.g., Geertz 1963; Boserup 1981; Dove 1985a). In contrast to this pattern, Bagak villagers are moving "away" from field/food-crop agriculture and "toward" the greater production of forests and agroforestry products. Over the past three generations, villagers have altered their hillside vegetation from a mixture dominated by swidden fields and fallows with patches of managed forests, to a heavily managed forest landscape dominated by useful economic trees. The villagers' increasingly intensive tree planting on village lands was stimulated not only by land scarcity engendered by enforced sedentarization and by the loss of their formal access (legal rights) to ancestral land when the colonial government carved a nature reserve from them, but also by the increased market access that resulted from road improvements, urbanization, population growth, and sedentarization. Moreover, their contemporary management activities build on traditional forest-management procedures and preferences.

The case provides evidence that fruit and forest product *production*—not unmanaged *extraction*—have been important elements of Bornean peoples' resource-management strategies for hundreds of years. Further, production of specific products has necessitated a form of ecosystem management or the manipulation—sometimes by tacit agreement among villagers, sometimes through conflict—of field and forest landscape components. The study, therefore, puts a different slant on much of the "extractive-economies"

Figure 28. Local durian trader buying fruits from local producers. Photograph by Nancy Lee Peluso.

literature that tends—often unintentionally—to underplay the purposive management roles taken by local people (see, e.g., Bunker 1985; cases in Nepstad and Schwartzman 1992; Dove 1995; cf., Hecht, Anderson, and May 1988; Padoch 1994).

The second surprise of this case has to do with the unintended outcomes and unanticipated impacts of government interventions on locally managed landscapes. Government land-management policies, sedentarization, changes in regional markets, and national political events initially caused multiple hardships for Bagak residents by creating new spatial land-use zones and redefining legal versus illegal land uses and access rights. Some interventions in local management procedures caused hardship and poverty. But by building on economic components of their previous land-use practice (mixed-fruit forests), adding other economic components (rubber gardens), and reinterpreting access rights to the nature reserve (creating a buffer zone of low-impact use), local people created a new and well-managed social and ecological landscape. The new forested landscape, and the buffer zone of useful/managed trees planted within the government-claimed territory of the reserve, can be seen as physical evidence of local resistance to, and counterappropriation of, government attempts to control the region's management and property rights. Every generation of villagers has come together in different ways to contest the boundaries of the government nature reserve, thus placing their own practices at the very heart of state–local struggles over resource control. In yet another context, then—one that was significantly altered by government intervention—the Bagak landscape serves as a living record of village history. The case illustrates the need to understand different versions of environmental and social history in order to be able to "read" a landscape.

The notion of temporal and spatial zoning produces different visions and scales of analysis. The Salako were forced by the Dutch to abandon their "traditional" landscape and significantly alter their ways of interacting with that landscape. They moved from grouped living arrangements (longhouses) to single-family homes—albeit ones large enough to accommodate some extended family members. Similarly, they were slowly pushed by circumstances to reconceptualize their resource rights and the spatial arrangement of their landscape—particularly its *extent*—moving toward a territorialization of these rights from an emphasis on temporal rights to products of the land—trees or crops. One could argue, perhaps, that these new landscape configurations and limits to access caused many to participate in the eviction of the Chinese from their farms in the 1960s. In other words, the political upheaval of that period was not simply about resource scarcity or a military-incited, anti-Chinese action, but a violent remaking of people's vision of their landscape (Peluso n.d.; Peluso and Harwell 2001).

In this study I have shown that notions of temporal and spatial zoning can be illustrated by the analysis of shifting property rights in long-living trees, and understood through the set of resource-tenure arrangements that people are engaged in at different points in their lives. As government officials and competing settlers changed the bounds and dimensions of local Salako swiddeners' territories, local people responded in various ways that created new spatial and temporal zones. By swiddening the native reserve during the Japanese occupation, and subsequently planting trees after the rice harvest, local people both pushed back the spatial borders of the reserve and created a long-term zone of de facto control for themselves. As their borders became increasingly fixed and the opportunities for moving or expanding territorially declined, people transformed the spatiotemporal zones of their swidden fallows at an increasingly rapid rate by planting rubber and fruit trees and enabling useful self-sown species to sprout and thrive. Depending on the species, and the family or individuals' decisions, these changes to the agro-economic forest created either more exclusive private-rights zones (as with rubber and some fruit), more inclusive common-rights zones (as with much fruit, especially durian), and some open-access zones.

This leads to a point about the relationship between biology, property rights, identity, and practice. It is hardly unusual to recognize that prices, policies, and legal systems affect formal property rights. I have argued that a tree's biological characteristics also influence access and rights. More important, however, durian trees' social values and meanings extend beyond economics, biology, and even the claims of the planter's descendants because the entire village views the trees as markers of settlement history and territorial claim. The case, then, shows how a historically grounded set of meanings attached to a resource can critically mediate both exclusionary and inclusive rights and access mechanisms. We saw first how a system of property rights in trees increased the number of rights-holders with each succeeding generation, again contradicting a stereotyped model predicting a linear procession of property relations from open access to common property to private property (Bromley 1989). Clearly, broader global trends and market or government incentives for privatization and individualization of resource access have not unilaterally transformed the common aspects of community and descent-group claims on property rights in trees. Although intensification of forest production and the improvement of market access creates strong pressures for people to privatize or individualize resource tenure, the social meanings of these resources and their links to villagers' collective and individual claims, memories, and social histories have caused many people to resist the divisive aspects of commodification and privatization. At the same time, other aspects of the colonial and contemporary state projects for allocating rights to land and resources—particularly the creation of allegedly non-indigenous others (Chinese, and later Madurese)—led to more intensely racialized patterns of landscape allocation (Peluso and Harwell 2001).

Finally, I have shown that the study of resource access and landscape as social processes interacting with ecological factors is much more conceptually complex than thinking of property and landscapes as inanimate objects. Moreover, if landscape is thought of—at least partially—as an artifact of human consciousness, and therefore something that is subject to multiple interpretations, visions, and memories (Schama 1995), it becomes ever more important to understand how the meanings and value of that landscape intersect with the processes of political economy, ecology, and institutions of access that affect it.

Notes

Many thanks to the friends and colleagues who commented on earlier drafts of this essay: Jill Belsky, Louise Fortmann, Bruce Koppel, Christine Padoch, Jesse Ribot, and Peter Vandergeest. A longer version of this paper was published in *Comparative Studies in Society and History*; it is partially reprinted here with their permission.

1 The term *nenek* in the Salako language, or "nek" for short, is used to refer to both grandmother and grandfather.

2 Salako, the ethnic group, and Selakau, the river, are spelled differently in this chapter because of differences in current practice. The Salako claim their origins lie along the Selakau River. On current Indonesian maps, the river is spelled Selakau.

3 That is, not by a specific government program.

4 The Confrontation was a "low-intensity conflict" between Malaysia and Indone-

sia which lasted from 1963 to 1966. Much of the conflict was staged from West Kalimantan and Sarawak.

5 Either rice self-sufficiency, or rice mixed with cassava and maize.

6 These rights were called *Huur Overencomst,* abbreviated H.O.

7 The name Patengahan still appears on Dutch maps from the 1930s.

8 To illustrate the contrast with previous interventions, the Chinese had moved into an ecosystem that was not at the time exploited by the mountain people of Bagak. When the Malays exacted tribute in the form of forest products, they did not move into the village and take over the territory within which these products grew. Even the missionaries were not interested in evicting local people from the lands they were most psychologically and physically dependent on. Under the Dutch, the Salako of Bagak were squeezed between state-appropriated and -controlled land and Chinese cultivators in the irrigated lowlands. The Dutch planned to let the watershed go back to "undisturbed" forest; the Chinese had already converted the swamp forest to wet-rice production.

9 This contradicts findings by Dove (1993b), who maintains that swidden production was preferred over rubber production as a means of resisting external control.

10 The complexities surrounding social and political relations of this violent period and the circumstances around the exile of the Chinese were difficult to research at the time this paper was written. Research or writing on ethnic conflict of any sort was forbidden by the Indonesian government. For more on the period, see Peluso (n.d.) and Peluso and Harwell (2001). See also, Somers-Heidhues (forthcoming).

11 Plans were eventually made to settle some four thousand Javanese families in a transmigration settlement on the lands of Maya Sopa.

12 Basal area is the area of a cross section of trees at breast height.

13 Land rights for forest clearance and swidden cultivation are well documented for Borneo; see Geddes (1954); Freeman (1955); Appell (1970); Weinstock (1983b); Padoch (1983); Dove (1985b, 1988); Rousseau (1990).

14 Fortmann (1985a: 220) refers to this as "the doctrine of labor creates rights"; Locke also saw labor as the critical motivator and confirmation of property rights. Interestingly enough, this "doctrine" seems to hold true in both Western and Eastern societies and has correlates in both ancient and contemporary property systems.

15 This pattern is common among many Dayak subgroups throughout Kalimantan and Sarawak: whichever child takes care of the parents until their deaths generally inherits the primary rights to control the swidden lands the parents cleared and the cash-crop trees, except fruit. In some Borneo societies, however, land and other resources are not passed through an intergenerational household unit, but are returned to the community's common pool when the household heads (husband and wife) pass away (Appell 1970). Rubber trees do not usually last through

more than two generations and therefore are not subject to the complex inheritance rights associated with fruit trees, especially durian.

16 In this, children can be said to have specific access rights to fruit, not unlike those described by Aschmann ([1963] 1988) in speaking of a "child's culture" of untrammeled claims by children of southern California in the 1930s to privately owned fruit growing in people's yards.

17 See Peluso and Padoch (1996).

18 According to Peter Ashton, durian has its origins in the northern part of Thailand.

19 Peter Brosius (n.d.) makes a similar point for the Penan of Sarawak, whose conception of the landscape revolves around the social-historical events that took place along rivers, forest paths between rivers, at the base of certain trees, and so on.

20 Of course, in practice this may be altered, say, if the child caring for elderly parents is unable to have children and no other children are able or willing to take on that role.

21 Illipe nut trees in some areas also represent common ancestry to co-heirs, but because most trees only fruit in cycles of four years or more, and because the nuts are not consumed en masse and on the spot, the experience (and the memories) are qualitatively different from durian trees. Illipe nut trees are not named. The low prices of illipe nuts, the uncertainty of their markets, and the usefulness of their wood for construction caused many Bagak villagers to cut them down. Few illipe nut trees remain on village lands or in the buffer zone between the village and the reserve.

22 This state of danger is called *kemponan* and is commonly accepted throughout Borneo as an outcome of refusing any food, cigarettes, or a betel chew.

23 A rapid survey of six other villages with similar resource-management traditions in 1991 (Padoch and Peluso, unpublished data), found in some places that durian trees can only be cut after ritual recognition of the planter and his or her descendants, and in others, that customary fines must be paid to the village and the descendants of the planter whenever durian is cut. I never came across such practices in Bagak.

24 At the time of this research, approximately 2,000 Rupiah = US$1.00.

25 Income from other fruits—particularly langsat and angkaham—varied and was not reported systematically.

26 In former days, much durian that could not be consumed was made into preserves called *tempuyak* or *lempok*, some of which was sold, some kept for later consumption. In 1991 I found only a few people who had made tempuyak; this changed in the bumper harvest of 1994, when a majority of the sample made and sold approximately 10 kg. of tempuyak per household (Simon Takdir, personal communication).

Reflections: Toward New Conceptions of Rights

Donald Brenneis

Underlying each of these chapters is a cluster of consequential and related questions: How might indigenous communities and persons survive in the rapidly changing circumstances of life in contemporary Southeast Asia, and how might their environments, both "natural" and patently human, most effectively be sustained? In more specific terms, how best might legitimacy be claimed for indigenous interests and futures, who might most effectively do the claiming, and to whom can or must such claims be made?

In a recent account of the discursive strategies of a tribunal organized by groups within the Hawai'ian sovereignty movement, Sally Merry has argued that "what they speak is law" (1997: 29), that is, that historically Western notions of legal rights now provide a framework at the same time universalizing and locally useful for particular indigenous communities. The attractions of such a strategy are considerable. Speaking—here, making claims and arguing cases—in terms of what are taken to be inherent individual and group rights provides an immediately recognizable translation of local crises into an increasingly widespread international legal language. Even if critical elements are missing—for example, sanctions to back up a particular decision or, at times, even a widely recognized forum within which such a decision might be made—such translation into universally based claims is significant in itself. It provides a compelling sense of transparency—that is, because of the legal discourse in which arguments are made, we feel we can more easily understand and, perhaps even more crucially, compare the strength of rival claims. Legal discourse, and especially that variety based on a strong notion of rights, draws its force not only from the strength of its ethical appeal but from its apparent clarity and from the comparison of competing claims that it appears to make possible.

At the heart of this volume lies the "question of rights," a question raised at several levels. In one sense, each article addresses the issue of what kinds of rights might most effectively be claimed by indigenous and other communities—and on what basis. In another sense, however, each of these essays also addresses rights discourse as a locally useful or ultimately effective way of conceptualizing the current situation. Drawing upon thoroughgoing field-work, these essays reveal some of the potentially problematic dimensions of rights discourse and point to alternative ways of thinking about how claims might be made. In many ways, and to varying degrees, these essays do what much good ethnography does: they jeopardize our preconceptions as read-ers and invite our reconsideration of local situations in local terms. None of these authors minimizes the complex and consequential relations between these communities and the larger national and international processes with which they are entangled. Indeed, this recognition shapes the urgency that all the contributors emphasize. At the same time, local practice and theory figure centrally in most of the articles. While no full-blown solutions are of-fered, these essays are good to think with. Not only do they enrich our under-standings of the Meratus Mountains, the Makassar Strait, and other "out-of-the-way place(s)" (Tsing 1993), they also jointly sketch an implicit and telling critique of how those of us who "speak law" use and understand that language.

In organizing my comments here, I draw upon the distinction Anna Tsing makes between "charismatic" and "bureaucratic" claims. For the Meratus Dayaks, she argues, successful honey gathering depends upon the individual exertions and attainments of particular men. While honey trees are consid-ered individual and inalienable property, as important as such ownership is to the ongoing "cultivation" of the trees, trees must not only be cleaned and maintained but visited and talked about. And they must be *convincingly* claimed. Trees are, further, singular and have their individual histories of be-ing attended and claimed. As such, they are difficult to consider and evalu-ate comparatively. Relationships of equivalence and comparability and the sense of shared and differentiating characteristics at the heart of bureaucratic classificatory schemata and authority are not at issue here.

Tsing's distinction shapes her account of the Meratus situation effectively. My principal concern here, however, is with the heuristic strategy it suggests for thinking about all of these cases. In the following discussion, I begin with a consideration of charismatic styles of claim-making, albeit with a light twist. This twist is to argue that charisma is not solely an individual accom-plishment. Rather, it is a performance requiring audiences whose interests and enthusiasms must be engaged and shaped. I will briefly consider some examples of charismatic claim-making in three of the studies here (Roseman, Zerner, and Tsing), paying attention to the style and strategy of such performances and to the complex audiences that they are used to influence. I'll then turn to a consideration of some of the recurrent bureaucratic forms and practices that play increasingly crucial roles, both in the current crisis and in our understanding of it. Here, the papers by Peluso, Fried, and Zerner figure more centrally. My goal in this latter discussion will be to examine such bureaucratic forms and practices as mapmaking in performative terms, that is, with an eye to implicit assumptions about audience, rhetoric, style, and the social relationships which they implicate.

Charisma as Contract

Critical to my understanding of how charismatic claims are effectively made is the question of audience. The person making charismatic claims necessarily takes his or her audience into serious account, shaping the validating performance to be as convincing and compelling as possible. Bauman's classic (1983) study of early Quaker ministers, for example, demonstrated how such speakers, caught between a theory of language that devalued religious speaking for which an immediate, divine origin was not apparent and the proselytic need to preach, developed strategies for authenticating both their message and its sacred source. And, equally important, Quaker members of their audience came to seek and recognize signs of inspiration in their speech. Ruth Borker's (1986) analysis of the effectiveness of church services among Scottish Brethren provides a comparable contemporary case. In Brethren breaking-of-bread services, it is the women of the congregation, sitting as silent but knowledgeable audience members, who evaluate how convincing and ultimately effective each particular service is.

Most scholarly considerations of charisma have focused primarily on the sender, the charismatic individual or group, often treating the effectiveness of their performances as more or less unproblematic. In reality, things seem to be somewhat more complicated. Early Quaker preachers, for example, had to convince a particular—and particularly complex—audience, some of whom were newly exposed to the faith (the primary audience, in rhetorical terms), but others who were already members (the secondary audience) and therefore held strong views on what could be heard as authentic "speaking in the light."[1] Both groups within the audience—those whom one wanted to convince and those for whom a continuing validation of divine inspiration was critical—shaped the message *and* were critical in helping effect the speaker's charisma. Beyond this, in both the Quaker and the Brethren cases, what the audience needed to be convinced of was the relationship between the speaker or performer and some unseen but highly significant, in these cases divine, entity who could not participate in the event in any unmediated way.

In thinking about charisma in this way, Bauman's (1977) definition of "verbal performance" as an activity that "involves on the part of the performer an assumption of responsibility to an audience for the way in which the communication is carried out, above and beyond its referential content" is particularly helpful.[2] The talk, verse, and song at the heart of the essays by Tsing, Roseman, and Zerner are more than about something: they are activities in themselves. That they concern claims made on nature or desired relationships with it is clearly significant. Equally important, however, is *how* these claims are made and how effectively claimants fulfill or surpass the expectations held by their audiences. What are the performances in these essays about, for whom are they staged, what kinds of stylistic characteristics mark them, and how does style map onto audience and intended outcome? The choice of performance genre is critical, as different genres afford different constraints and opportunities as well as being aimed at particular listeners and recipients.

For the kinds of charismatic claims noted in Tsing's essay to be effective and authoritative, various audiences must be captured and convinced. An individual tree "owner," for example, must make a compelling case to a human audience, assuring them that he has not forgotten or neglected his trees. In other instances, however, he must be able to court the bees themselves directly. Several things are particularly important in Tsing's treatment of "bee songs." First, they are not *about* the bees but addressed to them as interlocutors and potentially as an audience who will respond on the basis of how taken they are by the song. Second, while the lyrics are of some consequence, especially critical are the formal features that particular songs realize—and the specific kinds of social relationships that those formal features implicate. Through the shape of singing its organization "above and beyond its referential content," bees are treated, in various settings, as potential lovers or affines, or as children to be "pleased and calmed with a lullaby." That the songs are sung at night, as if by an intimate but unseen suitor or soothing parent, adds to their persuasiveness and further emphasizes the importance of the acoustic over the visual in such important engagements. How the song is performed is crucial in offering a desired social relationship to the bees; their implicit agreement to this offer is made evident in the success of the honey gatherer.

Zerner's study of the welter of sound on the Makassar Straits provides further vivid instances of performative engagements between humans and non-human nature. "Soundings" of several types are taking place: prayers, private spells uttered within the mouth and unheard by other fishermen, and public "callings," or ilongi. Spells demand secrecy, their effectiveness inversely proportional to how many men know and use them. Ilongi, on the other hand, are—at least on the sea—loudly called out, often overlapping and cascading over those of other men. One Mandar fisherman likened the sound of such spells to "stir-frying chili peppers in a wok,"—tumultuous, polyvocal, and crisply enticing. At the heart of Zerner's analysis is the importance of reciprocity as social practice and expectation, whether in the crucial role of exchange in the transmission of private spells or in the anticipated response of flying fish to particularly stylish and passionate entreaties. I'd like to suggest that often such reciprocity is speculative, that is, that fishermen hope for positive response but know that it is in large part contingent upon the quality of their performances. While, in contrast to the Meratus honey hunt, fishing may take place in daylight, sound rather than sight remains at the heart of the attractiveness critical to a successful trip.

Central to Roseman's account of Temiar relationships with the natural world is the notion of song as a principal medium for making "cartographic claims," for mapping out a complex web of human–tree ties, connections mediated through performance and the spirits. Songs are deeds within this landscape, the "paths" that give it shape, sustaining reciprocal relationships between Temiar and the trees so central to their physical and spiritual life, and providing a crucial form for their ongoing negotiation. At the heart of Temiar communal claims on trees is the issue of use rather than ownership per se. These claims are similar to those that Meratus Dayaks make through their displays of engagement and care. Temiar charismatic claims are made through performance and, more particularly, through individuals' use of songs associated with specific trees. As in Bauman's instance of the Quaker preacher, compelling songs are those for which a convincing source in the spirit world can be claimed and displayed. Genre and form are particularly crucial, as they play a large part in establishing a link with those trees and spirits that are simultaneously song source, song subject, and stylistic template. Here, it is the human authenticating audience that must be engaged and convinced rather than the trees themselves. A particular irony in contemporary struggles to maintain Temiar lands and forests is that those performances that are singularly convincing to Temiar listeners are not compelling for outside audiences, seeming particularly irrelevant to government officials charged with understanding and protecting local claims. Songs may chart and order the Temiar landscape for the Temiar themselves, but others often turn a deaf ear. Both the medium and the genre are unrecognizable.

Fried's account of Bentian Dayak authors provides a striking case of a community trying to make a generic translation from local forms of claim-making to those that might speak more effectively to—or more properly, be read by—an outside audience. Specifically, she is concerned with how local concerns are translated into the broader Indonesian development discourse, and she charts the rhetorical forms and the adopted language upon which the authors draw. How effectively these strategies work with the Bentian Dayak's external audience is uncertain, but their recognition of this audience and their attempts to perform in terms that it understands and values are striking.

The events central to Tsing's, Zerner's, and Roseman's articles fit Bauman's definition of performance very neatly. While these events often convey significant meanings, the competent and compelling execution of particular formal, stylistic, and interactional features is critical to their effectiveness. While in his charting of performance Bauman explicitly stresses the responsibility of performers toward their audiences, these three cases indicate that successful performance also obligates its auditors, enmeshing them in a reciprocal relationship with the performer. All of these instances suggest that something similar to a legal contract is being struck between performer and audience. Implicit in Bauman's notion are corollary practices to the three critical elements of legal contract—offer, performance, and consideration.[3] The "offer" is, literally, a matter of form. Performers take on a responsibility to others through the generic burden they assume by, for example, starting a song of a particular type. Their "performance," in the legal sense, lies in how they fulfill that initial promise. "Consideration" often is left implicit but assumed to be evident in a successful honey hunt without many stings, a net full of fish, or the willingness of one's fellows to grant rights to pick durian.

This perspective suggests that at the heart of charismatic claims lies something much like a contract. Charisma is not a fixed, enduring quality sited in a single actor. It is, rather, a matter of ongoing negotiation, enactment, and agreement. Very particular kinds of performances and the expectations that audiences, human and otherwise, are assumed to bring to them are critical in authenticating charisma. In the Meratus Dayak, Makassarese, and Temiar worlds, worlds shaped as much by the acoustic as the visual, such charismatic contracts are literally sound practice, relying upon the shape and style of talk, song, and chant for their force and for the reciprocity they aim to engender.

Bureaucratic Visions

In contrast to the often dark, intimate, face-to-face (or ear-to-ear) contexts within which charisma is effected, the world of bureaucratic claims-making is a public and visible one.[4] The association of the public with the observable is central to the Majene Court's decision that the sea is an *openlijk*[5] place (cf. Zerner, "Sounding," this volume) and to its extension of its own juridical power to the open seas of the Makassar Strait. The justiciability of cases "in the open" disrupts local understandings, at the same time enlarging the domain within which law is "spoken" and weakening earlier claims based on intimate understanding and connection.

The Coordinated Forest Land Use Planning Maps considered in an earlier article by Peluso (1995) analyzing forest practices in Kalimantan rely upon the assumption that what is crucial in decision-making can be seen and classified and that decisions can be made on the basis of the comparison of clearly defined and visually imaginable options. At the core of Peluso's critique is "what is left out of [maps]." That is, that which remains bureaucratically *invisible,* is often the most significant information: customary rights, village lands, and village-managed forests. As such, maps become the authoritative accounts shaping future policy and lawmaking, and that which is left invisible can become illegal. As Peluso noted, the cartographic grid provides a framework for "routinizing the flexible" and, in so doing, for editing out adat and customary rights. Implicit in Peluso's account is the strategic importance of getting such hidden but very consequential features of the Kalimantan human landscape "on the map."

Peluso's paper in this volume extends this consideration of landscape-making and mapping. Her account of the establishment of the boundaries of a conservation zone staked out in an area already shaped by existing Bagak Dayak villages, ancestral forests and lands, and former village sites demonstrates both local and bureaucratic imaginations at work. Peluso's fastidiously detailed examination is, in large part, a story of how different cultural conceptualizations of landscape and means of comprehending it have been at the core of a now seventy-year-long struggle.

The boundary marking the periphery of the Gunung Raya Pasi watershed protection area permitted Dutch officials an apparently clear topographic view of the West Kalimantan landscape that foregrounded colonial resource management policy concerns. But this culturally particular form of representation simultaneously rendered invisible the relations of local people with this landscape—their historical connections to it, their livelihoods, and their recently created new forest orchards and gardens—and the topomnemonic understandings within which they conceived it. Peluso shows that, over the past seven decades, local communities have scarcely accepted the implications and intrusions of this boundary and the zone it was meant to protect. Rather, they have contested this culturally particular form of place-making and landscape control by planting durian trees within the reserve, thus blurring the boundaries of nature and culturally managed and claimed territory.

Fried's discussion of the Bentian Dayak case further demonstrates the crucial role of the visible: the rattan gardens central to local economic well-being look like unruly jungle rather than productive, carefully tended plantations and so are fair game for more bureaucratically recognizable kinds of exploitation. In all three cases the extension of visual perception, whether literal or metaphoric, is exceptionally consequential. Judicial power, oversight, and surveillance expand to the open sea, and local sites and practices remain unseen and therefore unmappable.

If talk, song, and dance intended to compel and to connect humans with each other and with the non-human are at the heart of the charismatic claims discussed above, mapping, and especially the use of the cartographic grid, provide a widespread and consequential way of making bureaucratic claims. The notion that mapmaking is a far from neutral mode of representation, however, is most frequently examined, if at all, in terms of straightforwardly political practices, for example, leaving village fields out of the picture.[6] I want to argue that mapmaking is in itself a particular kind of per-

formance, one dependent upon epistemological assumptions about the pre-
eminence of the visual, intended to validate institutional choices in the eyes
of a diffuse audience, and involving a wide range of "authors" linked in a
highly conventionalized and interdependent variety of co-performance. In
making all else visible, or at least appearing to do so, mapping often succeeds
in making its own framework invisible; in this lies its particular power. As
Becker notes in his analysis of an Old Javanese tale, one of the crucial benefits
of scholarship is to "teach us to know those frames we look through and how
completely they bind us" (1995: 162) or, in this case, blind us. The following
brief excursion is intended to suggest some of the hidden performative dimensions of grid-based cartography.

In a provocative essay, David Turnbull quotes one of the earliest commen-
tators on grid mapping, the third-century Chinese cartographer Phen Hsui:
"When the principle of the rectangular grid is properly applied, then the
straight and the curved, the near and the far, can conceal nothing of their
form from us" (1993: 26). This revelatory capacity depends, argues Turnbull,
in part upon the fact that a "grid system . . . has to be *literally* conventional.
Grid systems require real conventions, negotiations and agreements. . . . The
power of maps lies not merely in their accuracy or their correspondence with
reality. It lies in their having incorporated a set of conventions that make
them combinable at one central place, enabling the accumulation of both
power and knowledge at that one center" (1993: 26, emphasis in original).
Such conventionality also makes possible commensurability, the measure-
ment and description in the same terms of many places that can always be located in relationship to each other. Two related features of such mapping-as-
performance, then, are that it requires and implies particular forms of social
organization and agreement and that its "texts" are shaped in an assumedly
clear and unambiguous "language." Closely linked to this assumption of referential transparency is the audience for whom such maps are intended,
a potentially universal readership for which the specifics of cultural back-
ground are thought to be inconsequential.

A further characteristic of mapping as performance has to do with the
question of perspective. The viewpoint on which grid maps depend is literally an extraterrestrial one; there is no central place from which what is represented can be seen. J. B. Harley has argued in Foucauldian terms that "cartog-
raphers manufacture power; they create a spatial panopticon" (1992: 244).[7]

It is the *fiction* of observability or, more exactly, the knowledge that such an imagined central vision makes possible that can lead to the determination of oneself and one's activities as being "out of place." Externally viewed, the world can best be described and categorized and its proper divisions and uses specified.

Harley has further suggested that, through maps, "the world is normalized" (1992: 245), a phrase here implying that a standard framework for description, comparison, and analysis has been provided. In a somewhat similar vein, the French social theorist François Ewald argues in his consideration of the rise of standard weights and sizes that such a shared system of measures and models makes possible the "institution of the perfect common language of pure communication by an industrial society, a language of precision and certainty, a language without puns, stylistic features, or interference" (1991: 151),[8] in short, a language of apparent pure reference. Such a means of representation is assumed, at least on some critical and consequential occasions, to be neutral, "outside" of politics or other situational concerns. It draws its power largely from its apparent transparency and from the invisibility which that engenders. Closely linked to the blandness of the bureaucratic discourse cited in all of these essays are the sentiments expressed by one civil servant to Zerner: "There are no rajas now." With democracy, the ideology replacing earlier princely power, public intelligibility and the possibility of equal participation, which that is thought to make possible, become critical, a point resonant with Silverstein's (1987) analysis of English Only and related movements for language standardization.

I want to offer two brief examples of how grid maps become normalized and the frame itself, as well as the political prerequisites it demands and reflects, effaced. The first is the cover of a book by Robert Ellickson, a scholar in the law and economics tradition. The book, *Order without Law: How Neighbors Settle Disputes,* draws upon ethnographic frameworks, comparative research, and formal modeling of bargaining behavior to demonstrate "how unimportant law is" (Ellickson 1991: vii) in the lives of ranchers near Mt. Shasta in northern California. Ellickson provides a stimulating, if not totally convincing, account of how rarely cattlemen resort to formal governmental or judicial agencies in managing their affairs with each other. At the same time, the design of the book cover itself features a USGS topographic map of the Mt. Shasta area, a grid that sets critical ground rules within which the cattlemen order their relations with neighbors. Similarly, a tax resisters' group in the town where I once lived refuses to acknowledge any municipal, state, or federal government. In its publications, the "real" address of the group is given in terms of township, range, and section numbers rather than street address (The Time Is Now Group 1994). As with the "natural" use of a topographic map to represent the cattlemen's territory, here again the frame vanishes, and the picture it shapes, whether graphic or expressed through cartographic coordinates, is taken as a neutral representation. Both of these examples speak to another of Foucault's claims about modernity, that contemporary state power lies not so much in its visible agencies such as police and courts as in the extension of nonjuridical power (1980c; see also Ewald 1991). In the more down-to-earth words of a character in a recent film, "Maps are the undergarments of a country" (*The Englishman Who Went Up a Hill but Came Down a Mountain*), unseen but indispensable. Grid-based mapmaking constitutes a critical site for bureaucratic performance, and central to the compelling power of such performances is just how unstaged they appear, in how effectively they appear to map the land but mask the mapping.

Mapping Memory

I want to return briefly to Roseman's observation that Temiar songs make cartographic claims. If the performances described by Roseman, Tsing, and Zerner constitute a charismatic cartography, they do so in a quite different way than does the grid system discussed above, as their goal is not so much topographic (literally, "writing place") as topomnemonic, that is both *remembering* place and remembering *through* place. The Temiar songs discussed by Roseman, for example, link individuals, spirits, trees, rivers, and other specific sites, conjuring up quite particularistic webs of association and interaction specific to and authenticating the claims and histories of particular individuals and groups. Steven Feld's detailed consideration of Kaluli song texts resonates here: the texts of the "sung-texted-weeping" through which women express and sympathize with grievous loss, and of the dance songs through which men evoke the sorrow of the bereaved, each chart a series of specific places heavy with the memory of being together with those individual kin or friends whom one has lost (1991; see also Feld 1984; Roseman 1984; Stewart 1996; Feld and Basso 1996). Along somewhat similar lines, dangers and regions important to Makassarese fisher folk serve to remind humans of particular points of past connection, sometimes successfully negotiated, sometimes not, but always implying reciprocal responsibilities and the perils of failure to perform appropriately.

Place and the specific memories with which it is entangled link past with present and human with the natural and supernatural. In all these cases, memory does not just exist; it must be refreshed—through talk, song, dance, and, in some communities and on some occasions, visual embodiment, although the visual is by no means the sole or invariably favored channel for such mapping.[9] A first difference with modern cartography, then, is that these performance practices topomnemonically call forth past interaction —incidental, ritual, aesthetic—and imply future interactional trajectories. Among those phenomena and practices encoded and exemplified in such local cartographic practices are the kinds of contractual connections suggested in the first section of this essay. The "map" is never static but always being shaped through ongoing activity.

A second crucial difference between Western mapping and these practices is that of perspective. The viewpoint implied by a topographic map is inherently imaginary, lying as it necessarily does outside of the region mapped. In contrast, the perspective apparent in the indigenous communities represented in this volume moves with the perceiver; it is individualized, changeable, and always located within particular contexts. The viewer is never himself or herself out of the picture. While there are clearly fixed points of reference to which descriptions can be pinned, the paths followed are multiple and, while often intersecting with those followed by others, shaped by individual movement and experience. In many ways, to borrow a term from linguistics, this is a strikingly *deictic* cartography, one in which meaning is heavily context-dependent and where those making meaning are always situated in very specific ways. Temiar songs point to particular places; but they also always point *from* particular places.[10]

Claiming Possibilities

This essay began with the notion of "speaking law" and the issue of rights, and it may seem that I have taken a very circuitous and perhaps unmappable route since then. In this conclusion, I return to my framing question: Drawing upon these provocative accounts, how best might legitimacy be claimed for indigenous interests and futures? Two general and often related strategies, one of contesting the terms in which arguments about environments, rights, and indigenous communities are conducted and the other of taking a thoroughgoing understanding of specific local legitimacies as a starting point, seem particularly relevant.

The first cluster of strategies, that of alternative discourses, has several variations. One involves taking the *form* of universal, administrative discursive practices such as mapmaking and uses those formal features to represent and highlight other information than that which is usually included, a practice I'll call "countermapping." Peluso's article, for example, lists a number of types of information—tended areas of jungle, villages, customary usufructory rights—which could be cartographically represented and, thereby, provide a very different picture of the same territory. Getting Bentian Dayak rattan gardens "onto the map" could be similarly helpful. Such countermapping has become a salient strategy among many North American environmentalists. Doug Aberley's notion of bioregional "mapping for local empowerment" (1993; 1994) and Dave Foreman and colleagues' ecosystem-centered remapping of wilderness preserves (Foreman, Wolke, and Koehler 1991) are particularly well-known examples.

A second kind of alternative discourse is one that goes off the grid and away from visual representation altogether. Among practitioners of this strategy, the notion of landscape is replaced, or at least challenged and supplemented, by that of soundscape, the acoustic surround that we hear and to which we ourselves contribute. Inspired in large part by the work of the Canadian composer and acoustician Murray Schafer (1977), a range of environmental activists, composers, ethnomusicologists, and others have worked both to record soundscapes and to create examples of what Alaskan composer John Luther Adams calls "sonic geography" (1994; 1996; see also Olwig 1993). Adams's own work draws upon field tapes of environmental sound, Western stringed instruments and percussion, Inupiat and Gwich'in performers, and texts, often simultaneous and multivoiced lists of place, animal, bird, plant, and weather names in Inupiaq, Gwich'in, Latin, and English. Field recordings rather than compositions, the discs produced by Steven Feld (1991) and Marina Roseman (1995) of Kaluli and Temiar soundscapes similarly both convey the assumedly natural environment and, by incorporating talk, chant, and song, locate humans within and in ongoing sonic interaction with "nature." In contrast to more usual environmental recordings, such works, both documentary and composed, do not see or, more appropriately, hear nature as lying wholly beyond or outside the human.[11] The engagement and assumed performative exchange figuring centrally in the essays in this volume are rhetorically salient in these sonic documents. Finally, it is important to point out that, as with the visible landscape, such soundscapes are always culturally inflected. In speaking with some of his Papago (O'odham) grammar-school students, for example, Gary Paul Nabhan once "asked them to contrast the city and the desert; they called the desert noisy" (1982: 51).[12]

These essays speak most directly to the second cluster of strategies, as each author clearly works to conceptualize and translate for a non-local audience those local idioms and practices through which legitimacy can be claimed and negotiated. One striking feature of all these studies is how far from static the worlds they represent are. Local claims are not considered to obtain from time immemorial but are rather under active negotiation with both human and non-human audiences. That these contracts are extended through aesthetically marked and charismatically compelling performance is significant. Ongoing work is involved, and audiences and interlocutors may not always be persuaded. The effectiveness of these essays derives in large part from the suggestive clarity with which they convey such events.

Coming to understand local conceptualizations is critical. A logically related issue, one for both indigenous communities themselves and for those of us who work with them, is that of translation. How best can the broader regional or global audience, and especially those who are empowered to make decisions of great consequence for such communities, come to understand local perspectives and practices and the logic and thought which inform them? Fried's and Zerner's studies document local attempts to translate the local into the languages and genres of more powerful speakers and readers, and each of these authors has necessarily translated the local for us as an academic audience. Such translation is, however, a very difficult task, and one for which the intended official audience often lacks patience. While all meaning is context-dependent, that represented on modern maps, for example, appears to be much less so than the highly particularistic and shifting information encoded in indigenous songs and stories. The fiction of transparency and the imagined external vantage point that makes it possible suggests a much clearer and more comprehensible one than that heard in the opaque evenings of a Meratus Dayak honey hunt or a Temiar healing session.

I'd like to conclude by turning to one of the classics of nineteenth-century anthropology, Sir Henry Maine's *Ancient Law* (1861). Central to Maine's argument was what he saw—in terms admittedly reflecting both social-evolutionary assumptions and a liberal sense of the importance and possibility of a freely made social contract—as a shift from status to contract at the heart of legal and social ideology and practice. These essays and the broader debates about indigenous rights in which they figure suggest that in fact something quite different is now taking place. The communities described here, deeply engaged as they are in the ongoing performative negotiation of their claims on and relations with the natural, live in a contractual world. This is particularly striking when compared with the rise of a politics of status, in this case, of one's status as "indigenous" or at least as a member of a historically resident group. Such a politics is shaped on the one hand by an extension of administrative classificatory, demographic, and mapping practices, and on the other by a discourse of indigenous rights in which claims of autochthony are taken to outweigh other considerations, including those that may well be more salient in local accounts. This volume argues strongly that local contracts and conceptualizations should be taken very seriously indeed. It also suggests that there may well be hidden costs in drawing solely upon a discourse of rights to sustain the local.

In the closing portion of Zerner's essay, he notes that a truly hegemonic system is not yet in place in the Makassar Straits, or elsewhere in Indonesia. There is, rather, a system of domination. There are ways in which the relationships among and, more specifically, the translations between the local, national, and the international could more effectively be made—and there may yet be time in which to make them. These polyvocal essays provide the surprise and challenge of the best ethnography. They enrich our sense of the complexities of local experience, illumine the hidden assumptions of and about an apparently bland bureaucratic world, and suggest promising ways of rethinking how most productively to engage and to make claims.

Notes

I am deeply indebted to Charles Zerner for his invitation to participate in the symposium which has led to this book and for his remarkable patience and enthusiasm over the course of the enterprise. Jane Atkinson, Anna Tsing, Nancy Peluso, and Marina Roseman have been exciting interlocutors, and I appreciate the subsequent opportunity to become familiar with Stephanie Fried's work. I also learned a great deal from the comments of members of the audience at the Wilson Center. Many thanks to Mary Bullock and the Woodrow Wilson Center staff for their hospitality and encouragement. Paul Faulstich and Wynne Furth provided timely and invaluable readings. This essay is in memory of my father, Andrew Brenneis, forest ranger and extraordinary reader of both maps and territories.

1   For a fuller discussion of primary and secondary audiences, see Brenneis (1978).

2   See also Hymes (1975).

3   I am indebted to Wynne Furth for her advice concerning legal definitions.

4   This discussion is indebted in part to Foucault's (1975; 1980a) claims concerning the rise of the visual episteme in the modern West.

5   My thanks to Rudi Volti for clarification of the connotations of the Dutch term.

6   Thongchai (1994) provides an exceptionally subtle, empirically grounded, and thought-provoking account of the complex historical relationships between cartography and nation-making in Thailand.

7   See also Harley (1988); Monmonnier (1991); Wood (1992). Recent work has considered in detail the role of different kinds of top-down perspective in mapping in a range of traditional societies. For detailed examples, see Woodward and Lewis (1998).

8   See also Brenneis (1994).

9   For particularly striking examples of visual topomnemonic practices, see the recent literature on Australian Aboriginal groups: Anderson and Dussart (1988); Faulstich (1998); Morphy (1991); Myers (1986); Turnbull (1993).

10 For lucid and thought-provoking discussions of *deixis* and its implications for linguistic, social, and cultural analysis, see Bachnik and Quinn (1994) and Hanks (1990). Brody (1982) and Pandya (1990) provide important considerations of how movement is taken to define space and place in several different non-Western communities.

11 An exemplary case of defining the world of natural sounds in terms of the absence of humans can be found in the recordings of Gordon Hempton ("The Soundtracker"), insightfully analyzed in Klein (n.d.).

12 For historically focused accounts, see Corbin (1998); Smith (1999).

Afterword. By Land and By Sea: Reflections on Claims and Communities in the Malay Archipelago

Jane Monnig Atkinson

In his insightful reflections, subtitled "Toward New Conceptions of Rights," Brenneis has gone to the "heart of this volume," what he terms "the question of rights" (see page 219) as they are being framed and asserted by different parties with interests in the forests and seas of insular Southeast Asia. Using the Weberian polarity of charismatic and bureaucratic authority, invoked here by Anna Tsing, he sketches an illuminating set of contrasts between the claims-making performances of Mandar fishermen, Meratus honey collectors, and Temiar singers, on the one hand, and bureaucratic modes of claims-making associated with state institutions, represented here by federal courts, forestry departments, and development seminars, on the other. The root question of these essays concerns the disjuncture between the claims over resources that local peoples are making and the rights to those same resources that state institutions are willing to recognize.

My contribution here will be to bolster Don Brenneis's focus on claims-making with some attention to commodity-making. After all, the discourses about rights that these papers examine concern rights to exploit environmental resources for various purposes, ranging from local subsistence to international trade. Claims to resources—honey trees, ironwood, and rattan gardens; tuna, shad, and flying fish—all entail assignments of value, from spiritual to monetary, being made at local, regional, national, and international levels.

Commoditization of forest resources has a long history in the archipelago; what has changed in recent decades is the fact that capital, technology, and the institutions that wield them are now extending state and corporate control over previously remote parts of Southeast Asia's forests and seas that were previously governable in name only. Centralized regimes, from sultanates to European colonial governments, have long asserted ownership of vast tracts of territory, but have lacked both the will and the means to control them directly. It is the presentation of the dilemmas posed for forest dwellers and local fishermen by the rapid expansion of wider economic and political interests into their previously remote domains that is the strong suit of this collection. Whereas subsistence farmers, armed with handmade axes (small iron blades hafted on rough wood handles and sharpened on stones) toil to clear small patches of forest to grow their crops, logging companies with trucks and machinery fell vast tracts of rainforest in an afternoon. On the open seas, gross differences in capital and technology not only put small-scale fishermen at a competitive disadvantage but also threaten to damage and exhaust marine resources. Maps deny the very existence of local inhabitants, let alone any stake they might claim in their environs. And the response (or lack of response) to local people's efforts to translate their claims into the authoritative discourse of state institutions suggests how difficult it is to challenge the collaboration of state and corporate interests.

There are no easy answers to be found in these essays. Policymakers looking for the "action clause" in this collection will be forced to wade through rich ethnographic detail before coming upon concrete proposals to ameliorate the problems described here. Implicitly or explicitly, all the essays call for fundamental changes in law and epistemology, not to mention significant changes in the exploitation of the archipelago's natural resources. The value of these essays lies less in the immediate practicality of the solutions they pose, and more in the challenging ways they illuminate questions of indigenous rights over environmental resources in contemporary insular Southeast Asia. They call on readers to acknowledge the constructed nature of the legal, economic, and political frameworks in which we operate. Anna Tsing, for example, notes that a way of thinking that restricts itself to exchange value, thereby suppressing other forms of value, is in itself a culturally constructed mode of thought that configures the world and motivates behavior within it. Taking the position that "it is impossible to separate nature from the cultural apparatus used to know nature", Tsing uses honey hunting as a way to show us how the rainforest is known and used by its Meratus inhabitants. Tsing and her colleagues offer a series of thought exercises that enable the reader to shed familiar epistemological frameworks and to try on those of Meratus honey collectors, Temiar singers, Bentian rattan farmers, and Mandar fishermen. The authors of these papers expect us to work at these exercises—to "stretch our ideas about resource claims rather than looking for easy matches with familiar international conventions" (see page 31).

Southeast Asian populations have long shared their sense of personhood with the plants, animals, and the seemingly inanimate features of their environment. In her analysis of the animation, if you will, of a Southeast Asian habitat, Roseman explores the kind of epistemological premises that underlie Meratus bee songs and Mandar fishermen's exhortations to spirits of the deep as well as Temiar dream songs. Common to many of the region's cultures has been the notion that activities like hunting, felling trees, and catching fish should be conducted properly as processes of ongoing exchange with these resources or the spirits associated with them. Imbalance in these exchanges can lead to illness or death—as in the case of a successful hunter who has not adequately compensated the spirit owners of the game he has killed. In retribution, those spirits may "take their share" by causing the hunter or members of his family to fall sick and die. This is not the place for a full review of the complex systems of exchanges between humans and spirits that have been described across a range of societies in the archipelago. Nor is it the place to consider the transformations monotheistic religions have wrought in these systems, some hint of which is evident in Charles Zerner's rich account of fishing spells in the Straits of Makassar. Suffice it to say, however, that these systems of exchange—call them cosmological—share with less spiritual forms of exchange a concern for "what a reasonable 'exchange of sacrifices' comprises" (Appadurai 1986a: 57).

Spirits, however, are not the only aliens with whom Southeast Asian forest dwellers are used to trading. Indeed, there is documentation for nearly two millennia's worth of experimentation on the part of upland populations who have tested the "commodity candidacy" (Appadurai 1986a:13) of a wide variety of forest products, ranging from fragrant woods, medicinal plants, rattans, and resins, to cultivated crops such as peppers, coffee, peanuts, and rubber, and even to human chattel, traffic in which became a growth industry in the region in the eighteenth and nineteenth centuries (see Bigalke 1981; Kuipers 1990, Reid 1983, Volkman and Zerner 1988). In his book *Early Indonesian Commerce* (1967), the eminent historian O. W. Wolters argues that the early maritime kingdoms of what is now western Indonesia developed their wealth not only by serving as entrepôts for trade between China, India, the Middle East, and the Mediterranean, but also by insinuating into that trade local products, initially as substitutes for foreign trade items (for example, Sumatran pine resin for frankincense, benzoin for bdellium myrrh), but later as desired commodities in their own right (dragon's blood and camphor). Forest dwellers comparable to the Temiar and Meratus, then, have been tied into global trade for many centuries. Typically, however, the forest producers have been involved only in the initial phase of commodity production, harvesting a product and conveying it to a trader (sometimes in the form of a chief or a raja) on the first leg of its commercial journey. Uplanders could participate in commodity production with ignorance of markets, money, and the ultimate destination or purpose of the commodity they provided. For example, "it is reasonably certain that traditional Borneo forest dwellers had relatively little idea of the uses to which the birds' nests they sold to intermediaries have played in Chinese medical and culinary practice" (Appadurai 1986a: 42). Likewise, contemporary rattan gatherers in the region may be unaware that there are retail stores in the United States, with names like "Malacca Rattan, Inc.," stocked with furniture made of the vines they gather. When Sulawesi highlanders pressed me about the uses to which local resins are put, they had no idea that the decline in the once thriving resin market in which they participated for most of this century was due in part to the development of synthetic substitutes for their forest product. And the denizens of a site called Ue nTaru, or Beeswax River, knew only that their forbears presented beeswax as tribute to the ruler of the coastal Sultanate of Tojo. What became of that wax they did not know. Was it carried off by Chinese junks that plied the coast of Tomini to be fashioned into Buddhist devotional candles, as one Southeast Asian historian suggested to me? Or was it used for loading shot into Portuguese firearms, as explained to me by an elderly civil servant in the Bay of Tomini?

In spite of their ignorance of wider market conditions, the initiative of forest dwellers in marketing forest products should not be underestimated. The spread of new crops with market potential through the tropical forests of Southeast Asia is well documented. From peppers and other spices, to coffee and coconuts, rubber and cocoa, subsistence farmers have been willing to experiment with a wide range of potentially marketable crops. It is telling that among the Galik of Kalimantan "enterprise plots,"—that is, gardens used for growing cash crops for market sales—are called by the same term, *usaha,* in both the local and national languages (Peluso, personal communication). Borrowed from the trade language of the region, the term bespeaks the market orientation of Galik farmers, not at all dissimilar to comparable populations throughout the archipelago.

Incentives for such experimentation include access to trade goods. Markets create desires, which over time become necessities. Longtime necessities, such as salt, metal tools, and cotton cloth are joined by other candidates—including sugar, dried fish, kerosene lamps, and medicines. New commodities replace old ones. For example, the popularity of manual sewing machines among forest dwellers has diminished somewhat due to floods of cheap factory-made garments that now appear in local Southeast Asian markets. Another incentive for market participation historically has been taxation, which has required subsistence farmers to sell farm or forest products to obtain cash to pay their taxes.

Both subsistence and market practices have caused ongoing physical transformations in local habitats. The widespread adoption of foodstuffs from the Americas over the past five centuries has transformed the gardens, diets, and health of even remote populations. The importation of livestock in some areas has contributed to widespread environmental degradation in certain parts of the archipelago. Development of large international markets for certain key crops—spices, rubber, and coffee, for example—has prompted subsistence farmers to alter their settlement patterns, concepts of ownership, and the nature of their labor. As has been noted by Geertz (1963), Dove (1985b), and others, the nature of swidden agriculture, with its relatively low investment of annual labor, offers farmers flexibility to cultivate cash crops and market forest products while continuing to produce their own food. Maintaining a balance between subsistence farming and marketing is a concern among many swidden farmers. Prosperous Wana farmers in Central Sulawesi, for example, admonish their young kin not to become so enamored with trade that they find themselves having to buy rice with the proceeds of their market sales.

The current nature and scope of economic and technological development in the twenty-first century makes rapid and radical environmental transformations far more possible and likely. Tsing disabuses us of the notion that local forest dwellers will automatically or inevitably function as "ecological geniuses destined to save the planet" (see page 48). High prices for resins in the late colonial period were enough to provoke uplanders in eastern Sulawesi to overtap damar trees until the quality of their product declined. With chainsaws, road access, and a market incentive, subsistence farmers can and do join in the destruction of their forest habitats. And travelers in the archipelago can see the damage done to coral reefs by local fishermen with access to dynamite. It would be an error to trust that cultural values alone will sustain sound and wise environmental practice. To do so is to idealize culture in the abstract, divorced from historical and material realities.

In Indonesia, particularly during the Suharto era, swidden agriculture has often been the object of negative, government-sponsored characterizations (Dove 1983). In addition to claims that swidden was environmentally destructive, critics have commonly asserted that rights to forests under swidden regimes could not be recognized because the practice failed to exhibit one of the key signs or indicia of property: continuous occupancy and use. Even mixed systems of agroforestry or forest gardening have been ignored or not recognized for what they are: complex, long-term systems of forest management resting on intergenerational labor and locally recognized as property (Rose 1994; Zerner 1990a, 1992a; Michon and de Foresta 2000; Fried 2000). Some scholars, and many environmental advocates working in Indonesia's richly complex brew of social movements, have demanded recognition of the customary rights of these forest-dependent groups and their inclusion in the institutional decision-making bodies with jurisdiction over forest use and planning (Michon and de Foresta 2000; Zerner 1994a,b; Lynch and Talbott 1995; Moniaga 1993; *Down to Earth* 1999).

During the past decade, many international conservation planners and project managers have proposed market-based solutions to forest management (Dove 1993a, 1994; Zerner 1999, 2000). Although the primary goal of these schemes is faunal and floristic conservation, many of them seek to improve the lot of local communities by focusing on livelihoods. They also propose the involvement of local people in forest management through the creation of incentives for the local population to conserve—and disincentives to squander—their forest resources (Brosius, Tsing, and Zerner 1998). With long-term interests guaranteed, so the theory goes, local populations would be in a position to make choices proactively, not simply reactively, and hence those choices would presumably be environmentally responsible ones. Given the relative poverty of most forest dwellers and the insatiability of markets for tropical hardwoods, however, one might well ask how a system of ecologically sensible incentives can be established and maintained in a way that ensures that short-term economic gain is not placed above long-term sustainability. One might well ask of these hybrid schemes, which goals are primary and which are subsidiary.

Which rights and which goals—property rights, cultural rights, rights to livelihood and societal well-being, biodiversity conservation, or habitat integrity—are vested with the power to trump other concerns and other claims? These questions are still being hotly debated. And in a moment of crisis and creativity in the post-Suharto era, a panoply of diverse schemes involving complicated mixtures of these concerns continues to be fashioned, deployed, and assessed in the field. These approaches invite a series of interesting questions about the institutional apparatus necessary to structure local forest management: the nature and kinds of knowledge—scientific, economic, legal, political—that would need to be merged and transmitted; and the conflicting interests and differences of power at and between every level—local, regional, national, and international—that would have to be balanced in order to achieve these goals. One might even ask, perhaps, whether the image of balance itself, or of balancing acts, is an apt metaphor to represent such unequal contests—of values, rights, and concerns—among such differently situated and differentially empowered communities.

If local people's rights could get on the map, so to speak, these populations would achieve legal standing and their claims would be defensible. Roseman and Tsing, however, point out just how incommensurable local claims might be to rights in bureaucratic legal systems. Local forms of "customary law" are the stuff of performance, rich with ambiguity, with ample room for outcomes that may defy legal logic but mediate the needs of communities and assertive personalities. Roseman suggests that governmental authorities mistrust the aural nature of ownership records because aurality, in dominant systems of knowledge, is "one step closer to the imaginary than writing." Recognition of customary law calls for transformation of performative practice into something quite different from the charismatic claims-making that typically goes on. But then, attempts to codify local forms of adat (customary law) have a long history in the region. And what passes as "local" adat in many interior populations is itself the product of negotiation with earlier forms of authorities, including colonial bureaucrats and regional elites. (Wana of Central Sulawesi, for example, claim to have imported their adat—that is, their system of legal payments for negotiating matters from marriage to murder—from the Sultanate of Bungku far to the south.) In the face of current threats to the world's forests—made possible by the flow of global capital and accompanying exploitative technologies—local systems of customary law will likely need to undergo a process of transformation and homogenization to bring them into conformity with wider bureaucratic discourses if local claimants are to exercise any rights at all.

Not prepared to yield so quickly to the imperatives of the world order, Roseman and Tsing want to make the case that the ways of being-in-the-world that the Temiar and the Meratus exemplify combine sophisticated knowledge of their habitats with poetic sensibilities about their place within them. One wishes that careful and persuasive ethnography by gifted interpreters like Roseman and Tsing will have a transformative effect on thoughtful scientists, planners, and policymakers. The more likely response is that authorities will, in Don Brenneis's words, turn a "deaf ear" to these performances, dismissing them as atavistic survivals from a premodern age—unless, I feel compelled to add, they see the entrepreneurial possibility for commodifying such performances for tourist consumption (cf. Acciaioli 1985; Picard 1990; Volkman 1984, 1990).

Roseman does not stop at a relativism that recognizes Temiar "imaginations of reality" as being on a par with those of more powerful people. Instead, she regards Temiar knowledge—at least that which concerns the rainforest—as superior to the toxicity of the dominant policies and interests threatening the Temiar way of life. Miners' canaries, rainforest mediums, the Temiar and others like them—in Roseman's argument—can be ignored only at the expense of the forests and, perhaps, global survival. In calling for recognition of Temiar concepts and local determination of forest use in such stark terms, Roseman does not speculate about the transformations such recognition and responsibilities might call for in Temiar forms of knowledge and lifeways—for example, in the inevitable written codification of land rights or in choices about the relative merits of a subsistence-based livelihood versus greater market participation. Absent from her stark picture are the accommodations and compromises on the Temiar side that could transform them—were the Malaysian government to allow it—from victims and visionaries to players in the Malaysian economic and political system. What is to guarantee that Temiar would retain their ecological knowledge and sensibilities if they were to gain more secure footing as Malaysian citizens? With education, health care, and economic opportunities, would many children forego the lifeways of their parents and lose the connections to the rainforest that Roseman so eloquently celebrates? Who is to say that the Temiar would remain

"Temiar," unless rigid conditions of their rights of ownership and management required them to "sustain their environments and chart their own course of development" in isolation from the rest of the nation-state. Is such a fiat desirable?

In contrast to those who call for recognition of customary rights within state frameworks of knowledge, Tsing would prefer a radical reconstruction of those frameworks. Tsing's project involves using local forms of knowledge to undermine and refashion the sciences of ecology and forestry, and the policies that they support. Tsing's essay also dwells on incommensurabilities rather than points of compromise and accommodation to get us out of the current dilemma. Her essay suggests the complexity of seeking recognition for local people's customary rights in the hope that putting their claims on the map will result in legal standing. Tsing's essay reveals how incommensurable locally defined rights might be to rights in the state's legal system. Her analysis of Meratus honey-collecting underscores the lack of transparency between Meratus concepts and those of dominant epistemologies of ecology, economics, and law. Any attempt at straightforward translation, one assumes, would result in distortion, most likely on the Meratus side. Tsing's valiant hope, one gathers, is that the more powerful side—made up of government officials, planners, corporations, and forest managers—could yield and learn from Meratus, rather than forcing Meratus to conform to alienating frameworks dictated by state interests and international capital. Short of that, one suspects, it is more practical to adapt the conservationists' strategy and argue for an arrangement, brokered perhaps by international environmental agencies and local NGOs, that would grant Meratus a role in forest management, although not on exclusively Meratus terms.

How difficult it might be to achieve such a compromise is suggested by Stephanie Fried's examination of Bentian efforts to stop the wholesale destruction of forests in East Kalimantan. Fried's paper offers the most dramatic account in this collection of the drastic effects of forest policy on local populations. She shows us, up close, the consequences of allocating forests to logging companies and large-scale plantations. Here, the excuse for deafness on the part of the government cannot be the opacity of local idioms or an epistemological gulf between cultures. Expressed in the national language, replete with commitments to the national project of development, the Bentian documents Fried presents have apparently been ignored or suppressed, not on account of their incomprehensibility, but rather on account of their incompatibility with the powerful economic interests that hold sway in the area.

The manner in which Fried casts her account is revealing of the rhetorical effects of different kinds of claims-making for different audiences, including ourselves. One is caught up short by the equivalence she drew between a rubber company's destruction of "1,000 hectares of mature rattan garden" and the "emptying, without permission or advance warning, [of] the back accounts containing the life savings of the local rattan farmers" (see pages 169–70). This account may in fact be more gut-wrenching to many readers than the notion that Temiar lifeways, for example, are threatened and on the wane. After all, the demise of the "Primitive" has long been predicted, but the injustice of property seizures hits likely readers of this volume where they live. Cast in the terms of an economic scenario that educated urban readers can understand and fear, it provokes identification and alarm rather than nostalgia for the passing of a romantic, but—by the standards of modern industrial society—outmoded and unviable societal form.

The Bentian case signals the problem of attributing homogeneity of interests and perspectives to an indigenous population. In the case of the Bentian, a considerable degree of social differentiation and assimilation with neighboring populations has occurred. One cannot speak of the Bentian in the homogeneous terms Roseman uses for Temiar. What is more, the Bentian are not exploiting the forest primarily for subsistence purposes, but for extensive cash-cropping. Most of the articulate spokespeople Fried cites are in fact educated town-dwellers employed in non-agricultural positions. Fried highlights a situation in which city-dwelling Bentian deploy their education and familiarity with national values and bureaucratic discourse to advance the case of Bentian land rights. More than differences in rhetoric, I suspect, distinguish the urban-based members of the Bentian Family Group (with its acceptance of the government premise that swidden farming should be eradicated) and the upriver rattan farmer who penned the "cry of pain and rage" that Fried presents as the final Bentian document in her essay. United in the cause of defending Bentian lands from incursions by the likes of Georgia-Pacific, these various authors might find socioeconomic, regional, and ideological divisions among themselves when it comes to charting a future for "the Bentian." Whether and how unification in the face of the logging crisis can be sustained and converted into a policymaking or decision-making body for self-identified Bentian at large remains to be seen.

There are challenges involved in defining and negotiating "indigenous" rights as local communities become socially more complex. Charles Zerner gives us the most explicit glimpse of ways in which class differences among local residents are a source of tension and even outright violence. It is not only "outsiders," but also "wealthy insiders . . . with grossly disproportionate gear and access to central governmental power and permissions" who are threatening Mandar fishermen with little wealth or clout.

> A fisherman's brother operating a roppong may be hurling rocks at a pagai owned by his government-employed sister, who works in the fisheries department. . . . She has a steady salary and can accumulate enough capital to invest in construction and operation of such an expensive vessel. (see page 106)

The same question holds for all the minority groups discussed in these essays. If state governments were to recognize them as full participants in the management of the natural resources located in their territories, mechanisms would have to be developed to enable these populations to reach informed decisions by representative means. The challenges of establishing such mechanisms might be different among populations like the Temiar and Mandar, where social stratification thus far seems less advanced, than in the Bentian and Mandar cases, in which societal differentiation is more firmly entrenched.

Charles Zerner's fishing companion, Pak Nihung, uses the metaphor of a radio broadcast to capture the complexity of discursive options available to the fishermen of Mandar. Indeed, the archipelago is abuzz with competing discourses, each associated with particular epistemological and institutional frameworks. The opportunities for code-switching provide actors with alternative sets of resources for advancing their interests. The choices they make can, over time, enhance or diminish the legitimacy and efficacy of those resources. For example, Zerner interprets Case No. 11/Criminal/B/1987 of the Majene District Court as a case of displacement of local jurisdiction by state authority. It is worth pointing out that the case was brought to court not by representatives of state or corporate interests, but by the nephew of "a retired Mandar investor"—not by a resident of Majene, but by an ethnic Mandar living several hundred miles away. Instead of reading the incident as an overreaching by the long arm of the state, we might see it as an instance of disputants "making a federal case" out of a matter that could have been settled

locally. Note how the existence of a federal court system offers local disputants the option of escalating their disagreement by "kicking it up a level."
Threatening to alert external authorities who are likely to operate on a different set of principles is often an effective way to persuade opponents to yield,
or at least to settle. Tsing (1993) offers some vivid examples of this tactic at
use among swidden farmers in Kalimantan, which I can match from comparable communities in central Sulawesi. In Tsing's examples, as in my own,
such threats were seldom acted upon because of the physical and social distance of the authorities from the contenders in a dispute. In Majene, however, it seems that access may incline disputants to increasing reliance on judicial resolution, furthering the erosion of customary law in favor of state
authority.

In many ways, the court case presented by Zerner epitomizes the theme of
this book. In the Majene courtroom we hear the clamor of competing claims
that cut across the divides of locality, ethnicity, class, and authority. The
court's ruling noted that science and technology are "so sophisticated," that
the sea and the heavens are no longer "closed." Indeed, "the sea is now a
lively crossroads," in the public eye, as it were. The high seas have become
visible not only to federal courts, but also to international sites of power and
courts of opinion. Likewise, the rainforests of Malaysia and Indonesia are
now open to the scrutiny of government, industry, and scientists not only in
country, but transnationally as well. The International Monetary Fund, the
World Bank, the United Nations, foreign governments, international agencies, multinational corporations, foundations, not to mention transnational
and national environmental organizations, are all involved in defining,
shaping, and implementing regional and national environmental policy.

Will exposure to multiple lines of vision grant clarity or confusion to the
picture? Will it lead to compromises and brokered solutions that permit responsible economic growth along with sustainable environmental policies?
Some observers find reasons to be hopeful about the development and implementation of environmental policy in the region, due in part to the combination of international scrutiny and in-country activism around environmental issues (see Sonnenfeld 1993). One might ask whether the future of
the region's rainforests and marine resources is less in doubt at this moment
than the continued viability of many local communities that depend on
them. With international focus on the survival of tropical environments, the

future of their least powerful inhabitants is often eclipsed. The virtue of this collection is to call attention to the interests, indeed the rights, of some of these people who depend for their lives and livelihood on the forests and seas of insular Southeast Asia.

Notes

My deepest thanks to Charles Zerner for his significant contribution to the development of my thoughts on these matters.

Works Cited

Aberley, Doug, ed. 1993. *Boundaries of Home: Mapping for Local Empowerment.* Gabriola Island, B.C.: New Society Publishers.

Aberley, Doug. 1994. "Mapping the Terrain of Hope." *Wild Earth* (summer): 62–63.

Acciaioli, Gregory. 1985. "Culture as Art: From Practice to Spectacle in Indonesia." In *Minorities and the State*, edited by Douglas Miles and Christopher Eipper. Special volume of *Canberra Anthropology* 8 (1/2): 128.

Adams, John Luther. 1994. "Resonance of Place." *North American Review* 279 (January/February): 8–18.

———. 1996. Composer's notes to *Earth and the Great Weather: A Sonic Geography of the Arctic.* New World Records, compact disc 80459–2.

Alcorn, Janis. 1981. "Huastec Noncrop Resource Management: Implications for Prehistoric Rainforest Management." *Human Ecology* 9 (4): 395–417.

Andaya, Barbara W., and Leonard A. Andaya. 1982. *A History of Malaysia.* London: Macmillan.

Anderson, Benedict. 1991. *Imagined Communities: Reflections on the Origin and Spread of Nationalism.* Rev. ed. London: Verso.

Anderson, Christopher, and Francois Dussart. 1988. "Dreamings in Acrylic: Western Desert Art." In *Dreamings: The Art of Aboriginal Australia*, edited by Peter Sutton, 89–142. New York: George Braziller.

Annandale, N. 1903a. "Primitive Beliefs and Customs of the Patani Fishermen." In *Fasciculi Malayenses: Anthropological and Zoological Results of an Expedition to Perak and the Siamese Malay States, 1901–1902, Undertaken by Nelson Annandale and Herbert C. Robinson*, 73–88. London: Longmans, Green.

———. 1903b. "Religion and Magic among the Malays of the Patani States." In *Fasciculi Malayenses: Anthropological and Zoological Results of an Expedition to Perak and the Siamese Malay States, 1901–1902, Undertaken by Nelson Annandale and Herbert C. Robinson*, 89–104. London: Longmans, Green.

Appadurai, Arjun. 1986a. "Introduction: Commodities and the Politics of Value." In *The Social Life of Things: Commodities in Cultural Perspective*, edited by Arjun Appadurai, 3–63. Cambridge: Cambridge University Press.

———. 1996. *Modernity at Large: Cultural Dimensions of Globalization.* Minneapolis: University of Minnesota Press.

——, ed. 1986b. *The Social Life of Things: Commodities in Cultural Perspective.* Cambridge: Cambridge University Press.

Appell, George. 1970. "Comparisons of Land Tenure Systems among the Dayak of Borneo." Unpublished manuscript, Brandeis University.

——. 1971. "Systems of Land Tenure in Borneo: A Problem in Ecological Determinism." *Borneo Research Bulletin* 3 (1): 17–21.

Aschmann, Homer. [1963] 1988. "Proprietary Rights to Fruit on Trees Growing on Residential Land." In *Whose Trees? Proprietary Dimensions of Forestry,* edited by Louise P. Fortmann and John W. Bruce, 63–68. Boulder, Colo.: Westview Press.

Atkinson, Jane Monnig. 1984. "Wrapped Words." In *Dangerous Words: Language and Politics in the Pacific,* edited by Donald Brenneis and Fred Myers, 38–68. New York: New York University Press.

——. 1989. *The Art and Politics of Wana Shananship.* Berkeley: University of California Press.

Attali, Jaques. 1989. *Noise: The Political Economy of Music.* Minneapolis: University of Minnesota Press.

Bachnik, Jane, and Charles Quinn, eds. 1994. *Situated Meaning: Inside and Outside in Japanese Self, Society, and Language.* Princeton, N.J.: Princeton University Press.

Bailey, Conner. 1988. "The Political Economy of Marine Fisheries Development in Indonesia." *Indonesia* 46 (October): 25–38.

Bailey, Conner, A. Dwiponggo, and F. Marahudin. 1987. *Indonesian Marine Capture Fisheries.* Studies and Reviews, no. 10. Manila and Jakarta: International Center for Living Aquatic Resources Management (ICLARM), Directorate General of Fisheries, and Marine Fisheries Research Institute, Ministry of Agriculture, Indonesia.

Bakhtin, Mikhail. 1981. *The Dialogic Imagination: The Four Essays.* Edited by Michael Holquist and translated by Caryl Emmerson and Michael Holquist. Austin: University of Texas Press.

Balée, William L. 1989. "The Culture of Amazonian Forests." In *Resource Management in Amazonia: Indigenous and Folk Strategies,* vol. 7, *Advances in Economic Botany,* edited by D. A. Posey and W. Balée, 1–21. New York: New York Botanical Garden.

——. 1994. *Footprints in the Forest: Ka'apor Ethnobotany—The Historical Ecology of Plant Utilization by an Amazonian People.* New York: Columbia University Press.

Bandjar, Hasmi, and Charles Zerner. 1996. "Breaking the Back of Sasi: Capital, Technology, and Property Rights in Haya Village, Indonesia." Paper presented at 6th Meeting of the International Association of Common Property, 5–8 June 1996, University of California at Berkeley.

Banuri, Tariq, and Frederique Appfel Marglin. 1993. "A Systems-of-Knowledge Analysis of Deforestation." In *Who Will Save The Forest?* edited by Tariq Banuri and Frederique Appfel Marglin, 1–23. London: Zed Press.

Basso, Keith. 1984. " 'Stalking with Stories': Names, Places, and Moral Narratives among the Western Apache." In *Text, Play, and Story: The Construction and Reconstruction of Self and Society. 1983 Proceedings of the American Ethnological Society,* edited by Edward Bruner, 19–55. Washington, D.C.: American Ethnological Society.

Bauman, Richard. 1977. "Verbal Art as Performance." In *Verbal Art as Performance,* edited by Richard Bauman, 3–58. Rowley, Mass.: Newbury House.

——. 1983. *Let Your Words Be Few: Symbolism of Speaking and Silence among Seventeenth-Century Quakers.* New York: Cambridge University Press.

Beccari, Odoardo. [1904] 1986. *Wanderings in the Great Forests of Borneo.* New York: Oxford University Press.

Becker, A. L. 1995. "Aridharma: Framing an Old Javanese Tale." In *Beyond Translation: Essays toward a Modern Philology,* edited by A. L. Becker, 37–81. Ann Arbor: University of Michigan Press.

Beinart, William. 1989. "Introduction: The Politics of Colonial Conservation." *Journal of African Studies* 15 (2): 143–62.

Bellwood, Peter. 1996. "Early Agriculture and the Dispersal of the Souther Mongoloids." In *Prehistoric Mongoloid Dispersals,* edited by T. Akazawa and E. Szathmary, 287–300. Oxford: Oxford University Press.

Benda-Beckmann, Franz von. 1992. "Changing Legal Pluralisms in Indonesia." *Yuridika: Majalah Fakultas Hukum Universitas Airlangga (Juridika: Journal of the University of Airlangga Law Faculty)* 4 (8): 1–23.

——. 1993. "Citizens, Strangers, and Indigenous Peoples: Multiple Constructions and Consequences of Rights, Resources, and Peoples." Paper presented at 13th IUAES International Conference, Commission on Folk Law and Legal Pluralism, 29 July–5 August, Mexico City.

Benjamin, G., compiler. 1983. "Map 37, Part 2: Peninsular Malaysia." In *Language Atlas of the Pacific Area,* edited by S. A. Wurm and S. Hattori. Pacific Linguistics Series C, no. 66. Canberra: Australian Academy of the Humanities and the Japan Academy.

Benjamin, Geoffrey. 1966. "Temiar Social Groupings." *Federated Museums Journal* 11: 1–25.

——. 1967a. "Temiar Religion." Ph.D. dissertation, Cambridge University.

——. 1967b. "Temiar Kinship." *Federated Museums Journal* 12: 1–25.

——. 1976. "An Outline of Temiar Grammar." In *Austroasiatic Studies,* edited by P. Jenner et al., 129–97. Honolulu: University of Hawai'i Press.

——. 1985. "In the Long Term: Three Themes in Malayan Cultural Ecology." In *Cultural Values and Human Ecology in Southeast Asia,* edited by Karl L. Hutterer, A. Terry Rambo, and George Lovelace, 219–78. Ann Arbor: University of Michigan Center for South and Southeast Asian Studies.

Benjamin, Geoffrey, and Cynthia Chou, eds. In press. *Tribal Communities in the Malay World: Historical, Cultural, and Social Perspectives.* Leiden: International Institute for Asian Studies.

Benjamin, Walter. 1969. *Illuminations: Essays and Reflections.* Edited by Hannah Arendt and translated by Harry Zohn. New York: Schocken.

Bentian Family Group. 1986. "A Program for the Implementation of the Planting of Sega Rattan and the Environmental Information Analysis." Unpublished manuscript, files of Stephanie Fried.

Berry, Sara. 1989. "Social Institutions and Access to Resources." *Africa* 59 (1): 41–55.

———. 2000. *Chiefs Know Their Boundaries: Essays on Property, Power, and the Past in Asante.* London: Blackwell.

Bigalke, Terrance. 1981. "A Social History of 'Tana Toraja,' 1870–1965." Ph.D. dissertation, University of Wisconsin, Madison.

Birkes, Fikret. 1989. *Common Property Resources: Ecology and Community as Bases for Sustainable Development.* London: Bellhaven Press.

Blagden, Charles Otto, and Walter William Skeat. 1906. "Taboo and Other Special Forms of Speech." In *Pagan Races of the Malay Peninsula,* 2:414–81. London: Macmillan.

Blaikie, Piers. 1985. *The Political Economy of Soil Erosion in Developing Countries.* London: Longman.

Blaikie, Piers, and H. Brookfield. 1987. *Land Degradation and Society.* London: Methuen.

Bock, Carl. 1985. *The Head-Hunters of Borneo: A Narrative of Travel Up the Mahakam and Down the Barito.* Singapore: Oxford University Press.

Booth, Wayne C. 1978. "Metaphor as Rhetoric: The Problem of Evaluation." In *On Metaphor,* edited by S. Sacks. Chicago: University of Chicago Press.

Borker, Ruth. 1986. "'Moved by the Spirit': Constructing Meaning in a Brethren Breaking of Bread Service." In *The Audience as Co-Author,* edited by Alessandro Duranti and Donald Brenneis. Special issue of *Text* 6 (3): 317–38.

Boserup, Esther. 1981. *Population and Technology.* Oxford: Blackwell.

Botkin, Daniel B. 1990. *Discordant Harmonies: A New Ecology for the Twenty-first Century.* New York: Oxford University Press.

Bourchier, David. 1997. "Totalitarianism and the 'National Personality': Recent Controversy about the Philosophical Basis of the Indonesian State." In *Imagining Indonesia: Cultural Politics and Political Culture,* edited by J. Schiller and B. Martin Schiller, 157–85. Monograph 97, Southeast Asian Studies. Athens: Ohio University Center for International Studies.

Bowen, John R. 1986. "On the Political Construction of Tradition: *Gotong Royong* in Indonesia." *Journal of Asian Studies* 45 (3): 545–61.

——. 1993. *Muslims through Discourse: Religion and Ritual in Gayo Society.* Princeton, N.J.: Princeton University Press.

Boyarin, Jonathan, ed. 1994. *Remapping Memory: The Politics of TimeSpace.* Minneapolis: University of Minnesota Press.

Brenneis, Donald. 1978. "The Matter of Talk: Political Performances in Bhatgaon." *Language in Society* 7 (2): 159–70.

——. 1994. "Discourse and Discipline at the National Research Council: A Bureaucratic Bildungsroman." *Cultural Anthropology* 9 (1): 23–36.

Brenneis, Donald, and Fred Meyers. 1984. *Dangerous Words: Language and Politics in the Pacific.* New York: New York University Press.

Brody, Hugh. 1982. *Maps and Dreams.* New York: Pantheon.

Bromley, Daniel W. 1989. "Property Relations and Economic Development: The Other Land Reform." *World Development* 17 (6): 867–76.

——. 1991. *Environment and Economy: Property Rights and Public Policy.* Cambridge, Mass.: Basil Blackwell.

Bromley, Daniel W., and Michael Cernea. 1989. *The Management of Common Property Natural Resources: Some Conceptual and Operational Fallacies.* World Bank Discussion Paper, no. 57. Washington, D.C.: World Bank.

Brosius, Peter. 1997. "Endangered Forest, Endangered People: Environmentalist Representation of Indigenous Knowledge." *Human Ecology* 25 (1): 47–69.

——. 1999a. "Analyses and Interventions: Anthropological Engagements with Environmentalism." *Current Anthropology* 40 (3): 277–310.

——. 1999b. "Green Dots, Pink Hearts: Displacing Politics from the Malaysian Rainforest." *American Anthropologist* 101 (1): 36–57.

——. Forthcoming. "The Forest and the Nation: Negotiating Citizenship in Sarawak, East Malaysia." In *Cultural Citizenship in Southeast Asia*, edited by Renato Rosaldo. Berkeley: University of California Press.

——. N.d. "Landscape and Society in Borneo: Penan Hunter-Gatherers of Sarawak." Unpublished manuscript, Anthropology Department, University of Georgia, Athens.

Brosius, Peter J., Anna Lowenhaupt Tsing, and Charles Zerner. 1998. "Representing Communities: Histories and Politics of Community-based Natural Resource Management." *Society and Natural Resources* 11 (2): 157–68.

Bryant, Raymond L. 1992. "Political Ecology: An Emerging Research Agenda in Third World Studies." *Political Geography* 11 (1): 12–36.

Bryant, Raymond L., and Sinéad Bailey. 1977. *Third World Political Ecology.* London: Routledge.

Brysk, Alison. 1994. "Acting Globally: Indian Rights and International Politics in Latin America." In *Indigenous Peoples and Democracy in Latin America*, edited by D. Cott. New York: St. Martin's.

——. 1996. "Turning Weakness into Strength: The Internationalization of Indian Rights." *Latin American Perspectives* 23 (2): 38–57.

Bunker, Stephen. 1985. *Underdeveloping the Amazon*. Chicago: University of Illinois Press.

Burns, Peter. 1989. "The Myth of Adat." *Journal of Legal Pluralism* 28: 1–126.

Butler, Colin. 1974. *The World of the Honeybee*. London: Collins.

Chanock, Martin. 1985. *Law, Custom, and Social Order: The Colonial Experience in Malawi and Zambia*. New York: Cambridge University Press.

Chew, Daniel. 1990. *Chinese Pioneers on the Sarawak Frontier*. Singapore: Oxford University Press.

Clifford, Sir Hugh. 1904. *Further India: Being the Story of Exploration from the Earliest Times in Burma, Malaya, Siam, and Indo-China*. London: Lawrence and Bullen.

——. 1929. *Bushwacking and Other Asiatic Tales and Memories*. London: Harper and Brothers.

Clifford, James, and George E. Marcus, eds. 1986. *Writing Culture: The Poetics and Politics of Ethnography*. Berkeley: University of California Press.

Colchester, Marcus. 1990. "A Future on the Land: Logging and the Status of Native Customary Land in Sarawak." *Ilmu Masyarakat* 19: 36.

Colfer, Carol, and Richard G. Dudley, with Herri Hadikusumah, Rusydi, Niken Sakuntaladewi, and Amblani. 1993. *Shifting Cultivators of Indonesia: Marauders or Managers of the Forest?* Community Forestry Case Study Series, no. 6. Rome: United Nations Food and Agricultural Organization.

Colfer, Carol, and Herwasono Soedjito. 1995. "Food, Forests, and Fields in a Bornean Rainforest: Toward Appropriate Agroforesty Development." In *Borneo in Transition: People, Forests, Conservation, and Development,* edited by Christine Padoch and Nancy Lee Peluso, 162–81. Kuala Lumpur: Oxford University Press.

Conklin, Harold. 1980. *Ethnographic Atlas of Ifugao*. New Haven, Conn.: Yale University Press.

Corbin, Alain. 1998. *Village Bells: Sound and Meaning in the Nineteenth-Century French Countryside*. New York: Columbia University Press.

Coville, Elizabeth. 1979. "Changing the World with Words: Fishing and Healing Ritual in Kelantan." Master's thesis, Department of Anthropology, University of Chicago.

Cronon, William. 1983. *Changes in the Land: Indians, Colonists, and the Ecology of New England*. New York: Hill and Wang.

——. 1995a. "The Trouble with Wilderness; or, Getting Back to the Wrong Nature." In *Uncommon Ground: Toward Reinventing Nature,* edited by William Cronon, 69–90. New York: Norton.

——, ed. 1995b. *Uncommon Ground: Toward Reinventing Nature*. New York: Norton.

De Palma, Brian. 1998. "Canadian Indians Win a Ruling Vindicating Their Oral History." *New York Times*, 9 February.

Denevan, William M., and Christine Padoch, eds. 1987. *Swidden Fallow Agroforestry in Latin America: Advances in Economic Botany*. Vol. 5. New York: New York Botanical Garden.

Dentan, Robert K. 1968. *The Semai: A Nonviolent People of Malaya*. New York: Holt, Rinehart and Winston.

——. 1991. "Potential Food Sources for Foragers in Malaysian Rainforest: Sagos, Yams, and Lots of Little Things." *Bidr. Taal-, Land- en Volkenk* 147: 420–44.

——. 1992. "The Rise, Maintenance, and Destruction of a Peaceable Polity: A Preliminary Essay in Political Ecology." In *Aggression and Peacefulness in Humans and Other Primates*, edited by James Silverberg and J. P. Gray, 214–70. New York: Oxford University Press.

Dentan, Robert K., and Ong Hean Chooi. 1995. "Stewards of the Green and Beautiful World: A Preliminary Report on Semai Aboriculture and Its Policy Implications." In *Dimensions of Tradition and Development in Malaysia*, edited by Rokiah Talib and Tan Chee Beng, 53–124. Kuala Lumpur: Pelanduk.

Dentan, Robert K., Kirk Endicott, Alberto G. Gomes, and M. B. Hooker, eds. 1997. *Malaysia and the Original People*. Boston: Allyn and Bacon.

Dentan, Robert K., and Bah Tony (Anthony) Williams-Hunt. 1999. "Untransfiguring Death: A Case Study of Rape, Drunkenness, Development, and Homicide in an Apprehensive Void." RIMA *(Review of Indonesian and Malaysian Affairs)* 33 (1): 17–65.

Diffloth, Gerard. 1975. "Les Langues Mon-Khmer de Malaisie: Classifications historiques et innovations." *Asie du Sud-Est et Monde Insulindien* 6 (4): 1–18.

Dixon, Anthony, Hannah Rodoti, and Lee Silverman. 1991. "From Forest to Market: A Feasibility Study of the Development of Selected Non-Timber Forest Products from Borneo for the U.S. Market." Harvard Business School, student paper, Project Borneo.

Djuweng, Stepanus. 1992. "Dayak, Dyak, Daya', dan Daya: Cermin Kekaburan Sebuah Identitas." *Kalimantan Review* 1 (1).

Dove, Michael R. 1983. "Theories of Swidden Agriculture and the Political Economy of Ignorance." *Agroforestry Systems* 1 (2): 85–99.

——. 1985a. "The Agroecological Mythology of the Javanese and the Political Economy of Indonesia." *Indonesia* 39 (April): 1–36.

——. 1985b. *Swidden Agriculture in Indonesia: The Subsistence Strategies of the Kalimantan Kantu*. Berlin: Mouton.

——. 1986a. "The Ideology of Agricultural Development in Indonesia." In *Central Government and Local Development*, edited by C. MacAndrew. Singapore: Oxford University Press.

——. 1986b. "Peasant Versus Government Perception and Use of the Environment: A Case Study of Banjarese Ecology and River Basin Development in South Kaliman-tan." *Journal of Southeast Asian Studies* 17 (3): 113–36.

——. 1988. *The Real and Imagined Role of Culture in Development.* Honolulu: University of Hawai'i Press.

——. 1993a. "A Revisionist View of Tropical Deforestation and Development." *Environmental Conservation* 20 (1): 17–24.

——. 1993b. *Rubber Eating Rice, Rice Eating Rubber.* Paper presented to the Agrarian Studies Seminar, Yale University, September.

——. 1993c. "Smallholder Rubber and Swidden Agriculture in Borneo: A Sustainable Adaptation to the Ecology and Economy of the Tropical Forest." *Economic Botany* 47 (2): 136–47.

——. 1994. "Marketing the Rainforest: 'Green' Panacea or Red Herring?" *Asia Pacific Issues* 13: 1–7.

——. 1995. "So Far from Power, So Near to the Forest: A Structural Analysis of Gain and Blame in Tropical Forest Development." In *Borneo in Transition: People, Forests, Conservation, and Development,* edited by Christine Padoch and Nancy Lee Peluso, 41–58. Kuala Lumpur: Oxford University Press.

Down to Earth. 1999. Special issue on Indonesia's Congress of Indigenous Peoples of the Archipelago. October. Penang: Asia-Pacific Peoples' Environment Network.

Doyle, Patrick. 1879. *Tin Mining in Larut.* London: E. and F. N. Spon.

Dunn, F. L. 1975. *Rain-Forest Collectors and Traders: A Study of Resource Utilization in Modern and Ancient Malaya.* Monograph no. 5. Kuala Lumpur: Malaysian Branch of the Royal Asiatic Society of Great Britain.

Echols, John M., and Shadily Hassan. 1989. *An Indonesian–English Dictionary.* Ithaca, N.Y.: Cornell University Press.

Edo, Juli. 1998. "Claiming Our Ancestor's Land: An Ethnohistorical Study of Seng-oi Land Rights in Perak Malaysia." Ph.D. dissertation, Australian National University.

Ellen, Roy. 1986. "What Black Elk Left Unsaid: On the Illusionary Images of Green Primitivism." *Anthropology Today* 2 (6): 8–19.

——. 1988. "Foraging, Starch Extraction, and the Sedentary Lifestyle in the Lowland Rainforest of Central Seram." In *Hunters and Gatherers,* vol. 1, *History, Evolution, and Social Change,* edited by Tim Gold et al., 117–34. Oxford: Berg.

Ellickson, Robert C. 1991. *Order without Law: How Neighbors Settle Disputes.* Cambridge, Mass.: Harvard University Press.

Endicott, Kirk. 1979a. *Batek Negrito Religion: The World-View and Rituals of a Hunting and Gathering People of Peninsular Malaysia.* Oxford: Clarendon.

——. 1979b. "The Impact of Economic Modernization on the Orang Asli (Aborigines) of Northern Peninsular Malaysia." In *Issues in Malaysian Development,* edited by James C. Jackson and Martin Rudner, 167–204. Singapore: Heinemann Educational Books.

———. 1983. "The Effects of Slave Raiding on the Aborigines of the Malay Peninsula." In *Slavery, Bondage, and Dependency in Southeast Asia,* edited by Anthony Reid, 216–45. Brisbane: University of Queensland Press.

Escobar, Arturo. 1995. *Encountering Development: The Making and Unmaking of the Third World.* Princeton, N.J.: Princeton University Press.

———. 1996. "Constructing Nature: Elements for a Poststructural Political Ecology." In *Liberation Ecologies: Environment, Development, Social Movements,* edited by Michael Watts and Richard Peet, 46–58. London: Routledge.

Evernden, Neil. 1992. *The Social Creation of Nature.* Baltimore, Md.: Johns Hopkins University Press.

Ewald, François. 1991. "Norms, Discipline, and the Law." In *Law and the Order of Culture,* edited by Robert Post, 138–62. Berkeley: University of California Press.

Ex, Juron. 1992. "Report on Social Forestry among Villagers in Sanggau." Unpublished manuscript, for Deutsche Gezellschaft für Technische Zusammenarbeit.

Fairhead, James, and Melissa Leach. 1996. *Misreading the African Landscape: Society and Ecology in a Forest–Savanna Mosaic.* Cambridge: Cambridge University Press.

Faulstich, Paul. 1998. "Mapping the Mythological Landscape: An Aboriginal Way-of-Being in the World." *Ethics, Place, and Environment* 1 (2): 197–221.

Feld, Steven. 1984. "Sound Structure as Social Structure." *Ethnomusicology* 28 (3): 383–409.

———. 1990. *Sound and Sentiment: Birds, Weeping, Poetics, and Song in Kaluli Expression.* 2d ed. Philadelphia: University of Pennsylvania Press.

———. 1991. *Voices of the Rainforest: Bosavi, Papua, New Guinea.* Rykodisc compact disc, RCD 10173.

———. 2000. "Sound Worlds." In *Sound: The Darwin College Lectures,* edited by Patricia Kruth and Henry Stobart, 173–201. Cambridge: Cambridge University Press.

Feld, Steven, and Keith Basso, eds. 1996. *Senses of Place.* Santa Fe, N. M.: School of American Research Press.

Firth, Raymond. 1946. *Malay Fishermen: Their Peasant Economy.* London: K. Paul, Trench, Trubner.

Fish, Stanley. 1980. *Is There a Text in This Class? The Authority of Interpretive Communities.* Cambridge, Mass.: Harvard University Press.

Fitzpatrick, Daniel. 1997. "Disputes and Pluralism in Modern Indonesian Land Law." *Yale Journal of International Law* 22 (winter): 17–212.

Foreman, Dave, Howie Wolke, and Bart Koehler. 1991. "The Earth First! Wilderness Preserve System." *Wild Earth* (spring): 33–38.

"The Forest and Land Crisis Occurring in the Bentian [Region] as a Result of the Logging Industry." 1992. Unpublished manuscript.

Fortmann, Louise P. 1985. "The Tree Tenure Factor in Agroforestry with Particular Reference to Africa." *Agroforestry Systems* 2: 229–51.

———. 1990 . "Locality and Custom: Non-Aboriginal Claims to Customary Usufructuary Rights as a Source of Rural Protest." *Journal of Rural Studies* 6 (2): 195–208.

Fortmann, Louise P., and John W. Bruce, eds. 1988. *Whose Trees? Proprietary Dimensions of Forestry.* Boulder, Colo.: Westview Press.

Foucault, Michel. 1972. *The Archaeology of Knowledge.* Translated by A. M. S. Smith. London: Tavistock.

———. 1975. *The Birth of the Clinic.* New York: Random House.

———. 1980a. *The History of Sexuality.* Vol. 1. New York: Pantheon.

———. 1980b. *Power/Knowledge: Selected Interviews and Other Writings, 1972–1977.* Edited and translated by Colin Gordon. Brighton, U.K.: Harvester.

———. 1980c. "Questions on Geography." In *Power/Knowledge: Selected Interviews and Other Writings, 1972–1977,* edited and translated by Colin Gordon, 63–77. New York: Pantheon.

Frank, Andre Gunder. 1998. *ReOrient: Global Economy in the Asian Age.* Berkeley: University of California Press.

Freeman, J. D. 1955. *Iban Agriculture: A Report on the Shifting Cultivation of Hill Rice by the Iban of Sarawak.* London: HMSO.

Fried, Stephanie G. 1992a. *Social and Economic Aspects of Rattan Production in the Middle Mahakam Region: A Preliminary Survey.* German Forestry Group Report 21 (November). Samarinda.

———. 1992b. *The Social Organization of Bentian Dayak Rattan Producers in East Kalimantan.* German Forestry Group Report 21 (November). Samarinda.

———. 2000. "Tropical Forests Forever? A Contextual Ecology of Bentian Rattan Agroforestry Systems." In *People, Plants, and Justice: The Politics of Nature Conservation,* edited by Charles Zerner, 204–33. New York: Columbia University Press.

Geddes, William. 1954. *Report on the Land Dayaks of the First Division.* Kuching: Colonial Printing Office.

———. 1957. *Nine Dayak Nights.* Melbourne: Oxford University Press.

Geertz, Clifford. 1963. *Agricultural Involution: The Processes of Ecological Change in Indonesia.* Berkeley: University of California Press.

Gianno, Rosemary. 1990. *Semelai Culture and Resin Technology.* New Haven, Conn.: Connecticut Academy of Arts and Sciences.

Goldman, Michael. 1997. "Customs in Common: The Epistemic World of the Commons Scholars." *Theory and Society* 26 (1): 1–37.

Gomes, Alfred. 1989. "Things Are Not What They Seem: Semai Economy in the 1980s." *Akademika* 35: 47–54.

——. 1990. "Confrontation and Continuity: Simple Commodity Production among the Orang Asli." In *Tribal Peoples and Development in Southeast Asia,* edited by Lim Teck Ghee and Albert G. Gomes, 12–36. Special issue of *Manusia and Masyarakat.* Kuala Lumpur: University of Malaya, Department of Anthropology and Sociology.

Griffiths, John. 1986. "What Is Legal Pluralism?" *Journal of Legal Pluralism* 24: 1–56.

Guha, Ramachandra. 1990. *The Unquiet Woods: Ecological Change and Peasant Resistance in the Indian Himalaya.* Berkeley: University of California Press.

Hale, Charles R. 1994. "*Wan Tasaya Dukiara:* Contested Notions of Land Rights in Miskitu History." In *Remapping Memory: The Politics of TimeSpace,* edited by J. Boyarin, 67–98. Minneapolis: University of Minnesota Press.

Hall, Stuart. 1996. "On Postmodernism and Articulation: An Interview with Stuart Hall." In *Stuart Hall: Critical Dialogues in Cultural Studies,* edited by D. Morley and K. Chen, 131–50. London: Routledge.

Hanks, William F. 1990. *Referential Practice: Language and Lived Space among the Maya.* Chicago: University of Chicago Press.

Haraway, Donna. 1989. *Primate Visions.* New York: Routledge.

——. 1991. *Simians, Cyborgs, and Women: The Reinvention of Nature.* London: Routledge.

Harley, J. B. 1988. "Maps, Knowledge, and Power." In *The Iconography of Landscape: Essays on the Symbolic Representation, Design, and Use of Past Environments,* edited by Denis Cosgrove and Stephen Daniels, 277–312. Cambridge: Cambridge University Press.

——. 1989. "Deconstructing the Map." *Cartographica* 26 (2): 1–20.

——. 1992. "Deconstructing the Map." In *Writing Worlds: Discourse, Text, and Metaphor in the Representation of Landscapes,* edited by Trevor J. Barnes and James S. Duncan, 231–47. London: Routledge.

Harrison, Regina. 1989. *Signs, Songs, and Memory in the Andes: Translating Quechua Language and Culture.* Austin: University of Texas Press.

Harrison, Robert. 1992. *Forests: The Shadow of Civilization.* Chicago: University of Chicago Press.

Hecht, Susanna, Anthony Anderson, and Peter May. 1988. "The Subsidy from Nature: Shifting Cultivation, Successional Palm Forests, and Rural Development." *Human Organization* 47 (1): 25–35.

Hecht, Susanna, and Alexander Cockburn. 1989. *The Fate of the Forest: Developers, Destroyers, and Defenders of the Amazon.* London: Verso.

Heryanto, Ariel. 1988. "The 'Development' of Development," translated by N. Lutz. *Indonesia* 46 (October).

Hibbets, Bernard J. 1992. "'Coming to Our Senses': Communication and Legal Expression in Performance Cultures." *Emory Law Journal* 41: 873–960.

Hodgen, Margaret T. 1964. *Early Anthropology in the Sixteenth and Seventeenth Centuries.* Philadelphia: University of Pennsylvania Press.

Hood Salleh. 1990. "The Orang Asli of Malaysia: An Overview of Recent Development Policy and its Impact." In *Tribal Peoples and Development in Southeast Asia,* edited by Lim Teck Ghee and Albert G. Gomes, 141–91. Special issue of *Manusia and Masyarakat.* Kuala Lumpur: University of Malaya, Department of Anthropology and Sociology.

Hood Salleh, and Hasan Mat Nor. 1984. "Roads Are for Development? Some Aspects of Jah Het Social Change." *Development Forum* 14 (1): 19–27.

Hooker, M. B. 1991. "The Orang Asli and the Laws of Malaysia: With Special Reference to Land" (English translation). *Ilmu Masyarakat* 18: 51–79.

Horridge, Adrian. 1985. *The Prahu: Traditional Sailing Boat of Indonesia Singapore.* Oxford: Oxford University Press.

Howell, Signe. [1984] 1989a. *Society and Cosmos: Chewong of Peninsular Malaysia.* Chicago: University of Chicago Press.

———. 1989b. "To Be Angry Is Not To Be Human, But To Be Fearful Is: Chewong Concepts of Human Nature." In *Societies at Peace: An Anthropological Perspective,* edited by Signe Howell and Roy Willis, 45–59. London: Routledge and Kegan Paul.

Hymes, Dell. 1975. "Breakthrough into Performance." In *Folklore: Performance and Communication,* edited by Dan Ben Amos and Kenneth Goldstein, 11–74. The Hague: Mouton.

Jessup, Timothy, and Nancy Peluso. 1986. "Minor Forest Products as Common Property Resources in East Kalimantan, Indonesia." In *Proceedings of the Conference on Common Property Management,* 505–31. Washington, D.C.: National Academy Press.

Johannes, Robert E., and Michael Riepen. 1995. *Environmental, Economic, and Social Implications of the Live Fish Trade in Asia and the Western Pacific.* Consultants' Report to the Nature Conservancy and the South Pacific Forum Fisheries Agency.

Jones, Alun. 1968. "The Orang Asli: An Outline of Their Progress in Modern Malaya." *Journal of Southeast Asian History* 9 (2): 268–92.

Kallo, Abdul Majid. 1988. "Penguasaan Laut Di Teluk Mandar, Periode 1950–1975: Kasus Desa Labuang, Kecamatan Banggae, Kabupaten Majene" (Sea Control in the Mandar Gulf, Period 1950–1975: The Case of Desa Labuang, Banggae District, Majene Regency). Unpublished manuscript, Ujung Pandang, Proyek Pengkajian Dan Pengembangan Masyarakat Pantai (Social Science Institute, Hasanuddin University).

———. 1990. *Nelayan Mandar: Suatu Studi Tentang Organisasi Kerja Nelayan Di Keluruahn Labuang Kabupaten Majene (Mandar Sailors: A Study of Sailors' Labor Organizations in Labuang Area, Majene Regency).* Ujung Pandang: Hasanuddin University.

Keck, Margaret. 1995. "Social Equity and Environmental Politics in Brazil: Lessons from the Rubber Tappers of Acre." *Comparative Politics* 27 (4): 409–24.

Keck, Miriam, and K. Sikkink. 1998. *Activists beyond Borders: Activist Networks in International Politics.* Ithaca, N.Y.: Cornell University Press.

Keil, Charles, and Steven Feld. 1993. *Music Grooves: Essays and Dialogues.* Chicago: University of Chicago Press.

Kessler, Clive S. 1978. *Islam and Politics in a Malay State: Kelantan, 1838–1969.* Ithaca, N.Y.: Cornell University Press.

King, Victor T. 1993. *The Peoples of Borneo.* Oxford: Blackwell.

Kingsbury, Benedict. 1998. "Indigenous Peoples in International Law: A Constructivist Approach to the Asian Controversy." *The American Journal of International Law* 92 (3): 414–57.

Klein, Deborah. N.d. "Listening to the Land: The Politics of Representing Soundscapes." Unpublished manuscript, Department of Anthropology, University of California at Santa Cruz.

KUD. 1990. "Bentian Rattan Proposal," 5.

Kuipers, Joel. 1990. *Power in Performance: The Creation of Textual Authority in Weyewa Ritual Speech.* Philadelphia: University of Pennsylvania Press.

Kuletz, Valerie. 1998. *The Tainted Desert: Environmental and Social Ruin in the American West.* New York: Routledge.

Laderman, Carol. 1981. "Symbolic and Empirical Reality: A New Approach to the Analysis of Food Avoidances." *American Ethnologist* 8 (3): 468–93.

Lahjie, Abubakar M., and Bertold Seibert. 1988. *Agroforestry: Untuk Pembangunan Daerah Pedesaan di Kalimantan Timur.* Proceedings of Forestry Seminar held 19–22 September, at Fakultas Kehutanan, Universitas Mulawarman, Samarinda, East Kalimantan, with GTZ (German Technical Assistance), German Forestry Group. Pontianak: Deutsche Gezellschaft für Technische Zusammenarbeit.

Lambut, M. P. 1992. "Perlukah Mendayyakkan Orang Dayak?" *Kalimantan Review* 2 (1).

Leach, Melissa. 1995. *Rainforest Relations: Gender and Resource Management among the Gola of Sierra Leone.* Washington, D.C.: Smithsonian Institution Press.

Leach, Melissa, and Robin Mearns, eds. 1996. *The Lie of the Land: Challenging Received Wisdom on the African Environment.* Bloomington: Indiana University Press.

Leach, T. A. [1919] 1988. "Date-Trees in Halfa Province." In *Whose Trees? Proprietary Dimensions of Forestry,* edited by Louise P. Fortmann and John W. Bruce, 43–48. Boulder, Colo.: Westview.

Leaman, Danna J., Razali Yusuf, and Harini Sangat-Roemantyo. 1991. *Kenya Dayak Forest Medicines.* Jakarta: World Wide Fund for Nature/Indonesia Programme.

Leary, John D. 1995. *Violence and the Dream People: The Orang Asli in the Malayan Emer-*

gency, 1948–1960. Monographs in International Studies, Southeast Asia Series, no. 95. Athens: Center for International Studies, Ohio University.

Lev, Daniel. 1972. "Judicial Institutions and Legal Culture in Indonesia." In *Culture and Politics in Indonesia,* edited by Claire Holt. Ithaca, N.Y.: Cornell University Press.

———. 1976. "Origins of Indonesian Advocacy." *Indonesia* 21 (April).

Levang, P., and Riskan Marten. 1984. *Agro-Economic Survey of a Transmigration Center on South Kalimantan.* Jakarta: Indonesia–Orston Transmigration Project.

Li, Tania Murray. 2000. "Constituting Tribal Space: Indigenous Identity and Resource Politics in Indonesia." *Comparative Studies in Society and History* 42 (1): 149–79.

Lindblad, J. T. 1988. *Between Dayak and Dutch: The Economic History of Southeast Kalimantan, 1880–1942.* Dordrecht: Foris Publications.

Lopa, Baharuddin. 1982. *Hukum Laut, Pelayaran Dan Perniagaan (Law of the Sea, Sailing and Trade).* Bandung: Penerbit Alumni.

Lowe, Celia. 1997. "Conservation in a Trans-locality: Mobility and Sea Cucumber Harvests in Sulawesi." Paper presented at panel of the American Anthropological Association: Space, Identity, and Natural Resource Politics in Southeast Asia, Washington, D.C.

———. 2000. "Global Markets, Local Injustice in Southeast Asian Seas: The Live Fish Trade and Local Fishers in the Togean Islands of Sulawesi." In *People, Plants, and Justice: The Politics of Nature Conservation*, edited by Charles Zerner. New York: Columbia University Press.

———. Forthcoming. "The Magic of Place: Sama at Sea, on Land in Sulawesi." *Journal of Southeast Asian Studies.*

Lynch, Owen. 1992. "Securing Community-based Tenurial Rights in the Tropical Forests of Asia." *Issues in Development Report.* Washington, D.C.: World Resources Institute.

Lynch, Owen, and Kirk Talbott. 1995. *Balancing Acts: Community-based Forest Management and National Law in Asia and the Pacific.* Washington, D.C.: World Resources Institute.

Magenda, Burhan. 1991. *East Kalimantan: The Decline of a Commercial Aristocracy.* Cornell Modern Indonesia Project, monograph no. 70. Ithaca, N.Y.: Cornell Modern Indonesia Project.

Maine, Sir Henry. 1861. *Ancient Law.* London: Murray.

Malaysia. Department of Statistics. 2000. *Yearbook of Statistics, Malaysia.* Kuala Lumpur: Malaysia Department of Statistics.

Malkki, Lisa. 1992. "National Geographic: The Rooting of Peoples and the Territorialization of National Identity." *Cultural Anthropology* 7 (1): 24–44.

Manguin, Pierre-Yves. 1993. "The Vanishing Jong: Insular Southeast Asian Fleets in Trade and War (Fifteenth to Seventeenth Centuries)." In *Southeast Asia in the*

Early Modern Era: Trade, Power, and Belief, edited by Anthony Reid, 197–213. Ithaca, N.Y.: Cornell University Press.

McKay, Bonnie M., and James M. Acheson. 1987. *The Question of the Commons: The Culture and Ecology of Communal Resources.* Tucson: University of Arizona Press.

Merry, Sally. 1988. "Legal Pluralism." *Law and Society Review* 22 (5): 869–96.

——. 1996. "Legal Vernacularization and Ka Ho'okolokolonui Kanaka Maoli, the People's International Tribunal, Hawai'i, 1993." *PoLAR (Political and Legal Anthropology Review)* 19: 68.

——. 1997. "Legal Pluralism and Transnational Culture: The Ka Ho'okolokolonui Kanaka Maoli Tribunal." In *Human Rights, Culture, and Context: Anthropological Perspectives,* edited by Richard A. Wilson, 28–48. London: Pluto Press.

Meyer, Judith. 1989. *Rattan Cultivation, Family Economy, and Land Use: A Case from Pasir, East Kalimantan.* Forestry and Forest Products, GFG Report 13 (June).

Michon, Genevieve, and Hubert de Foresta. 2000. "The Damar Forests of Krui, Indonesia: Justice for Forest Farmers." In *People, Plants, and Justice: The Politics of Nature Conservation,* edited by Charles Zerner, 159–203. New York: Columbia University Press.

Mitchell, W. J. T., ed. 1994. *Landscape and Power.* Chicago: University of Chicago Press.

Moniaga, Sandra. 1993. "Toward Community-based Forestry and Recognition of Adat Property Rights in the Outer Islands of Indonesia: A Legal and Policy Analysis." In *Legal Frameworks for Forest Management in Asia: Case Studies of Community–State Relations,* edited by Jefferson Fox, 131–50. Program on the Environment, Occasional Paper no. 16. Honolulu: Environment and Policy Institute, East-West Center.

Monmonnier, Mark. 1991. *How To Lie with Maps.* Chicago: University of Chicago Press.

Moore, Sally Falk. 1986. *Social Facts and Fabrications: "Customary" Law on Kilimanjaro, 1880–1980.* Cambridge: Cambridge University Press.

Morphy, Howard. 1991. *Ancestral Connections: Art and an Aboriginal System of Knowledge.* Chicago: University of Chicago Press.

Myers, Fred R. 1986. *Pintupi Country, Pintupi Self: Sentiment, Place, and Politics among Western Desert Aborigines.* Washington, D.C.: Smithsonian Institution Press.

Myers, Norman. 1992. *The Primary Source: Tropical Forests and Our Future.* New York: Norton.

Nabhan, Gary Paul. 1982. *The Desert Smells Like Rain: A Naturalist in Papago Indian Country.* San Francisco: North Point Press.

——. 1997. *Cultures of Habitat: On Nature, Culture, and Society.* Washington, D.C.: Counterpoint.

Nasir, Josia. 1991a. *Bertanam Rotan Menurut Tradisi Petani Bentian.* Gaharu Bulletin 2. Samarinda, East Borneo: PLASMA.

——. 1991b. *Tradisi Pemilikan dan Pengolahan Tanah Pada Masyarakat Dayak Bentian.*

Gaharu Bulletin 2. Samarinda, East Borneo: Lembaga Pengembangan Lirakungan dan Sumbodaya Monusia (PLASMA).

National Research Council. 1986. *Proceedings of the Conference on "Common Property Resource Management."* Washington, D.C.: National Academy Press.

Nedelsky, Jennifer. 1990. "Law, Boundaries, and the Bounded Self." In *Law and the Order of Culture,* edited by Robert Post, 162–90. Berkeley: University of California Press.

Nepstad, Daniel, and Stephen Schwartzman. 1992a. "Non-Timber Forest Products as Sustainable Management Strategies." In *Non-Timber Forest Products from Tropical Forests: Evaluation of a Conservation and Development Strategy,* vol. 9, *Advances in Economic Botany,* edited by Daniel Nepstad and Stephen Schwartzman, 3. New York: New York Botanical Garden.

——, eds. 1992b. *Non-Timber Forest Products from Tropical Forests: Evaluation of a Conservation and Development Strategy.* New York, N.Y.: New York Botanical Garden.

Neumann, Roderick. 1992. "The Political Ecology of Wildlife Conservation in the Mount Meru Area of Tanzania." *Land Degradation and Rehabilitation* 3 (2): 85–98.

——. 1995. "Ways of Seeing Africa: Colonial Recasting of African Society and Landscape in Serengeti National Park." *Ecumene* 2: 149–69.

——. 1996. "Dukes, Earls, and Ersatz Edens: Aristocratic Nature Preservationists in Colonial Africa." *Society and Space* 14: 79–98.

Ngo, T. H. G. Mering. 1992. "Inilah Peladang." *Kalimantan Review* 2 (1).

Nicholas, Colin. 1990. "In the Name of the Semai? The State and Semai Society in Peninsular Malaysia." In *Tribal Peoples and Development in Southeast Asia,* edited by Lim Teck Ghee and Albert G. Gomes, 68–88. Special issue of *Manusia and Masyarakat.* Kuala Lumpur: University of Malaya, Department of Anthropology and Sociology.

——. 1997. *The Orang Asli of Peninsular Malaysia.* http://www.xlibris.de/magickriver/oa.htm.

Noone, H. D. 1936. "Report on the Settlement and Welfare of the Ple-Temiar Senoi of the Perak-Kelantan Watershed." *Journal of the Federated Malay States Museums* 19 (part 1): 1–85 and map.

Oakerson, Ronald J. 1986. "A Model for Analysis of Common Property Problems." In *Proceedings of the Conference on Common Property Management,* edited by Panel on Common Property, 3–30. Washington, D.C.: National Academy of Sciences.

Obi, Chinwuba. 1963. *The Ibo Law of Property.* London: Butterworths.

Okoth-Ogendo, H. W. O. 1989. "Some Issues of Theory in the Study of Tenure Relations in African Agriculture." *Africa* 59 (1): 6–17.

Olwig, Kenneth R. 1993. "Harmony, 'Quintessence,' and Children's Acquisition of Concern for the 'Natural' Environment." *Children's Environments* 10: 60–71.

———. 1995. "Reinventing Nature: Yosemite and Mount Rushmore—A Meandering Tale of a Double Nature." In *Uncommon Ground: Toward Reinventing Nature,* edited by William Cronon, 379–408. New York: Norton.

Ong, Walter J. 1977. *Interfaces of the Word: Studies in the Evolution of Consciousness and Culture.* Ithaca, N.Y.: Cornell University Press.

———. 1982. *Orality and Literacy: The Technologizing of the Word.* New York: Methuen.

Ostrom, Elinor. 1990. *Governing the Commons: The Evolution of Institutions for Collective Action.* New York: Cambridge University Press.

Padoch, Christine. 1983. *Migration and Its Alternatives Among the Iban of Sarawak.* The Hague: Martinus Nijhoff.

———. 1994. "Woodlands of Tae: Traditional Forest Management in Kalimantan." In *Forest Resources and Wood-based Biomass Energy as Rural Development Assets.* New Delhi: Oxford University Press.

Padoch, Christine, and Nancy Lee Peluso. 1995. "Changing Resource Rights in Managed Forests of Kalimantan." In *Borneo in Transition: People, Forests, Conservation, and Development,* edited by Nancy Peluso and Christine Padoch, 121–33. Singapore: Oxford University Press.

Padoch, Christine, and Charles Peters. 1993. "Managed Forests of West Kalimantan, Indonesia." In *Perspectives on Biodiversity: Case Studies of Genetic Resources for Conservation and Development,* edited by Christopher S. Potter, Joel I. Cohen, and Dianne Janczewski, 167–76. Washington, D.C.: American Association for the Advancement of Science.

Padoch, Christine, and Miguel Pinedo-Vasquez. 1996. "Managing Forest Remnants and Forest Gardens in Peru and Indonesia." In *Forest Patches in Tropical Landscapes,* edited by John Schelhas and Russell Greenberg, 327–42. Washington, D.C.: Island Press.

Pandya, Vishvajit. 1990. "Movement and Space: Andamanese Cartography." *American Ethnologist* 17 (4): 775–97.

Pantir, Titus. 1988. "Abandoned Lands, Productive Lands, and Shifting Cultivation in East Kalimantan." *Manuntung.*

———. 1990. "Hak Milik Menurut Hukum Adat Ditinjau Dari UUPA No. 5/1960" (Ownership Rights According to Adat Law as Viewed from [National] Basic Agrarian Law No. 5/1960). Manuscript prepared for seminar Adat Masyarakat Dayak Kabupaten Kutai, Tenggarong.

Parmentier, Richard J. 1987. *The Sacred Remains: Myth, History, and Polity in Belau.* Chicago: University of Chicago Press.

Pearce, Roy Harvey. [1953] 1988. *Savagism and Civilization: A Study of the Indian and the American Mind.* Berkeley: University of California Press.

Peluso, Nancy L. 1983. "Markets and Merchants: The Forest Products Trade of East Kalimantan in Historical Perspective." Master's thesis, Cornell University.

——. 1992a. "The Ironwood Problem: (Mis) Management and Development of an Extractive Rainforest Product." *Conservation Biology* 6 (2): 210–19.

——. 1992b. "The Political Ecology of Extraction and Extractive Reserves in East Kalimantan, Indonesia." *Development and Change* 23 (4): 49–74.

——. 1992c. "Rattan Trade in East Kalimantan, Indonesia: Can Extraction Be Reserved?" In *Non-Timber Products from Tropical Forests: Evaluation of a Conservation and Development Strategy*, edited by Daniel C. Nepstad and Stephen Schwartzman. New York, N.Y.: New York Botanical Garden.

——. 1992d. *Rich Forests, Poor People: Resource Control and Resistance in Java.* Berkeley: University of California Press.

——. 1993. "Coercing Conservation: The Politics of State Resource Control." *Global Environmental Change* 4 (2): 199–218.

——. 1995. "Whose Woods Are These? Counter-Mapping Forest Territories in Kalimantan, Indonesia." *Antipode* 27 (4): 383–406.

——. 1996. "Custom, Property, and Forestry in Southeast Asia." Paper presented at 6th Meeting of the International Association of Common Property, 5–8 June 1996, University of California at Berkeley.

——. Forthcoming. "Weapons of the Wild: Violence and Wildness in the Rainforests of Indonesian Borneo." In *In Search of the Rainforest,* edited by Candace Slater. Durham, N.C.: Duke University Press.

Peluso, Nancy Lee, and Emily Harwell. 2001. "Territory, Custom, and the Cultural Politics of Ethnic War in West Kalimantan, Indonesia." In *Violent Environments,* edited by Nancy Lee Peluso and Michael Watts. Ithaca, N.Y.: Cornell University Press.

Peluso, Nancy L., and Timothy C. Jessup. 1985. "Ecological Patterns and the Property Status of Minor Forest Products in East Kalimantan, Indonesia." Paper presented at BOSID–NRC Conference on Common Property Resource Management, Annapolis, Maryland.

Peluso, Nancy Lee, and Christine Padoch. 1996. "Changing Resource Rights in Managed Forests of West Kalimantan." In *Borneo in Transition: People, Forests, Conservation, and Development*, edited by Christine Padoch and Nancy Lee Peluso. Kuala Lumpur: Oxford University Press.

Peluso, Nancy Lee, and P. Vandergeest. 2001. "Genealogies of the Political Forest and Customary Rights in Indonesia, Malaysia, and Thailand." *Journal of Asian Studies* 61 (3): 761–812.

Peluso, Nancy L., and Michael John Watts, eds. 2001. *Violent Environments.* Ithaca, N.Y.: Cornell University Press.

Pemberton, John. 1994. *On the Subject of "Java."* Ithaca, N.Y.: Cornell University Press.

Peters, Charles. 1994. *A Practitioner's Guide to Tropical Forest Ecology.* Washington, D.C.: World Wildlife Fund Biodiversity Support Network.

Peters, Pauline. 1992. "Manoeuvres and Debates in the Interpretation of Land Rights in Botswana." *Africa* 62 (3): 413–34.

Picard, Michel. 1990. "Cultural Tourism in Bali: Cultural Performances as Tourist Attraction." *Indonesia* 49 (April): 37–74.

Pickett, Steward T., V. Thomas Parker, and Peggy L. Fiedler. 1992. "The New Paradigm in Ecology: Implications for Conservation Biology above the Species Level." In *Conservation Biology: The Theory and Practice of Nature Conservation, Preservation, and Management,* edited by D. Fiedler and K. Jain, 66–88. New York: Chapman and Hall.

Pollan, Michael. 1991. *Second Nature: A Gardener's Education.* New York: Atlantic Monthly Press.

Posey, Darrell. 1985. "Indigenous Forest Management among the Kayapo." *Agroforestry Systems* 3 (2): 132–58.

———. 1989. "Forest Islands." In *People of the Tropical Rainforest,* edited by Julie Denslow and Christine Padoch. Berkeley: University of California Press.

Pospisil, Leopold. 1971. *The Anthropology of Law: A Comparative Theory at Law.* New York: Harper and Row.

———. 1981. "Modern and Traditional Administration of Justice in New Guinea." *Journal of Legal Pluralism* 19: 93–116.

Potter, Leslie. 1987a. "Banjarese Swidden Cultivators in South Kalimantan." In *Land Degradation and Society,* edited by Piers Blaikie and Harold Brookfield. London: Methuen.

———. 1987b. "Land Degradation, Innovation, and Social Welfare in the Riam Kiwa Valley, South Kalimantan, Indonesia." In *Land Degradation and Society,* edited by Piers Blaikie and Harold Brookfield, 164–75. London: Methuen.

Priasukmana, S., Amblani. 1988. "Budidaya Rotan Sega di Daerah Bentian, Kalimantan Timur." *Wanatrop* 3 (2): 55–72.

Proctor, James D. 1995. "Whose Nature? The Contested Moral Terrain of Ancient Forests." In *Uncommon Ground: Toward Reinventing Nature,* edited by William Cronon, 269–97. New York: Norton.

Putusan Perkara Pengadilan Negeri Majene (PPPNM) (Case Decision of the Majene District Court). 1987. No. 11/Pid/B/1987/PNM. Kabupaten Majene, Sulawesi Selatan.

Rachagan, S. Sothi. 1990. "Constitutional and Statutory Provisions Governing the Orang Asli." In *Tribal Peoples and Development in Southeast Asia,* edited by Lim Teck Ghee and Albert G. Gomes, 101–11. Special issue of *Manusia and Masyarakat.* Kuala Lumpur: University of Malaya, Department of Anthropology and Sociology.

Rambo, W. E. 1899. "Apis Dorsata Caught at Last." *Gleanings in Bee Culture* 27 (1 June): 425.

Rashid, Razha, ed. 1995. *Indigenous Minorities of Peninsular Malaysia: Selected Issues and Ethnographies*. Kuala Lumpur: Intersocietal and Scientific Association.

Reid, Anthony. 1983. *Slavery, Bondage, and Dependency in Southeast Asia*. St. Lucia, Australia: Queensland University Press.

———. 1988. *Southeast Asia in the Age of Commerce 1450–1680*, vol. 1, *The Lands Below the Winds*. New Haven, Conn.: Yale University Press.

———, ed. 1993. *Southeast Asia in the Early Modern Era: Trade, Power, and Belief*. Ithaca, N.Y.: Cornell University Press.

Riker, James V. 1994. *State–NGO Relations and the Politics of Sustainable Development in Indonesia: An Examination of Political Space*. Working Paper Series on Development at a Crossroads: Uncertain Paths to Sustainability, no.15. Global Research Program, University of Wisconsin, Madison.

Roosevelt, Anna Curtenius. 1980. *Parmana: Prehistoric Maize and Manioc Subsistence along the Amazon and Orinoco*. New York: Academic Press.

———. 1997. *The Excavations at Corozal, Venezuela: Stratigraphy and Ceramic Seriation*. Yale University Publications in Anthropology, no. 83. New Haven, Conn.: Department of Anthropology and Peabody Museum, Yale University.

———. In press. "The Lower Amazon: A Dynamic Human Habitat." In *Pre-Columbian New World Ecosystems*, edited by M. Heckenberger. New York: Columbia University Press.

Rosaldo, Michelle Z. 1975. "It's All Uphill: The Creative Metaphors of Ilongot Magical Spells." In *Sociocultural Dimensions of Language Use*, edited by M. Sanches and B. Blount, 177–202. New York: Academic Press.

Rose, Carol M. 1994. *Property and Persuasion: Essays on the History, Theory, and Rhetoric of Ownership*. Boulder, Colo.: Westview Press.

Roseman, Marina. 1980. "Malay and Orang Asli Interactions: Views from Legendary History." Unpublished manuscript, Department of Anthropology, Cornell University.

———. 1984. "The Social Structuring of Sound." *Ethnomusicology* 28 (3): 411–45.

———. 1991. *Healing Sounds from the Malaysian Rainforest: Temiar Music and Medicine*. Berkeley: University of California Press.

———. 1995. *Dream Songs and Healing Sounds: In the Rainforests of Malaysia*. Smithsonian Folkways Recordings, SF CD 40417.

———. 2000. "Shifting Landscapes: Mediating Modernity in a Malaysian Rainforest." *Yearbook of Traditional Music* 32: 31–66.

———. 2001. "Making Sense Out of Modernity." *New Horizons in Medical Anthropology: Essays*, edited by Mark Nichter and Margaret Lock. New York: Routledge.

———. In press. *Engaging the Spirits of Modernity*. Berkeley: University of California Press.

Rousseau, Jerome. 1990. *Central Borneo: Ethnic Identity and Social Life in a Stratified Society*. Oxford: Clarendon Press.

Salafsky, N., O. L. Dugelby, and J. W. Terborgh. 1993. "Can Extractive Reserves Save the Rainforest? An Ecological and Socio-Economic Comparison of Non-Timber Forest Product Extraction Systems in Peten, Guatamala and West Kalimantan, Indonesia." *Conservation Biology* 7 (1): 39–52.

Sather, Clifford. 1993. "Trees and Tree Tenure in Paku Iban Society: The Management of Secondary Forest Resources in Long-established Iban Country." *Borneo Review* 1 (1): 16–40.

Schafer, R. Murray. 1977. *The Tuning of the World.* New York: Knopf.

Schama, Simon. 1995. *Landscape and Memory.* New York: Knopf.

Schieffelin, Edward L. 1976. *The Sorrow of the Lonely and the Burning of the Dancers.* New York: St. Martin's Press.

——. 1979. "Mediators as Metaphors: Moving a Man to Tears in Papua New Guinea." In *The Imagination of Reality: Essays in Southeast Asian Coherence Systems,* edited by A. L. Becker and A. Yengoyan, 127–44. Norwood, N.J.: Ablex.

Schirmer, Jennifer. 1994. "The Claiming of Space and the Body Politic within National Security States: The Plaza de Mayo Madres and the Greenham Common Women." In *Remapping Memory: The Politics of TimeSpace,* edited by J. Boyarin, 185–220. Minneapolis: University of Minnesota Press.

Schroeder, Richard A. 1993. "Shady Practice: Gender and the Political Ecology of Resource Stabilization in Gambian Garden/Orchards." *Economic Geography* 69 (4): 349–65.

Scott, Anthony. 1973. *Natural Resources: The Economics of Conservation.* Toronto: McClelland and Stewart Press.

Scott, James C. 1976. *The Moral Economy of the Peasant: Rebellion and Subsistence in Southeast Asia.* New Haven, Conn.: Yale University Press.

——. 1985. *Weapons of the Weak: Everyday Forms of Peasant Resistance.* New Haven, Conn.: Yale University Press.

——. 1990. *Domination and the Arts of Resistance: Hidden Transcripts.* New Haven, Conn.: Yale University Press.

——. 1998. *Seeing Like a State: How Certain Schemes to Improve the Human Condition Have Failed.* New Haven, Conn.: Yale University Press.

Shipton, Parker, and Mitzi Goheen. 1992. "Understanding African Landholding: Power, Wealth, and Meaning." *Africa* 62 (3): 307–27.

Siegel, James T. 1986. *Solo in the New Order: Language and Hierarchy in an Indonesian City.* Princeton, N.J.: Princeton University Press.

Silverstein, Michael. 1987. "Monoglot 'Standard' in America: Standardization and Metaphors of Linguistic Hegemony." Working Papers of the Center for Psychosocial Studies, no. 14. Chicago: Center for Psychosocial Studies.

Smith, Bruce R. 1999. *The Acoustic World of Early Modern England: Attending to the O-Factor.* Chicago: University of Chicago Press.

Smith, Neil. 1984. *Uneven Development: Nature, Capital, and the Production of Space.* Oxford: Basil Blackwell.

Soekanto, Soerjono. 1985. *Meninjau Hukum Adat Indonesia.* Jakarta: C. V. Rajawali.

Sonnenfeld, David A. 1993. "Conflict and Innovation: Social Movements' Influence on Adoption of Environmental Technologies." Chapter in "The Pulp and Paper Industries of Southeast Asia and Australia." Ph.D. dissertation, University of California at Santa Cruz.

Spyer, Patricia. 1996. "Diversity with a Difference: Adat and the New Order in Aru (Eastern Indonesia)." *Cultural Anthropology* 11 (1): 25–50.

Stewart, Kathleen C. 1996. *A Space on the Side of the Road: Cultural Poetics in an "Other" America.* Princeton, N.J.: Princeton University Press.

Talbott, Kirk, and Owen J. Lynch. 1995. *Balancing Acts: Community-based Forest Management and National Law in Asia and the Pacific.* Washington, D.C.: World Resources Institute.

Taylor, Diana. 1997. *Disappearing Acts: Spectacles of Gender and Nationalism in Argentina's "Dirty War."* Durham, N.C.: Duke University Press.

Tennant, Chris. 1994. "Indigenous Peoples, International Institutions, and the International Legal Literature from 1945–1993." *Human Rights Quarterly* 16 (1): 1–57.

Thompson, E. P. 1975. *Whigs and Hunters: The Origin of the Black Act.* London: Allen Lane Press.

The Time Is Now Group. 1994. *Setting the Agenda for a Peaceful Transition.* Claremont, Calif.: The House of Time.

Towne, William, and Wolfgang Kirchner. 1989. "Hearing in Honey Bees: Detection of Air Particle Oscillations." *Science* 244 (12 May): 686–88.

Triwahyudi, M. A. Muhshi, and H. A. Farchad (Tim Studi WALHI [Indonesian Environmental Forum Study Team]). 1992. *Peran HPH Dalam Pembangunan Ekonomi Regional Kalimantan Timur (The Role of the Forest Concession Right [HPH] in the Regional Economic Development of East Kalimantan).* Jakarta: WALHI.

Tsing, Anna L. 1984. "Politics and Culture in the Meratus Mountains." Ph.D. dissertation, Stanford University.

——. 1988. "Gender and Performance in Meratus Dispute Settlement." In *Power and Difference: Studies of Gender in Island Southeast Asia,* edited by J. M. Atkinson and S. Errington, 95–125. Stanford, Calif.: Stanford University Press.

——. 1990. "(Com)posing the Last Rainforest Peoples." Paper presented at the annual meeting of the American Anthropological Association, New Orleans, November.

——. 1993. *In the Realm of the Diamond Queen: Marginality in an Out-of-the-Way Place.* Princeton, N.J.: Princeton University Press.

——. 1994. "Magic and Management in Indonesia's Rainforests." Paper presented at the conference on Human Impacts on Global Environmental Change, University of Georgia, Athens, April.

———. 1995. "Empowering Nature, or, Some Gleanings in Bee Culture." In *Naturalizing Power,* edited by Carol Delaney and Sylvia Yanagisako, 114–43. New York: Routledge.

———. 1999. "Becoming a Tribal Elder and Other Green Development Fantasies." In *Transforming the Indonesian Uplands: Marginality, Power, and Production,* edited by Tania Murray Li, 159–202. Amsterdam: Harwood Academic.

———. 2002. "Land as Law: Negotiating the Meaning of Property in Indonesia." In *Land, Property, and the Environment,* edited by John Richards, 94–137. Oakland, Calif.: Institute for Contemporary Studies Press.

Turnbull, David. 1993. *Maps Are Territories: Science Is an Atlas.* Chicago: University of Chicago Press.

Urban, Greg. 1988. "Ritual Wailing in Amerindian Brazil." *American Anthropologist* 90 (2): 385–400.

Vandergeest, Peter. 1996. "Mapping Natures: Territorialization of Forest Rights in Thailand." *Society and Natural Resources* 9 (2): 159–76.

Volkman, Toby A. 1984. "Great Performances: Toraja Cultural Identity in the 1970s." *American Ethnologist* 11 (1): 152–69.

———. 1985. *Feasts of Honor: Ritual and Change in the Toraja Highlands.* Urbana: University of Illinois Press.

———. 1990. "Visions and Revisions: Toraja Culture and the Tourist Gaze." *American Ethnologist* 17 (1): 91–110.

———. 1994. "Our Garden Is the Sea: Contingency and Improvisation in Mandar Women's Work." *American Ethnologist* 21 (3): 564–85.

Volkman, Toby A., and Charles Zerner. 1988. "The Tree of Desire: A Toraja Ritual Poem." In *To Speak in Pairs: Essays on the Ritual Languages of Eastern Indonesia,* edited by James J. Fox, 282–305. Cambridge: Cambridge University Press.

Vollenhoven, Cornelius van. 1981. "Het adatrecht van Nederlandisch-Indie." In *Van Vollenhoven on Indonesian Adat Law,* edited and translated by J. F. Holleman. The Hague: Matinus Nijhoff.

Wan Hashim. 1988. *Peasants under Peripheral Capitalism.* Bangi, Selangor: Universiti Kebangsaan Malaysia.

Weiner, James F. 1991. *The Empty Place: Poetry, Space, and Being among the Foi of Papua, New Guinea.* Bloomington: Indiana University Press.

Weinstock, Joseph A. 1983a. "Kaharingan and the Lawangan Dayaks: Religion and Identity in Central-East Borneo." Ph.D. dissertation, Cornell University.

———. 1983b. "Rattan: Ecological Balance in a Borneo Rainforest Swidden." *Economic Botany* 37 (1): 58–68.

——. 1989a. "Shifting cultivation and agro-forestry in Indonesia, some notes and data." *Proceedings of the Joint Seminar on Watershed Research and Management.* Bogor and Balikpapan, Indonesia.

——. 1989b. *Study on Shifting Cultivation. Phase I and II.* Jakarta: FAO.

Wilkinson, R. J. 1959. *A Malay–English Dictionary.* 2 vols. London: Macmillan.

Williams, Raymond. 1973. *The Country and the City.* New York: Oxford University Press.

——. 1976. *Keywords: A Vocabulary of Culture and Society.* New York: Oxford University Press.

——. 1982. *Problems in Materialism and Culture.* London: Verso.

Winichakul, Thongchai. 1994. *Siam Mapped: A History of the Geo-Body of a Nation.* Honolulu: University of Hawai'i Press.

Wolf, Eric. 1982. *Europe and the People without History.* Berkeley: University of California Press.

Wolters, Oliver W. 1967. *Early Indonesian Commerce: A Study of the Origins of Srivijaya.* Ithaca, N.Y.: Cornell University Press.

——. 1982. *History, Culture, and Region in Southeast Asian Perspectives.* Singapore: Institute of Southeast Asian Studies.

Wood, Denis. 1992. *The Power of Maps.* New York: Guilford Press.

Woodward, David, and G. Malcolm Lewis, eds. 1998. *Cartography in the Traditional African, American, Arctic, Australian, and Pacific Societies,* vol. 2, bk. 3, *The History of Cartography.* Chicago: University of Chicago Press.

World Bank. 1994. *Indonesia, Environment, and Development: Challenges for the Future.* Environmental Unit, East Asia, and Pacific Region. March.

Worster, Donald. 1990. "The Ecology of Order and Chaos." *Environmental History Review* 14 (1/2): 1–18.

Wright, Michael, and David Western, eds. 1994. *Natural Connections: Community-based Resource Management.* Washington, D.C.: Island Press.

Yamada, Yoichi, ed. 2000. *Sound of Nature, Sound of Culture: Resounding with Environment.* Human Being and Environment Series, vol. 11. Kyoto: Shouwado Press.

Young, Oran. 1981. *Natural Resources and the State: The Political Economy of Resource Management.* Berkeley: University of California Press.

Zawawi Ibrahim. 1995. *Regional Development in Rural Malaysia and the "Tribal Question."* Hull, U. K.: Center for South-East Asian Studies, University of Hull.

——. 1996a. "The Making of a Subaltern Discourse in the Malaysian Nation-State: New Subjectivities and the Poetics of Orang Asli Dispossession and Identity." *Southeast Asian Studies* 34(3): 568–600.

——, ed. 1996b. *Kami Bukan Anti-Pembangunan! (Bicara Orang Asli Menuju Wawasan 2020).* Kuala Lumpur: Persatuan Sains Sosial Malaysia.

Zerner, Charles. 1981. "Signs of the Spirits, Signature of the Smith: Iron-forging in Tana Toraja." *Indonesia* 31 (April): 88–112.

——. 1987. "The Flying Fishermen of Mandar." *Cultural Survival Quarterly* 11 (2): 18–22.

——. 1990a. *Community Rights, Customary Law, and the Law of Timber Concessions in Indonesia's Forests: Legal Options and Alternatives in Designing the Commons.* Forestry Studies UTF/INS/065. Jakarta: Ministry of Forestry, Government of Indonesia and Food and Agriculture Organization of the United Nations.

——. 1990b. "Marine Tenure in the Makassar Strait: The Mandar Raft Fishery." Paper presented at 1st Annual Meeting of the International Association for the Study of Common Property, Duke University, Durham, N.C.

——. 1991a. "Key Issues in Indonesian Fisheries Law and Institutional Development: Implementation, Environmental Management, and the Rights of Small-Scale Fishers." Report for the Central Fisheries Research Institute, Ministry of Agriculture, Jakarta.

——. 1991b. "Sharing the Catch in Mandar: Social and Economic Changes in an Indonesian Raft Fishery (1970–89)." In *Sociocultural Aspects of Small-Scale Fisheries Development,* edited by R. Pollnac and J. Poggie, 42–70. Kingston: International Center for Marine Resource Development, University of Rhode Island.

——. 1992a. "Indigenous Forest-dwelling Peoples of Indonesia's Outer Islands: Livelihood, Rights, and Resource Management Institutions in the Era of Industrial Forest Exploitation." Forestry Sector Monograph. Washington, D.C.: World Bank.

——. 1992b. "Capital and Control Rights in Indonesian Fisheries: Javanese Cage Culture, Rock Wars in Sulawesian Seas, Mollusk Extraction in the Maluku Islands: Voices from South Sulawesi." Paper presented at 3rd Annual Meeting of the International Association for the Study of Common Property, Washington, D.C.

——. 1994a. "Through a Green Lens: The Construction of Customary Environmental Law and Community in Indonesia's Maluku Islands." *Law and Society Review* 28 (5): 1079–1122.

——. 1994b. "Transforming Customary Law in the Maluku Islands, Indonesia, 1870–1992." In *Natural Connections: Community-based Resource Management*, edited by M. Wright and D. Western. Washington, D.C.: Island Press.

——. 1994c. "Telling Stories about Biological Diversity." In *Valuing Local Knowledge: Indigenous Peoples and Intellectual Property Rights,* edited by Stephen Brush and Doreen Stabinsky. Washington, D.C.: Island Press.

——. 1996. "Of Men, Mollusks, and the Marine Environment in the Maluku Islands: Customary Law and Institutions in Eastern Indonesia." In *Nature and the Orient: Essays on the Environmental History of South and Southeast Asia,* edited by Richard Grove, Vaneeta Damodaran, and Satpal Sangwen, 534–72. Oxford: Oxford University Press.

——. 1997. "Shares, Sites, and Property Rights in Mandar: Changes in an Indonesian Deep Water Raft Fishery (1970–1989)." In *Fish Aggregating Devices in Developing*

Fisheries: Potentials and Pitfalls, edited by R. Pollnac and J. Poggie. Kingston: International Center for Marine Resource Development, University of Rhode Island.

———. 1998. "Moving Translations: Representing Communities in Indonesian State Law and Customary Law." Paper presented at Annual Meeting of the Law and Society Association, Aspen, Colo.

———. 1999. *Justice and Conservation: Insights from People, Plants, and Justice.* New York: The Rainforest Alliance.

———, ed. 2000. *People, Plants, and Justice: The Politics of Nature Conservation.* New York: Columbia University Press.

Zimmerer, Karl. 1994. "Human Geography and the 'New Ecology': The Prospect and Promise of Integration." *Annals of the Association of American Geographers* 84 (1): 108–25.

———. 1998. *Nature's Geography: New Lessons for Conservation in Developing Countries.* Madison: University of Wisconsin Press.

List of Contributors

Jane Monnig Atkinson is Professor of Anthropology at Lewis and Clark College, where she currently serves as Vice President and Provost. She is author of *The Art and Politics of Wana Shamanship,* and coeditor of *Power and Difference: Gender in Island Southeast Asia.* Her published work has explored facets of religion, ritual, gender, and dynamics between political centers and peripheralized populations in Indonesia.

Don Brenneis is Professor of Anthropology at the University of California at Santa Cruz. He is currently working in two major research areas, a discourse-centered ethnography of federal social-science funding and a book on the anthropology of sound. Recent publications include "New Lexicon, Old Language: Negotiating the 'Global' at the National Science Foundation," in George Marcus, ed., *Critical Anthropology Today.*

Stephanie Fried is a senior scientist in the International and Oceans Programs of Environmental Defense, a nonprofit environmental organization, based in Hawai'i. Her work focuses on environmental and social dimensions of development in the Asia-Pacific region, including indigenous peoples and their rights to natural resources. Her recent work examines the impacts of programs in Indonesia funded by Export Credit Agencies, the World Bank, and the Asian Development Bank. Working with a broad coalition of native Hawaiian cultural practitioners, fishermen, and environmentalists, she has played a key role in the establishment of the largest marine protected area in U.S. jurisdiction, the Northwestern Hawaiian Islands Coral Reef Ecosystem Reserve.

Nancy Lee Peluso is Professor of Environmental Social Science and Policy in the Department of Environmental Science, Policy, and Management, University of California at Berkeley. She is also Chair of the UC Berkeley Workshop in Environmental Politics, an interdisciplinary group of faculty and students for UCB and other universities in the Bay Area. Her work on forest and agrarian politics in Indonesia, and more recently, Sarawak, began in 1979. Her publications include *Rich Forests, Poor People: Resource Control and Resistance in Java; Borneo in Transition: People, Forests, Conservation and Development* (co-edited with Christine Padoch); and *Violent Environments* (co-edited with Michael Watts). She is currently engaged in a long-term collaborative project with Peter Vandergeest on histories and formations of political forests in Malaysia, Indonesia, and Thailand.

Marina Roseman is Associate Professor and Clinical Research Coordinator at Pacific Graduate Institute, Santa Barbara, California, and a Research Associate on the faculty in the Department of Anthropology at Indiana University. Recipient of fellowships from the Guggenheim Foundation, National Endowment of the Humanities, Asian Cultural Council, and the Social Science Research Council, she has conducted long-term research among the Temiar people of peninsular Malaysia. Her publications include *Healing Sounds from the Malaysian Rainforest: Temiar Music and Medicine*; *Performances of Healing: Engaging the Spirits of Modernity* (co-edited with Carol Laderman); the compact disk *Dream Sounds and Healing Sounds: In the Rainforests of Malaysia*; as well as articles in *American Anthropologist, Social Science and Medicine, Yearbook for Traditional Music,* and *Ethos.*

Anna Lowenhaupt Tsing teaches anthropology at the University of California at Santa Cruz. She is the author of *In the Realm of the Diamond Queen: Marginality in an Out-of-the-Way Place*, and coeditor (with Paul Greenough) of *Nature in the Global South: Environmental Projects in South and Southeast Asia*. Her current research focuses on environmental debates and dilemmas in Indonesia.

Charles Zerner is the Barbara B. and Bertram J. Cohn Professor of Environmental Studies at Sarah Lawrence College and Co-Director of the interdisciplinary colloquium series *Intersections: Boundary Work in Science and Environmental Studies*. Formerly the director of the Natural Resources and Rights Program of the Rainforest Alliance, an international non-governmental organization, he has written on cultural, legal, and political dimensions of environmental issues and has conducted research in Sulawesi, Java, Sumatra, Kalimantan, and the Maluku Islands of Indonesia. He is the editor of *People, Plants, and Justice: The Politics of Nature Conservation* and co-editor, with Anna Tsing and Peter Brosius, of *Representing Communities: Politics and Histories of Community-based Natural Resource Management*. His current research focuses on environmental risk and rhetorics linking disease, invasive organisms, and immigration.

Index

Aberley, Doug, 230

Acciaioli, Gregory, 19n. 2, 105n. 42, 242

Acheson, James, 24n. 22

Adams, John Luther, 231

Adat law: of Bentian Dayaks, 15, 20n. 3, 150–51, 160–62, 165–68, 180n. 9; codification of, 241–42; discourse with government on, 158–77, 224, 231, 243–44; the Dutch and, 15, 20n. 3, 24n. 23, 150–51

Alcorn, Janis, 22n. 15, 186

Amblani, 152

Anderson, Anthony, 186, 214

Anderson, Benedict, 111, 180n. 3

Anderson, Christopher, 234n. 9

Annandale, N., 102n. 19

Appadurai, Arjun, 237

Appell, George, 200, 217nn. 13, 14

Aschman, Homer, 218n. 16

Atkinson, Jane, 46, 55n. 24, 101nn. 14, 16, 103n. 27, 105n. 41

Attali, Jaques, 19n. 2, 100n. 6

Authority: of Mandar fishermen, 21n. 4, 62, 99n. 5, 101n. 17; spirits, 11, 62, 66–69, 71, 72–74, 101nn. 16, 17, 102n. 18, 237; of state legal system, 84–90, 103nn. 30, 31, 104nn. 32, 34, 105nn. 40, 41, 43, 106n. 44

Bachnik, Jane, 234n. 10

Bagak Dayaks: boundaries of, 197; Chinese settler evictions by, 195–96, 217n. 10; durian trees, 11, 184–85, 202–11, 218nn. 21, 22, 23, 26; landscape changes and, 192–95, 217n. 8; longhouses, 191–92, 193; relocations of, 192–94, 214–15, 217n. 8; rubber cultivation by, 194; swidden agriculture of, 190–92

Bagak Sahwa, 189–90, 196

Bagak Salako. *See* Bagak Dayaks

Bailey, Connor, 99n. 3, 107n. 49

Bailey, Sinéad, 188

Balée, William, 186

Bandjar, Hasmi, 105n. 42

Banuri, Tariq, 51n. 4

Basic Agrarian Law (Indonesia), 176

Basso, Keith, 19n. 2, 101n. 15

Bauman, Richard, 221–22, 224

Becker, A. L., 227

Beinart, William, 99n. 4

Benjamin, Geoffrey, 60, 124, 127, 128

Benjamin, Walter, 18

Bentian Dayaks: adat law of, 15, 20n. 3, 150–51, 160–62, 165–68, 180n. 9; Bentian Family Group (BFG), 157–60, 162–63, 244; citizenship of, 158–59, 163–64, 175–76; discourse strategies of, 158–77, 224, 231, 243–44; environmental preservation program, 158–59, 171; history of, 152–53, 171–73, 181n. 13; industrial forest plantations,

Library of Congress Cataloging-in-Publication Data
Culture and the question of rights : forests, coasts, and seas in
Southeast Asia / edited by Charles Zerner.
Includes bibliographical references and index.
ISBN 0-8223-2802-X (cloth : alk. paper)
ISBN 0-8223-2813-5 (pbk. : alk. paper)
1. Human ecology—Asia, Southeastern. 2. Ethnology—Asia,
Southeastern. 3. Land tenure—Government policy—Asia, Southeastern.
4. Right of property—Asia, Southeastern. 5. Civil rights—Asia,
Southeastern. 6. Conservation of natural resources—Asia, Southeastern.
7. Asia, Southeastern— Social life and customs. 8. Asia,
Southeastern—Environmental conditions. 9. Asia, Southeastern—Politics
and government. I. Zerner, Charles.
GF668 C87 2002   333.7'2'0959—dc21   2001007926